Tries & Prayer

A Rugby League Journey

Bill Ashurst

With Steve Manning

London League Publications Ltd

Tries & Prayers
A Rugby League Journey

Cover design © Stephen McCarthy.

Front cover photo Bill scoring a try for Great Britain against France in 1972. (Courtesy *Rugby League Journal*). Back cover photos: left: Bill's visit to Penrith in 2006; right: Bill on the attack against Rochdale Hornets with support from Bill Francis and Geoff Lyon at Central Park.

A CIP catalogue record for this book is available from the British Library.

First published in Great Britain in September 2014 by London League Publications Ltd, P.O. Box 65784, London NW2 9NS.

ISBN: 978-1909885-06-6.

Cover design by Stephen McCarthy Graphic Design, 46, Clarence Road, London N15 5BB.

Layout by Peter Lush.

Printed and bound in Great Britain by Charlesworth Press, Wakefield.

"This book is dedicated to my wife and family. I love you all."

Bill Ashurst

Foreword

Rugby league has continuously developed over the years so the game that is played today differs immensely to that of the one played a decade ago, let alone 40 years ago. These days, the game is a full-time professional sport which uses a range of tools such as sports psychologists, GPS, video analysis, controlled weight training, and speed and agility training to attain the best from each individual.

Back in the 1970s however, rugby league was part-time. It was the thing players would look forward to after a long day's work. Training would consist of three sessions per week and then a beer with your mates. Generally, teammates lived and worked within the local community and would regularly spend time together away from football.

So, to compare players from different periods, I believe, is unreasonable. However, each era has seen many great players whose skill, talent and ability has been ahead of their time. One such player was **Bill Ashurst**.

The Penrith Panthers had not long been introduced into the competition and were not consistently competitive. Being based in Western Sydney, the club struggled to attract star Sydney players and decided to expand its recruitment to include England. There, the club managed to sign two internationals, Bill Ashurst and Mike 'Stevo' Stephenson. The signings added a captivating dimension to the existing team and suddenly everyone was aware of the Penrith Panthers.

Bill and Mike both brought creditability to the Penrith Panthers. They instilled confidence within the playing group, especially the younger players. Their influence greatly improved the team's results, which in turn assisted in recruiting other elite players including English international David Topliss and the club's first Australian international prop forward Bob O'Reilly.

Bill was tall, strong, quick, aggressive and skilful. He had the skills of a centre, which he had played in his younger days, and the footwork and acceleration to worry any defence. He had the ball skills before the line and in the line, which was something you didn't see too often in the forwards. His hand-eye coordination was exceptional; he had the cut out pass, the around-the-corner pass and then, of course, there was the famous 'chip n chase'.

I saw these skills come to the fore in a midweek AMCO Cup game in 1974. The same game resulted in Bill not only winning a colour television for man-of-the-match, but also an Alfa Romeo for 'Try of the Year'. The memorable story is that Bill was so sure he'd win man-of-the-match that he offered to sell the colour television before we went out to play. Barry Walsh, who was a club director at the time, said he'd buy it – I think this was just to get Bill to shut up. Bill was then cheeky enough to negotiate the price.

Bill's 'Try of the Year' involved a chip kick over the frontline defence, then a chip over the full-back to score under the posts. I remember it was a 60 or 70 metre effort and Stevo saying as we walked back to halfway 'I think we'll give Bill the ball tonight'. I replied 'Yeah, I think that'd be a good idea Mick'. Bill had an extraordinary game and led the team to victory.

We eventually advanced through to the final of the AMCO Cup. Bill did not play in the final however. He was injured the week before, having played a starring role against a Jack Gibson coached Roosters team full of Australian internationals who went on to be the back-to-back Premiers for 1974 and 1975. We narrowly lost the final 6–2. Bill's influence on our games each week was such that I'm sure, had he played in the final, the result would have been reversed.

If Bill's passing and running skills weren't impressive enough, he also had the general kicking skills of a half-back that in today's game would have made him a 40/20 specialist. He was also one of the first around-the-corner goalkickers to play in Australia.

I recall Bill's kicking genius in a game against a strong Western Suburbs at Lidcombe Oval. Just before half-time, and leading by only a couple of points, we received a penalty on halfway. Bill wanted to kick for goal, but Stevo didn't because of the distance. The two argued until big Bob O'Reilly went over and said to Stevo, 'Just give him the beep beep ball'. Bill then put it down and slammed it over with such force that the ball went into the crowd behind the posts on the full. We were all were amazed by Bill's kick and as we ran into the sheds, Bill said to Stevo 'I told you I could kick it!' – Bill's way of reminding Stevo that when he asked for the ball he should be given the ball.

Unlike today, the game in the 1970s allowed forwards to get involved on either side of the ruck, which suited Bill's game. He was able to move around the field, engage in and produce brilliant plays. Bill was probably the most naturally talented forward I played with during my 13 year career. His talent was such that in his 46 games he scored 19 tries, kicked 51 goals and six field goals. Even after 30 years of coaching, I would find it difficult to name another forward as gifted as Bill.

As a testament to his ability, Bill was included in the 2006 Penrith Panthers' Team of Legends for the club's 40th anniversary. There isn't much footage available of Bill in those times, which is a shame, but

I'm sure he will always be remembered by his teammates, his fans and the Penrith community who witnessed many of his great games.

Bill had a big influence on my career both as a player and as a coach. I enjoyed playing an attacking style of football alongside Bill. He read the game well and I remember marvelling at his speed, footwork and his ability to use the short ball or the cut out pass, all skills that are still very relevant in today's game. Years later as a coach, Bill still has an influence on some aspects of my attacking game plans.

After all these years Bill and I remain good friends. He is a great character and was an even greater player.

Tim Sheens

Tim Sheens played 166 first team games for the Penrith Panthers from 1970 to 1982, scoring 11 tries. At all grades, he played a club record 258 games. Initially a second-row forward, he played the latter half of his career at prop.

He then went on to have a very successful coaching career, including with the Panthers, the Canberra Raiders, North Queensland Cowboys and Wests Tigers. Since 2009 he has been the Australia national coach, and guided them to victory in the World Cup in 2013.

About the co-author:

Steve Manning is a retired police officer who attended St Helens College as a mature student and gained HND qualifications in Radio Journalism and Creative Writing. He became a rugby league producer and presenter on the College radio station. From there he gravitated to freelance work for the BBC before being involved with Radio City 96.7 and currently its sister station City Talk 105.9 on long running weekly *In Touch* with Lauren Moss.

For over the last decade he has been a freelance rugby league writer for various publications, including *League Weekly,* where he covers Leigh Centurions and co-wrote the highly acclaimed *Biting Back – The Mike Gregory Story* in 2006.

He dipped his toe into the world of cable television with Channel One Liverpool and Channel M where he coproduced and presented the successful two series of *Code 13 Grassroots*. Since then he has commentated for the partially sighted and blind at St Helens RLFC for a number of years.

Steve has been involved in BARLA (British Amateur Rugby League Association) for over a decade. He first commentated on video for games before becoming its Media Manager and touring the world. He was appointed onto the Board and is the current Vice Chair as well as chair of WARLA (Women's Rugby League Association).

He lives in sunny St Helens with his wife Diane. He has three children from his previous marriage: Louise, Gareth and Alexander; and two grandchildren Broadie and Caelan.

Steve supports an array of other sports, but knows nothing about football because he is a supporter of Bolton Wanderers FC.

A message from Steve:

"I would like to thank Stuart Prior for the conversation I had with him in 2011. I went to Cumbria one Sunday afternoon which led to him arranging for me to meet with Bill. Initially this was to talk about his career in the game and this story came to light, warts and all. Without that and further meetings with Bill there would have been no book.

I would also like to thank Peter Lush and Dave Farrar of London League Publications Ltd for giving their blessing for the publication of the book and the support that they have given both Bill and I in producing it. The book has been a pleasure to write. I hope you enjoy reading it as much as I enjoyed writing it, which at times wasn't easy."

Thank you
London League Publications Ltd would like to thank:
everyone who supplied photos for the book;
Steve McCarthy for designing the cover;
David Middleton for his help with Bill's time at Penrith; and
the staff of Charlesworth Press for printing the book.

Contents

The Ashurst family: Back: Carl, Billy, Graham, Kathleen;
front row: Laura, Bill, Sheila, Leeane, Andrew.

1. Early years in Wigan

I was 10 years old and it was Saturday 10 May 1958, a day I'll never forget which was to change my life forever and has seen my involvement in the rugby league for over 55 years as a player, coach, after dinner speaker about the game and Christianity. Even though I was from Ince in Wigan I had never seen a game of rugby league and never watched a game of rugby league as we had no telly.

We pestered and pestered my mam – 'get a rented telly' – and there used to be the most famous shop in Wigan then called Bullough's Rentals. My mam got a black and white rented telly which was being delivered on this Saturday morning, it was one of the best things that she ever did. Well, we were excited, we couldn't go out, we were waiting for this telly to come and it did at half past one. The bloke came in with the telly, by the time he had set it up, Wigan were just kicking off against Workington Town on BBC in the 1958 Challenge Cup Final at Wembley.

I watched that game that day; Wigan won 13–9. Rees Thomas, the Wigan scrum-half, got the Lance Todd Trophy. I'm not sure I would be far off now in naming that team. I was soon hooked on rugby league: the occasion, the speccies and the players that distinctively stuck in my mind from then. Boston, Ashton, Sullivan, Brian McTigue, John Barton, Bill Sayer, Terry O'Grady, the team of that era Norman Cherrington, Frank Collier and Rees Thomas. I was absolutely hooked, I said to my mam that day: "Mam, mam I'm going to play at Wembley and I'm going to lift that cup." I'll never forget that day. Sadly it didn't come to fruition. I played there twice; got beat in both, so didn't get the chance to lift it.

I wanted to be that guy I had been watching on that telly, it was the toughness of it, one-on-one combat, wanting to be better than him; he's not going to overcome me. I wanted to be Brian McTigue or Eric Ashton and from watching that game my hero was Eric Ashton as I started to go to watch Wigan. Never did I think that one day I would play with him, he was absolutely awesome. I think it was a penny to go and watch in the pen then. I started to go and watch my heroes live rather than on the telly.

From watching that game though I had the mental attitude there's nobody going to do what I am going to do on the pitch, I want to be the best and that was from such an early age. You'll see later on when I put on a pair of boots whatever it took, there was nobody going to beat me. If they wanted to out-abuse me, out-call me, or to out-fight me, there was nobody going to be better than me.

My mates and I started going to Central Park. We walked from where we lived; it was only a couple of miles and me mam used to make sure I had tuppence on a Saturday on a match day, a penny to get in and a penny for some toffee, and over the next two years I started idolising Eric Ashton and Wigan. I was fortunate that my school, Rose Bridge Secondary Modern, took us to our first Rugby League Challenge Cup Final. It was one of the best games I've ever seen, Wigan and St Helens in 1961. I think it was a hundred and odd in the shade that day. If I hadn't have been hooked then I would have been after that final, a far cry from when I was born.

My sister Isobel told me the tale of how I was born on Monday 12 April 1948 and like my life for the last 66 years, it wasn't a run-of-the-mill birth as you tend to get these days. Believe it or not I don't think anyone knew my mam was pregnant. She never told anybody, it wasn't noticeable and everybody was shocked when I arrived.

My mam, Mary Anne Ashurst, was working at the cotton factory at Empress Mill at the time, which was in Higher Ince, Wigan. She had had stomach pains and they sent for an ambulance which took her from the factory and should have taken me to Wigan Infirmary.

It didn't get that far because when we got to King Street in Wigan, which was a lot busier than it is now, the ambulance pulled up outside the County Picture House which was on the left hand side before you got to the traffic lights. My mam held up a bit of the traffic and I was born in the ambulance in Wigan town centre – a true Wiganer – and I came out at five pounds five ounces.

I remember being brought up by my three sisters; Jean 14 the eldest, Isobel 11 and Agnes 10. They used to slip these snippets in while my mam was at work. We lived in Bell Green Lane, Ince until the family moved into a new council house in Derwent Avenue when I was two. Because my mam never got married to my dad I was brought up mostly by my sisters in my early years and I eventually found out why I was in their care.

At the time of writing, Jean is still alive, touching 78; Isobel died about 11 years ago and Agnes, who we don't keep in touch with much, is 76. She's about 10 years older than me, so you can say I suppose that I was a big mistake.

Jean and Isobel were from my mam's first marriage and Agnes from her second. I was told when I was younger that he drowned trying to save someone in the canal.

As far as I can remember my dad didn't come onto the scene until I more or less started school. My mam did everything; she was a mam, dad, worked and used to do the loving, smacking and chastising. I used to be glad when she had gone to work because my sisters didn't do that – only on odd occasions. My mam couldn't afford a lot, but fortunately we got by and I wasn't wearing everybody's hand-me-downs.

I had a fabulous early childhood; my sisters could never do enough for me. I started school when I was four at Bell Green Infants School. Isobel, who had left school by then, used to take me in the morning and pick me up at night. She did this for 12 months.

She wasn't in good health and only had half a lung. Isobel was the closest of my sisters. She had bronchitis and everything, I remember later on they told her she didn't have long to live, but she went on Guinness and got another 10 years, so she did well.

By the time I moved up to Bell Green Primary School, Isabel was working and Agnes had left school and started working at Rappaports Factory. Jean had married a fabulous husband called Joe; he was a brilliant bloke, absolutely brilliant. I was lucky a lot of the time, they had a house around the corner from Bell Green School and I would sometimes go straight from school around to Jean's at night and then walk the mile back home.

So I used to have to do everything, get myself up for school as my mam and other two sisters had all got up and gone to work. As you can imagine there were a lot of mornings when I didn't go because I couldn't get myself up. I was lucky at school; I never came home for dinner because I used to get free school dinners because my mam was on a low income. I would come home at teatime and sometimes our Bel (Isobel) would be home, sometimes she wouldn't so I'd let myself in and the house was mine till everyone came in

When I was at home I was used to my mam and sisters, there was no bloke knocking about the house. My mam was like a dad anyway in a lot of respects. I remember once as a kid I'd been fighting with my mate, a lad called Peter Lowe, across the road and his dad come knocking on our door. I'll never forget it; he said "I want your Bill to come out here". Me mam had her apron, I'm hiding behind it and I remember her saying "Go away from my door". He said "I'm not going until you send your Bill out here", She said "I'll count to three and if you don't go away…" Anyway, he didn't move and she counted "One, two, three", thumped him and broke his nose. I was just stood there behind her pinny shouting "Go on mam, go on".

He went off, but my I didn't get it off my mam. But I got what I deserved if I did something wrong, she would paste me, she had the fastest shoe in Wigan and it could turn corners because she never missed with her shoe. I used to love my mam; the expressions that she would use were unbelievable. She would get ready to give you a smack and then she would say to me "Now this is going to hurt me more than it's going to hurt you".

Then she would hit you with every word 'Don't (smack) do (smack) that (smack)'. I thought mam you're as thick as I am; your vocabulary's not good enough. That's what my mam was like, but afterwards when she had given me a good hiding she would sit me on her knee and give me a hug after. My mam was hard, but fair. Bringing me up she would give me so much leeway, but when I knew I was getting it I was getting it because she could leather me. She was a big woman then, later in life obviously she wasn't, she eventually died of cancer at 86, but she was a great mam.

Bell Green Primary School in Higher Ince was a great school. The headmaster was Mr Barnes; the teachers were Mr Woodward, Mr Fearnley and Mr Wood who was great. It was Mr Woodward who used to have a stick, not a cane, which he called Excalibur and we knew when he used to say he was going to get Excalibur that someone was in for it.

I used to go on school trips every year to Rhyl. I remember getting on the bus at Bell Green; we had a song and would scream it "We are the Bell Green Laners, everybody knows, we save our tanners, we have our manners, we are respected wherever we go" that used to echo all the way from Bell Green Lane to Rhyl because we never shut up singing it.

Mr Fearnley was great; he was our football teacher with Mr Baldwin and it was through them that I started getting involved in football when I was nine. We played the local schools, Ince Central and St Williams. We used to walk from school about two miles away as the pitch weren't near our school. We used to play on like a bowling green dugout thing, there were no goals, we'd just put our jackets down, whatever, and that's how I got

3

involved in playing football. I remember my sister buying me my first pair of boots, leather boots with big cork studs, when I was nine.

We had to put dubbin on the boots to make them a bit softer. We used to play with those big leather balls and in the rain we would be left with a lace impression on our foreheads. I played with my mates in that team and we all grew up together going to the same high school.

I didn't have a position; we just run all over the pitch, got to the ball and tackled whenever we could. There was no structure to it because I would be sat back one minute; that side one minute then on the wing so everybody was everywhere really. It was a matter of just stop them scoring and score yourself, it was very competitive and we used to kick lumps out of each other. Many years ago I watched people like Norman Hunter at Leeds United, but he never kicked anyone as hard as we kicked each other. We were alright – we'd win games, we'd lose games, but it didn't really matter. It was about having fun and enjoying ourselves; it wasn't about how many goals we scored and how many weren't scored; it was about getting full of mud, kicking lumps out of each other and as I say just having fun really.

Ince Central and St Williams were within walking distance at the bottom of Bell Green Lane so playing at their places we would walk there and back with our teacher. When we were aged 10 he would let us walk it on our own because we were old enough. We would walk up Branch Brew before all the houses and estates were built over the old pits and the railway line. That was our domain, our castle and we were kings of that, the teacher would let us do our own thing after the game.

From nine years old I was all sport orientated. In our local park in summer we'd play the sport in the seasons. In Ince Park in the summer we played tennis and cricket with a dustbin as a wicket. We marked out a chalk line where we bowled from. In winter we would just play football in the park. Later on, we played rugby league in the park in winter when I went to Rose Bridge Secondary Modern School.

When I went into school I wasn't bad. I used to do my exams and come in the middle in class and I remember at the age of 11 I did pass the 11-Plus exam to attend grammar school. I couldn't go though as there was no such thing as free uniforms and help with paying for them. Because we couldn't afford the uniform my mam said that I would have to go to Rose Bridge Secondary Modern School. It probably was for other people, but not for me. All my mates I played football with 99.9 per cent were on the same intellectual level as me. They were all going to Rose Bridge so I was pleased in the end that I didn't go to the grammar school and could go to the secondary modern school with them. I'd known them from being six and we just carried on at Rose Bridge as we had from being young kids. I had a fabulous education, not just learning wise, but growing up wise

As it turned out, it was the best thing I ever did really going there. I wouldn't say I was thick, I always tell this story, when I was little the teacher would find out who was the thickest in class. The teacher would say "I'm going to give you all 20 questions and we'll find out who the thickest is". We did this test and he pulled me in and said, "Bill you're the thickest." I said "Why", he said "Well look at this you copied off him". I said "What do you mean I copied off him?" He said "Well, look Bill for 19 questions you have both got them all right, but on question 20 he's put 'I don't know' And you have put 'Neither do I'." This is anecdotal, I wasn't thick!

Being serious though, I was gobsmacked I'd passed the 11-Plus, never mind surprised. I knew I wasn't any Einstein, and I didn't copy when I was doing the exam by the way. My sisters were all pleased and my mam was always very proud of me and proud of me passing the 11-Plus. It was hard times, I remember she tried to scrimp and scrape, but at the end of the day the rent, gas and electricity was far more important than buying me all the uniform I would need to go to grammar school.

From being eight years old and growing up, I remember that most of the stuff we got was on 'tick'. I remember going to the local shop, walking about a mile from our house. Scott's off licence – me and my sister had to go on Saturday morning, we would have a shopping list off me mam and we always got the stuff. We didn't have any money, my mum wouldn't get paid until the week after, but she would always go in and pay it then and that's how things worked in those times. I know that we had no telly until I was 10 and we used to listen to the radio in our bedroom and that's how it was at that time.

All the families from a working class area where we lived at the time did exactly the same as us. There was no such thing as credit ratings. An area of pits, mills and factories with plenty of work available; everybody was busy in the bustling town of Wigan. Growing up my mam had always worked in the cotton industry: Trencher Field, Eckersley's and Empress Mills. That was the community then; people could leave a job and go straight into another one.

Life and early childhood was hard and good. I mean I didn't miss my dad who I didn't know then, I had my mam, my sisters, spoiled by all three of them, disciplined by me mam. Every childhood's rough and smooth with no dad and illegitimacy. It had a stigma in those days, though I don't recall anything being said. We, as a family, and me growing up, had a close knit mates' society thing, lads who stuck together. We very rarely at that age ventured outside our comfort zone and I don't recall being called a bastard or whatever. I know that there was a stigma attached, to someone who had a child and was not married. I never looked it as a detriment, I was just happy living with my mam and my sisters.

I recall though being chased by some bullies when I was at primary school. I was always, how shall I put, it a soft arse really when I was younger. I don't know whether I had been pampered or overly protected by my sisters, but I used to always get chased by these three lads when I was about eight, just before I started playing football for the school. I remember being chased one night at Bowness Place. I'll never forget that place, Bowness Place, where I stopped it. This woman, Mrs Kilgannon, was at the gate and I remember stopping, I was thinking will she stop it; will she stop them hitting me if I stop? Anyway I just turned round to my chasers and said "That's it, I've had enough, I'll take all three of you." I remember just cracking the first couple and the third ran off, so that was it. I was never bullied again after that and I've hated bullies all my life.

The watching Mrs Kilgannon clapped and said "Well done Bill, they'll not do that again", because it was a close knit community and everyone knew each other. We had a couple of days of us avoiding each other after I stood my corner and we began being on nodding terms before becoming mates.

We just took care of ourselves really. I remember I did tell my mam and her words back were "Look just turn around and just crack them back and get on with it", that must have sunk in because that day I did turn around and crack them back and I never had any more problems after that. Ironically, I later played with two of the lads in the school rugby league team at Rose Bridge Secondary Modern, although they were older than me.

They ended up in the senior side before me, a lad called Jimmy Ellis and a lad called Brian Willetts. I see Jimmy these days when I attend funerals. We have been the best of friends for a lot of years and he said to me at the last funeral I saw him at "I always regret doing that Bill" and I said to him "It's water under the bridge mate. It doesn't make any difference. We grew up with it and we got on with it and that's what it's all about."

I tell my kids it was the same when growing up with me mam "Put it to bed and don't bear any grudges" and that's how I tried to bring my kids up as I was brought up: get it sorted, it's gone and put to bed and there's no animosity after. I stuck up for myself, my mates and classmates, and in our close friendship community you helped each other. We didn't let other people pick on our mates, but with bullies later in life I've always got in trouble sticking up for people and sometimes avoided big trouble because I was a rugby league player.

2. The dark side of life

As I said, I had a happy childhood in my early years, but from being six to 13 I had a nightmare growing up even after the elation of watching my first Challenge Cup Final when I was 10 and knowing what I wanted to do. I told my mam that, but I couldn't tell her this secret in the dark side of my life in those years.

My dad's name was Frank Goulding. I don't remember how old I was, I was young, and he came to see me at weekends. I didn't go with him then when he came to my mam's. I was about six when my mam told me I was going to go and stay at his house at weekends and spend time with him as they would say now. I didn't know any different then, he had got so much custody or whatever and I think he was paying my mam half a crown a week. That was an absolute fortune then, when he did pay it, and so I was made to go and stay at his house at weekends.

Everything was good in the daytime initially; I had some good times with him, even some great times with him. He would take me to Blackpool; we'd go to Liverpool and jump on a ferry to New Brighton which had a massive funfair at the time. We did lots of things together during the day.

He lived about a mile and a half from where we lived in Derwent Avenue, a place called Cambridge Street in Wigan which was not far from Wigan St Patricks Rugby League Club, where I was involved as a coach until 2011.

He lived there with my uncle Tommy, my grandma and granddad. My grandma, she was a lovely woman and I didn't really know her long because when I started going there she started getting gangrene in her legs and eventually she had to have three, four, five amputations. She eventually died. Granddad died not long after. Sadly I can't remember their names, but they were good people.

I made a lot of friends there; it was like when you opened the backdoor it was like a big square yard, toilets outside. All the neighbours lived back to back in terraced houses so you all used the same toilets. I remember becoming friends at that time with Ian Lenagan the now chairman and owner of Wigan Warriors, we used to play in that square at the back outside, outside the back door when we were kids. You just played your little games, I mean we used to play with the girls who lived there playing hop scotching, piggy were you hit the stick, hoopla with hoops, we played everything.

Sometimes during the daytime on a Sunday we would be lookouts because the men would go playing pitch and toss on Branch Brews. We would get two bob for looking out for the bobbies. I can remember those times and they were good times, I mean we never looked out; we were playing while they were playing pitch and toss. If any bobbies had come we would never have seen them.

There must have been about 25, 30 men on a Sunday, every Sunday afternoon playing pitch and toss just over the corner were William Foster playing fields are now; it used to be chock-a-bloc with men; me, uncle Tommy, uncle Jonnie and my dad. They – and all these blokes – lived in the same vicinity, Silver Street, John Street all within three streets.

When I slept there, the sleeping arrangements were I had my own room and I had my own little bed, the abuse only started when my grandma and granddad had died. It was always when my uncle Tommy, who lived at the house, had gone to bed; it just left me with my dad.

It was in the front lounge on the lounge chair or in the front place on the rug on the floor or then later in the front lounge, it was never upstairs as Uncle Tommy was always upstairs. So whether he was scared of being found out, I don't know. I do know later on in life many, many years ago after that I know and believe that he got done for molesting some other kids.

It was always downstairs at night time when it, when the abuse started it was, you know, when the lights went out and the gas mantle was turned low, there was no electric then, that's when it all started all then the abuse. When it first started you know I didn't know what it was and then eventually when I got a bit older I eventually got terrified of that darkness.

If it helps somebody else then that's why I want the truth to come out I mean I was scared, after the fifth or sixth time it happened he used to say to me that if I ever said anything, I'd get took away from my mam and from everybody else; and I'd get more blame for it than him. It was hit and miss for the first few years, but I was frightened and just couldn't say a word. It was a night time thing and even when I went, it always happened at night time.

I think first time, it's so vivid in my memory really "Come and sit on my knee". There was no telly or radio on, silence – peace and quiet. The next thing he was doing was he started touching me sexually abusing me, although I didn't know that at the first time it was happening, it was so strange as I was wondering what the heck was going on. It was him on me, always him on me, and then later on I had to do to him what he had been doing to me that first time and all those other times.

I didn't know it was wrong until he threatened me not to say anything but I still really didn't know anything was wrong then. I had never been brought up like that at me mams, with me mam and three older sisters; I had never seen anything like that that had happened to me. There was no telly and no explicit programmes as there are now and there was certainly nothing on the radio about it then.

I assumed, I suppose, possibly that it was his love for me because you know what I mean that it was on an intimate basis with me sat on his knee while he was doing it. It was only later on some of years that it had been going on that I had started growing up and listening to things at school that I knew what he was doing wasn't right for a dad to do to his son.

I couldn't understand it, it's so hard to explain, and I see people today who have gone through the same thing, I see things on telly and cry. It's so sad awful; I cry today, it's something that will never, never leave me. I've lived with it all my life, it affects you, there are so many triggers that make you feel so low, down, and I still get depressed today.

There's only Sheila knows and I don't talk to her about it, I never told Sheila until it just come out one day in September 2011 and I said it, I was having an argument with her about something and it just happen to come out "That you don't know what the hell people go through". She said "What do you mean?" and bang I put it to her and told her the truth and I just have to live with it and get on with it.

There are times when the kids will say what are you depressed for when I've seen something on the telly and its triggered it off and I just can't explain it to them. I can't tell them and it's a dark side of my life that I wish had never happened, but it happened for so long but thank God I had outlets in the daytime and we had fantastic outlets in daytime with my friends and my rugby league. It was just that Friday and Saturday, those two nights, that I dreaded, absolutely dreaded.

I don't know why my mam never twigged because when it came to going I kept saying "I don't want to go again, I don't want to go again", but the initial thing was "Well, your dad's paying towards you, so you have got to go" but to this day I don't know why nobody twigged what was going on. Like I said night times was terrible.

Some weekends it didn't happen because like I said I had some fabulous times with him I mean like if we went away. To Blackpool or to New Brighton or wherever we would most of the times stay overnight and nothing ever happened then. The time when you knew you weren't going anywhere or stopping overnight that was when trepidations started and my fear started of what was to come. I knew when I was going away and staying away that nowt would happen. So I suppose it was when he felt like it I suppose.

I never asked him why he did these things to me; I don't know why whether because of the fear of the comebacks on me or not I don't know. All I know is that we weren't brought up like that and I have spoken about it on one occasion, I don't know why, but I remember I was doing a Christian meeting and it came out in my testimony.

I told people and amongst them there was a young girl who was heartbroken and she came to me and said to me 'I could never tell anybody it happened to me exactly how it happened to you and I have had such a release after you spoke about what happened to you', all that guilt came out of me and it was the same for her. It makes you feel the guilty one, not the person that has sexually abused you.

You're in a Catch 22; you're the victim, you're the cause, it doesn't work like that in the present day; we're talking about 40, 50 years ago – the late 1950s and beginning of the 1960s, when it was a lot different then. I can't remember but I know we were brought up in a respectable decent family; we didn't talk about sex or anything like that.

It's scary absolutely scary I think the number of times sat at the table with my mam and it's on the tip of your tongue and then the feeling don't say anything or else you won't see your mam or three sisters again. I mean there's so many times when you want to tell people and at the back of your mind if you tell them you won't see them again. The fear of losing my family but then the more I was growing up is the fear of what people would say about me.

The blame would be more on me than me mam, it became a personal thing then and what people would think of me, they'd call me homosexual or taunt other names, call me everything you know what I mean. It's me who would take the can rather than him. I mean it's like the old comedy thing 'If I tell you I'll have to kill you', it wasn't and it's not a nice situation.

Why did I let it happen, how can you not let it happen, and I was in the situation where I would have said that me mam told me to go from the start. But I would never blame my mam she didn't know what he was doing it's not her fault. I got on with it because me mam said I had to go and obviously I told you about my mum breaking that blokes nose she'd a killed him me mam, at the end of the day the fear factor was absolutely shocking.

That's why I probably grew up with no fear factor when I went on a rugby field. Because I'd pent up all that fear as I said at 10, 11, 12 and 13 years old when I started playing rugby league. At that age and at daylight times I could get rid of all those emotions against somebody I was playing against, or scoring a try or kicking a goal everything that night time thing would just go, disappear, it was all revelling on what I was doing on that pitch.

It was a lot more regular for three years from the age of 10 years old to 13 and it was at that time when I was brave enough to stand up for myself. Not in a way of telling people because the stigma would be on me and it would have been on my family, people like my sisters and my mam who didn't deserve it and eventually I kept saying "I hate it I'm not going anymore".

It got worse long beyond him touching me and me touching him there was a lot of buggery if you want to put it when I was little. It was the opposite way, the opposite way but thankfully there was no penetration it was just the position, that's all that it was, that wasn't as often as just the masturbating thing, but the other thing did happen on a lot of occasions. There but for the Grace of God...

Again by that stage you realise that from going back all the pressure is being put on you and he is going to say it's your fault and coming to the age between 10 and 13 you're at school, kids alright are not as streetwise as they are now you're at that stage when it's all happening you realise it's wrong and it shouldn't be happening your threatened and you can't do anything about it, it's all about emotion isn't it

I pent up my feelings and it was getting more vociferous 'that I wasn't going I hate him' and then this particular Friday night when I was 13 I had a rugby final the day after, so I wasn't staying at his place that night I was supposed to go on the Saturday that weekend.

I got myself into a situation where I could get out of something. He was at my place that night, as was my sister Jean who had come to see me my mam, but as luck would have it my mam was out.

I was getting ready to go to bed and wouldn't get ready. I knew he would try and get me ready because he was touchy, feely and anyway as he pulled my jumper I did something. He cracked me across the back of my head in front of my sister Jean. Our Jean just jumped in and smashed him across the face with some force behind the crack and said "That's the last time you ever lay a finger on him and it's the last time you ever pick him up again, you don't ever come and see this lad again."

I did expect Jean to react as she did, she never liked him, I don't know why. Probably though because it wasn't her own dad and our Jean was my eldest sister. Like I said earlier, they were all my mum to me, so if anybody put their hands on me our Jean was straight in there.

My mam came home later and he was still there and she backed our Jean. Her words were "There's no-one hits him, only me". There was a shouting match between them all but me mam like I say got angry. There was nobody tougher than me mam and he couldn't stand up to my mam and my mam backed our Jean. She said "I've had enough of it anyway, don't bother coming back for him again"; so that was it.

I never stayed and I never went again, I thought thank god for that and from that day I didn't have to go again. Once he'd been told I disowned him physically and mentally. When people used to say whose your dad I used to say he's dead I've got none.

Many years later, while married to Sheila, we bumped into him at Blackpool and it was still there inside my head, believe it or not he had met a woman. He came to our house a couple of times; he asked me if I would give him permission to marry this other woman. I was gobsmacked I said "No, we are not interested". I didn't want him in our house because I had young children and I didn't want him near the place.

It finished up he actually died worth a fortune, he got all his back pay from his career in the army, he got shot in Korea, he got back pay from all his war pensions. He used to buy gold, bought a big house in Torquay and when he died I was told by a friend of mine on the Wigan board of directors that I was entitled to half of what he had left. I said what the guy did for me in life, I don't want a penny in death so I never contested the will.

Before that I recall reading in the *Wigan Evening Post* that he had been convicted of sexual abuse molesting children, although he had done it previously it hadn't been proved. I was elated because he had got caught ... shattered because he was my dad. The elation was more important than the other side of it because now he wouldn't do it again with other kids, he had probably done it to other kids before that but he got caught. That's the type of person that he was.

I do have regrets, obviously you do have regrets that it happened to other people but at the end of the day I wasn't a Christian when it happened. That was many, many years later when I became a Christian, so self preservation was more important than other people then. I'm at the stage of my life now that other people are more important than my life now. Do you understand? It's the only way that I can explain it.

Self was more important, the stigma attached to what it was and it wasn't just me who would be attached to the stigma it would have been all my family. Now it doesn't matter because the reason I want to put this in is because everybody doesn't have to have this stigma of what's happening to them.

It's not their fault, they are not at fault they are innocent it's the guilty ones which should be punished not them. I suppose another way of putting it is if someone reads this book, kids read this book and its happening to them, the message is tell somebody don't feel you're the victim. You are a victim but it's not your fault and something needs to be done. Tell somebody, open your gob man, because don't let it go on, it has got to stop

I have had this on my mind and consciousness for over 50 years and the only person who knows this is Sheila, my sister Agnes and I don't get on now, we've drifted apart. I'm still close to our Jean and thankful for what she did all those years ago, I suppose our Jean will go mad but we'll find out then. I have no fear factor anymore and the reason I'm putting it in the book is to let other people know you don't have to put up with it

Finally looking back on that dark side and bringing it back to today: the daytime stuff at the start of getting to know him was good. In today's terms in the daytime I was groomed and at night time... you know what I mean. That's the way I've looked at it ever since, I was groomed during the day with sweet things and then at night time the sour stuff.

1959 Ince Boys Brigade football team.

Ince Parish Church football team. Bill is second from the left on the back row.

13

Top: Bill's mum 'The best ever'

Bottom: Carl Roden and Bill, captain and vice-captain of the Wigan Schools team.

14

3. Thank you, Mr Purcell

So when I was aged 11 I went to Rose Bridge Secondary Modern School with most of my mates though Jed Byrne and John Colborn didn't. As they were Catholics they didn't go to Belle Green they went to St Williams. When they went to the big school they went to Cardinal Newman.

I stayed at school until I was 15 and each year we had a different form teacher, the first year we had Mr Hurst, second year Mr Birtwhistle, third year Mr Purcell, and the final year I think we had Mr Ockleshaw.

I had different teachers for other lessons Mr Arkwright, English, Mr Hurst, Science, Mr Wren for Woodwork, I remember them all Mr Arkwright for Geography, Mr Brown for Music.

Finally, the most important person in my school life, a fantastic teacher and rugby league coach, was Mr Alan Purcell our PE teacher and rugby league teacher. He coached me all the way through school. I think Mr Ockleshaw originally was our football teacher initially because I played both for the rugby and the soccer teams. It was Mr Purcell though and the rugby team which had the biggest influence on my life

In my first year at school Mr Purcell started a rugby league team and we had a good side. Most of the lads I think all of the lads that came from Belle Green School got in the rugby team Kenny Dumican, Carl Roden he was my best mate of all, in fact my eldest son is named after him, Carl Riding, Roy Fraser, Billy Cottam, Wilf Holland, William Ashurst the same name as me, which is why I got known as 'WF' as my middle name was Frank.

I remember when I was 11 years old, we were playing a game one day and there was a kid who was called Joe Atkinson and what a character Joe was. It's a cup game and threequarters through the cup game all of a sudden Joe ran to the side of the pitch and said to Mr Purcell "What time is it Sir?"

I think he might have said "Twenty past four Joe. Why?"

"I have go" and he ran off the pitch with his gear on and ran home.

As he was running off the pitch we said "Where are you going Joe?"

He said "I'm missing *Doctor Who".* It was so funny; unbelievable, but we won the game with 12 men anyway.

That first year was the first time I had played the game with a rugby ball and as part of a team. Before that I had watched that cup final and got a new hero in Eric Ashton. We played tick-and-pass in Windermere Road. We couldn't get a full game because that was the bus terminus and when the bus came we had to stop. We didn't have a ball, we had rolled up newspaper wrapped round with Sellotape. That was our rugby ball when I played tick-and-pass as a 10-year-old.

When I first met Mr Purcell at school for rugby league I took to it straight away. He began coaching us. It wasn't coaching as it is today, but we did some passing, catching and kicking.

What he did then was, we had four houses, colours, Arley Wood, Borsden Wood, Deane Wood and Haig Wood after all the woods in Wigan. I was in Arley 'Red' and we played games against the other colours. From that Mr Purcell got us all playing together and organised our school rugby league team.

I was picked at right centre. Mr Purcell said to me 'You're going to be a centre because you're robust and fast.' I held that position for the next few years. Even when I signed for Wigan I was in that position.

Apart from playing centre in my own age group, I was playing so well that I played in the age group two years older than me, the 'Seniors' with those two bullies I mentioned earlier. I was on the wing for those games because they said that the opposition players were too big for me if I played at centre.

In the late 1950s and 1960s there was no such thing as kid's rugby league. It was just schools, there were more schools playing rugby league at that time than now because there were no junior clubs. Every school in Wigan had a rugby league team: Rose Bridge, Aspull, All Saints, Thomas Moore, Cardinal Newman and Pemberton. There aren't as many now as then. It was through the schools that players learned their trade and education at rugby league.

I was fortunate I had it, it just came easy to me and I'll say how lucky I was. Luck does play a part in life, I remember aged 11, I had just started playing rugby league and there were trials for Wigan Schoolboys team. I wasn't picked to go for these trials; Carl Roden, Kenny Dumican, Bill Ashurst, Carl Riding and Roy Fraser were picked from our school.

Mr Purcell just said to me it was at Cale Lane, New Springs, Wigan where they had them. He said "Just take your boots Bill, someone might not turn up." So I took my boots up to Cale Lane and went with all my mates to watch them play.

The bloke who was taking the trials said "Do you want a game?", and he stuck me on the wing. Three of my mates didn't get picked, but Carl Roden and I got picked for Wigan Schoolboys Intermediates. I was on the wing, my first representative honour and I shouldn't have even been in the trial. The team was made up of first and second years and there was Wigan Schoolboys Seniors made up of the third and fourth year lads.

I didn't ask Mr Purcell why I hadn't been picked. It's not something you did in those days in case you got a clip round the ear. How times have changed. I wasn't bothered it wasn't the be-all and end-all; it was just a game of rugby. My mates were playing so I went and watched because I would have been with them anyway.

Jack Keen was the Wigan Schoolboys coach, who later was a director at Wigan. I don't know if he had a clue though as he said Andy Gregory would never be big enough, look were Andy Gregory ended up, so you can imagine now why I got picked.

I was lucky in my first school year; I played for the school teams at Intermediates (11 and 12s) and Seniors (13s and 14s) at rugby league and football for the Intermediates as well as the Wigan Schoolboys Intermediate rugby league and football teams. Later as a Senior I continued playing for both town teams as well as my school sides at rugby league and football.

I was a busy bee so on schools rugby league match days I would never go to school in the mornings, because I knew we had a game at night. I would turn up at school just before dinner to make sure I was in time for my free dinner. I would go into the classroom for my lessons. Mr. Purcell would say "Where have you been WF?"

I'd say "There's a game on tonight, I've been resting."

So every game that we had and that I played in I never went to school in the morning and Mr. Purcell used to go berserk and I used to walk in the afternoon and he would say "Have you been resting WF?" I would say "Yes Sir". You could get away with it then, there was no qualifications unless you was a swot and you got your 'O' and 'A' levels like you do today. At 15 you left school to start work.

It went full circle though when I was coaching the kids at Wigan St Patricks Alan's (Mr Purcell) grandson Joe Davies, Joe Smith now as he's known, as his mam has got married again. He came in late for training at the club one day and I said "Where have you been Joe?" After a couple of seconds he said "Bill, me granddad said I've been resting", and we both burst out laughing.

I used to love science at school but we got done one day when we took it to an extreme. We did bisection and we had to use chloroform to knock these frogs out. Me and my mate Wilf Holland we nicked some of this chloroform and I think we knocked four or five lads out and sent them to sleep, put them to sleep. We got six strokes of the cane on each hand but we thought it was funny like, we could have killed them but we didn't realise it and how strong this chloroform was.

I had a few run-ins with the cane, stick and whatever else they used for corporal punishment and discipline back then. If your mates did something and you were with them you'd get done just the same so you kept your gob shut and just accepted it.

They were strict at sport. With Mr Ockleshaw when it came to the summer and football and rugby league had finished we did athletics. I didn't want to run in athletics and do athletics full stop. But I was a flyer, fast I remember the schools houses Arley and Borsden were running against each other and I didn't want run in this 100 yards.

I'm just taking my time and next thing this cricket wicket with the steel thing to put in the ground came flying past my head and Mr Ockleshaw said 'You, stop racing, you better try again.' I tell you what I finished first 20 yards in front of everybody else because I didn't want to get it and I finished up running for the school, for the town, for the county, so summer was all took up with athletics then. I did the 100, 200 yards and relays because I was pretty fast.

Athletics was a bonus. I loved playing rugby league; football took up a lot of my life as well, because when I played for Wigan Schoolboys at senior level we had some cracking times. We had a good team; we played at grounds such as like Old Trafford, Maine Road [then home of Manchester City], Burnden Park [then home of Bolton Wanderers] and Springfield Park [then home of Wigan Athletic]. We were playing all the top quality school teams from round here, it was absolutely fantastic.

I played at centre half, Peter Birtwhistle in goal and Kenny Dumican played. It was a cracking team, but eventually we got knocked out of the cup competitions. Then the Wigan Schoolboys rugby league coach picked me and I played for town team. I didn't do them both at the same time, I chose soccer first, but when we were knocked out of the soccer cups I'd go back to rugby league.

When I wasn't playing football for the schools I joined the local Boys Brigade for a couple of years, I only joined it mainly for the football team as all my mates had; we had a good football team. I didn't get a bugle or a trumpet or anything like that, but I did some marching around churches. I used to go and march around Liverpool once a year to the cathedrals at Liverpool, our master was a former sergeant major called Wally Blake.

We did have a very good schools rugby league team but there was always one team better school than us at that time and that was Thomas More from New Town in Wigan. They always seemed to beat us in finals but at senior level when I played two years above my age limit we had a good team as well. Peter Magnall was a big guy, Brian Boyd, Dickie Holland, Denis Nicholson, Jimmy Moore, people like that good players. Denis Nicholson is dead now he died of cancer. I won more cups with them at that level than I did at Intermediate level.

I played in lot of finals, there used to be one called Charlie Seeling Trophy, that particular trophy at the time was named after a former Wigan player who gave an Intermediate Cup to the school. We won that on two occasions at intermediate level in my first and second year.

At senior level we won a lot of trophies although I remember costing them one trophy though at Knowsley Road St Helens. We were losing by two points, I was on the wing for the Seniors and I remember Ken Ratcliffe got the ball. It was the final minutes and I only had to catch the ball to score. I dropped it.

Mr Purcell has never let me live it down from that day to this present day. He always says "Do you remember that dropped pass at Knowsley Road?"

I always say "I do sir". I still call him 'sir' after all those years.

As well as Knowsley Road when I played for the Wigan Schoolboys, we also played at Leigh and other grounds like that, but mostly Wigan Town teams played at Coronation Park which was just outside of Wigan. That was the place where I had the biggest injury of my rugby league career.

When I was playing rugby league for these school and town teams, and thought 'I'm good at this', I was never made captain of any of the sides. I was never bothered about it. To me it was always about playing, it wasn't about captaincy.

I believe that when you have got a pair of boots on, everyone is the captain because you would never shut your mouth when you were on the rugby pitch anyway. We were that closely knit that no-one insulted each other, it was just said and we all got on with it.

Mr Purcell was a very good coach, every training session was the same it was mostly based on tick-and-pass, there wasn't the skills training there are today, we were sent into any grids, it was tick-and-pass and play rugby league against each other. When I played as a kid and as a professional you learned the tackling techniques, you were told 'put your head on the right and be careful how you stand when you're going in'.

At the end of the day it was knock his head off, so there was no tackling techniques as such, just get them down the best way you could. Make sure you hurt him when you put him on the floor as aggressively as you can. It was dog-against-dog and we wanted to be top dog whoever we tackled. That's what it was all about. It was just something about rugby league. That's how I was brought up and it served me well throughout my career.

As well as the sport and Boys Brigade, I had a great social life at school, with the youth club which was at the school as well on Wednesday and Friday nights at school between six o'clock and eight o'clock as well. We had some great times, got into all the musical evenings, all the lads would meet the birds. I appeared in many plays there.

Mr Shenton wrote a school play called *The Bean and the Jack Stalk*. I was the fairy queen, absolutely fantastic, my mam made me a tutu I wore big steel toe cap boots, little tights and we had our final rehearsal. Those tosser mates of mine went off with my clothes, I had to go home in a tutu: I've never ran as fast in my life. But overall I had a fantastic time at school.

I used to love playing in the games whether it was rugby league or football for the school. I had such a great time; I got away with a lot of school work because of it. I was with my friends all the time and was learning how to be a winner whether it was football or rugby. I was dedicated to each sport I did.

I'd always wanted to play for Wigan from being 10, but there was a chance later on when I was 15 and 16 playing professional soccer for Blackburn Rovers. At the end of the day I'm just glad that when I was thinking about it, I had to pack it in, and because of that rugby league eventually was what my life was all about. As I said, it's all about luck.

I was lucky with my more late starts than on time starts because of my sport. My mam didn't know half the time because she and my sisters were working. I didn't tell her because what I didn't tell her wouldn't hurt her, we didn't get any letters or visits off the 'wag' man. It wasn't that I played truancy so I didn't get in trouble, I just didn't go in in the morning.

I used to get pulled in occasionally by Mr Winstanley, the headmaster but no-one came knocking on the door. Once my mam said "Don't do this anymore". Knowing my mam she would have probably broken my nose too, as she did to that bloke, if she had known how many times I went in late.

The school reports I got it never used to mention my attendance record, it used say from every teacher 'excels at sport, but could do better in his other subjects'. Believe it or not my last school report I filled it in myself. There was me and Wilf, we got our report and it looked as if we could unglue a page so I just put A, A plus, B, B plus. I'll tell you what, after filling it in and showing my mam, I think I got a fiver

We didn't have careers peoples or careers offices then. Wigan was still an industrial town with lots of job opportunities for young kids, different to today. As I was leaving school on that Friday I knew my sister Agnes had got me a job at Rappaport's, a local factory just across the way from Rose Bridge Secondary Modern School. No rest, no gap year for me; leave school on Friday and start work there on a Monday.

We had just got knocked out of the town soccer cups and I was told to turn up for training in midweek for Wigan Schoolboys rugby league team. They had a final against Widnes Schoolboys at Coronation Park and there was a chance I might be selected.

I got selected at centre and during the first half I got in a tackle position with my foot stuck in the mud. This big kid completely fell on my right knee and it shot backwards. I had never been in so much pain in all my life, it was enormous. Mr Purcell, who was at the game, got an ambulance to take me to Wigan Infirmary where my knee was X-rayed.

I was told "It's not broken, you can go home". Mr Purcell took me home and I was crying and crying all night. I must have cried for over eight hours, the pain was horrendous; we didn't have a telephone, although the next door neighbour did.

Mr Purcell had left his number in case he was needed, so my mam rang him around six o'clock the following morning. He came and picked me up and took me back to the hospital. My leg was dangling and every time I moved it either way the pain was excruciating. He got me a wheelchair and somebody there had the sense to put a splint board under the leg.

The pain was still bad, but when they x-rayed me again they said "I'm sorry you have snapped the epiphysis of the femur." Apparently the femur grows onto the knee cap but it grows over this little thing. I had snapped this little thing, plaster wouldn't fix it. I had to go into hospital with traction weights on my foot. I was there for 18 weeks. My only consolation was that we won the cup and I had a medal.

Until then I'd never had any major injuries playing sport, the only worst injury was when I lost my teeth. I had one tooth knocked out playing rugby league for the school. I went down in a tackle to the ground and somebody came in and kicked me in the mouth and the teeth just came flying out. I just sponged and then got up and carried on. You could say that he got his comeuppance before I went to the dentist. When somebody did something like that to one of your teammates or yourself, it wasn't just you who sought retribution, it was all your team as well.

My mam had got me my first brand new bike. I'd had it a day and I hit a pothole, went over the handlebars straight onto the kerb with my teeth. It knocked one backwards. Back to the school dentist who cut my gum and got the tooth out, that was it. Within two days I had lost both teeth, to this day they are still missing.

4. Oops – growing up in hospital

When I was told what was wrong with me and what they were going to do I asked about playing rugby league and other sports again. I was told that I might struggle to play; it didn't worry me then because I always overcame adversity. Probably the way I was brought up having to do a lot of things for myself, with my mam and sisters at work.

I never looked on the negative side of things; I've never been a negative person. I knew that as soon as I got out of hospital I would be back in the park playing tick-and-pass with me mates. I knew that I didn't care what everybody told me, it's what I wanted to achieve that was the most important thing.

I couldn't wait to get back playing tick-and-pass and rugby. I had no negative attitude, if they had come there and said 'I'm sorry Bill you'll not walk again' obviously that would have been it, when there's optimism there's always hope. That's the way I've always looked at things.

Here I was in North Ward, Wigan Infirmary 15 years old with traction weights for 18 weeks. I'd always been homesick even when I was little; it was a case of not being able to go home I think that was the biggest shock not the injury. I mean I could overcome the injury once they had put the splint on and the weights on, the pain had gone, I was getting pain killers no more crying from me. That had shifted; it was the sadness of not being able to go home for 18 weeks.

North Ward was a men's ward I'll never forget it, I was right in the corner of the ward and it was all men. I was the youngest there; there were some men 20, 30 odd, a few motor bike accidents in there and initially a strict ward. The sister she was, wow unbelievable you couldn't turn over, she would know all about it. Very strict but eventually we got around the sister becoming part of the family.

Being in so long you could smoke in the hospital then, I didn't smoke, during my time in hospital until Jimmy Tomlinson from the same village was put in a bed next to me. He had been involved in a motor bike accident and it was him who offered me a cigarette. Then I started smoking with Willy Woodbines, so it's Jimmy's fault and I've never stopped since.

Neither my mam or sisters tried to stop me, I mean the era was different then it was my choice. I finished up going out with my sisters who used to smoke, so I think that must have been the norm in those days, a lot of people smoked then. My mam also used to smoke but she stopped eventually.

Because of how I was lay in the bed I was introduced to bedpans and urinating in a bottle both skilled feats in their own making. At least then you could get one straight away when you asked or shouted for one not like these days if everything you read is right. Having mastered the art we finished up having fun with those bottles though.

Jimmy was a harem scarem; he didn't give a monkey's really, one time his wife had bought him an apple drink in, he loved apple drinks. He asked sister for a bottle, he wanted to use the bottle, so he poured an apple drink in it. When the sister came in for it she was disgusted, said "James, this is rather cloudy what have you been eating?"

Jimmy said "Just let me have a look, sister". She handed it to him and with a grin he said "I'd better recycle it" and he drank it. She ran out, she was heaving, that's the way it was we used to have fun.

Alcohol and beer on the wards was that strictly taboo and Jimmy never had any, god knows how that would have looked in a bottle or if it had been tested they would have thought one of us needed a new liver.

I looked forward to visiting time, but there weren't any afternoon visits apart from Saturday and Sunday. It was just an hour at night time and I used to get quite a few people coming, strict hospital rules only two visitors for five minutes, they would have to go, then somebody else for five, that's the way it was then a culture shock.

My mam and my family eased it a lot coming during the week and my mates at weekend. I got a lot of chances to see my mates as well so it broke it up a bit, I could get bored when my mam come. I loved her but I couldn't talk on her level, I was okay when my mates came we were all on the same level.

As patients we tried to plan our weeks out not to get bored with a couple of more young uns coming in, still older than me though 20 odd. We had loads of fun throwing grapes at each other and we would amuse ourselves with our own quizzes and being jokers. The sisters became good because if there was something good on telly they moved all the beds together so you could watch telly.

The first time Wigan played Wakefield Trinity in the Challenge Cup Final at Wembley, all the beds into the main ward, sadly Wigan lost. I really hated Wakefield at that time for the way they battered Wigan; ironic because later I played for and coached Wakefield. Then Manchester United played Leicester City and beat them in the FA Cup Final. When there were big matches the ward sister was alright, she showed her soft side by then after we'd been in there so long.

It was different watching it hospital with men rather than the first one at home in 1958 and with mates in 1961 when we went to Wembley with the school. Mr. Purcell took three or four of us on a school trip, the St Helens game, 90 odd degrees in the shade and defeat. The other one I remember vividly was when Wigan created a record points score against Hull in 1959, 30–13.

While I was in hospital all that time I developed a chronic disease growth therapy. It was a shocker I couldn't believe it, it wasn't just healing therapy it was growth therapy they must have put my legs in a grow bag.

I went in the hospital that Saturday morning believe it or not I was 5 feet 10 inches and within the period of my leg healing and when I come out of bed for the first time I was now 6 feet 1 inch. When I stood up and also realised how tall I had become my mam went berserk when I told her the good news. There was only my mam working then, she had to buy me new pants and everything so she was a little bit mad at me.

Then 18 weeks into recovery the doctor came in and told me I was going to be discharged me, although I felt like part of the furniture being in that length of time. I had some great times in there with other patients, including Jimmy, but I couldn't wait to get out. The shock was when I got up and can't walk, I mean I've heard people tell stories of having sea legs, but I had bed legs. It was three or four days before I could get the circulation back and everything else, it was a shock.

I had an extra week learning how to use the crutches and having constant physio. I learned straight away more or less how to get on the crutches, and did a lot of work with the physio in hospital. By the end of the week I was virtually running on the crutches.

I came out of hospital on crutches, but wasn't on them for long because with the daily physio I was receiving the muscles strengthened up. After about three weeks the physio said I could throw them away.

Mr Purcell used to take me, or my sister would take me on the bus, to the physio at Wigan Infirmary. The bloke who did my physio was at that time – and I didn't know until I signed – was the physio at Wigan Rugby League club. He was Jack Halstead – absolutely cracking person, no sense of humour, he wouldn't accept a joke.

I could play tricks with him; he wouldn't accept it, but was a cracking physio. Although he didn't remember me when I was 15, I remembered him when I signed for Wigan and he was at the club all the time that I was there. He did see me again when I had my operations and physio at the club. At that initial meeting he had got notes of what had happened to me, he never once mentioned that he was physio at Wigan.

He just said 'I'm involved in rugby'. He was a typical 'Wiganer'. His favourite expression every time I went was 'Don't worry it'll be reet.' That's all I used to get from him, there was no negativity. I don't know with Jack he put so much confidence in saying, making you work, making you get better, and he didn't push you in a physical way.

He gave me little thoughts in my head. 'If you think you can do this you can'; I remember one expression that I have used my entire career in my playing side of it, in my coaching side of it. He used to say to me and I got it from him all those years ago "Listen young man, there's no 'T' on the end of can, never say you can't"; and I've used that all through my career and it's so true. When Jack told me I could throw those crutches away, I was discharged. I was elated.

With his and my positive attitudes it was back to normal, playing tick-and-pass rugby with me mates in the park, football, meeting all the girls and lads together, our musical evenings as we used to call them then, just doing what we normally did and I was able to walk properly. It was great, freedom. I wasn't going back to where I was fastened in a bed anymore: pull yourself up, no more bed pans, no more bottles. I could go to the loo anytime I wanted; freedom.

I kept in touch with Jimmy because he lived in the same village; he was a lot older than me, about 20, and lived at the top of Belle Green Lane. I lived just around the corner, I would pass his house give it a knock and see if he was in. He had a lovely family, but I lost contact, the shops and houses where he used to live were knocked down. Everyone drifted off in their own ways, I don't know where Jimmy finished up or whether he is still alive.

After I was discharged from hospital, it was time to find work. The job I should have gone to when I was injured had fallen through. I was told that there was a job going at a fish shop in Wigan and I went there. It was called William Davies, Bill Davies in Commercial Yard in Wigan. It's not there anymore, it's now The Galleries. I went to the shop and asked for the job and he said "Can you start on Monday?" So my first ever job was working in a fish shop.

I became a fishmonger. I learned how to fillet and gut fish, I used to burn my fingers every day. I used hot ice and I used to forget to put my gloves on. Sometimes I would burn the tip of my fingers on hot ice. Summer it was good, winter was shocking because I was the lad who had the bike, delivering the fish to Wigan Infirmary. Absolutely freezing, my fingers turned blue. Imagine riding a bike up and down the hills in and around Wigan. Snowing away, we didn't take them in a car or van, I was the delivery fish boy.

I was biking up and down the hills, brows and streets of Wigan not on a mountain bike like today, but on an old fashioned bike; bog standard, no gears, just hard peddling and a tin at the front where I put the fish. The biking helped me; it built up the muscles in my leg that had wasted away in hospital. I didn't think about it that way then; it was hard work up and down in all weathers.

I was there just over a year and loved it though with Johnny, Tom and Big Ben. I'll never forget the lads who I had my first job with. One was enormous he was a John Barton and Brian McTigue put together was Benny, but he was funny. It was good, women came in the shop, we met young girls coming into the shop and I think that working in the shop with customers gave me more confidence.

There was a lot of healthy fish eating in the Ashurst family with me working at the fishmongers. I got it cheaper but not free. Mr Davies was a great boss, but he was tight as well. We had to pay for everything that we had, but I had a lovely 12 months; he was a good boss.

The staff were great, we had fun times as well. I mean things that we could do sticking our hands inside a fish head, we had more puppets in that fish shop than soft mick. It was great, but I left for the simple reason that I got the chance to work where my wife to be, me new girlfriend was working.

I was on £3 a week, which was good money. It was different to today what I did with the money. I took all my wages home and gave them to my mam and then got some back for the week. I had started drinking, I'd get about six pints, 10 Woodbines and some chips for going home and still have plenty of change. I was brought up from leaving school to tip up my wages to my mam and did the same when I was married.

It didn't happen like that with everyone. I knew people when I was a kid, the dads had just gone out and spent their wages before they came 'wom'. The thing was then, that's different from today, there was a community that was so close, if somebody didn't have a loaf someone would make sure that they had some bread. Some dads would get away with it because neighbours would rally round and help. It's changed now, for better or worse.

I went to work at Empress Mill, Higher Ince which was a cotton mill. It was next door to the factory I should have started at when I first left school. I worked in the warehouse. I was there for about three years and then moved on from job to job. There was always work in Wigan.

I worked on the railways, a pickle factory, Gallagher's Pickles, and I worked on building sites. When I signed for Wigan I didn't have jobs for long periods, I used to get sacked. The simple reason was we played on a Sunday. I never went to work on a Monday, I was always tired.

I remember one boss, Bill Kay, when I was working on a Platt Bridge building site. He said "Look, you're not putting enough time in; you're having too many Mondays off. Before you get your cards tell me why you only do four days a week?"

My simple answer was "Bill, because I can't live on three days a week." I always got sacked with humour whatever happened, happened.

Never mind the government's three day week[1] it was the Bill Ashurst four day week. I used to play hard on a Sunday and have what I called a 'key day' on Monday. I had a few bob in my pocket and went round for a few pints with everybody and it would last all day.

It was a different era of rugby league. Now we have full-time pros, semi pros and non pros, this was a time when it didn't matter whether you played rugby league or not, you still had to earn a living working as well. Until I signed for Wigan I used to work five days a week and sometimes six when I worked with Sheila.

The beauty of it then is that there was a lot of work out there if people wanted to find it. People could go from one job into another if they got off their backsides and went looking. We even swapped from job to job, then looked for jobs. We would go out and ask, no Job Centres, no computers, people would pass things on by word of mouth. Go there straight away and ask if there was any chance of a job, whereas now there's still a lot of work out there but I think that a lot of people don't want to find it.

The only thing then was 'UEB' the Unemployment Assistance Board which was mostly for married families and was in King Street in Wigan. Before I signed for Wigan we used it a couple of times because I was in-between jobs. If you had a family you'd take the kids, a bit like Social security today. The odd times I finished up there I would queue up at a window and get a few bob to get by on until I was okay.

---

[1] In 1974, the government introduced a three day week for factories and offices during a national miners' strike.

Left: Bill says: "My beautiful wife Sheila who deserved a dress like this; a beauty for a beauty."
Right: Teenage sweethearts – Bill and Sheila aged 16. The baby is Mary's first child, Bill's niece Lynn.

5. Booze, girls, the love of my life

Although I picked up some bad habits in hospital, I had already discovered drinking earlier. I was 14; we used to go to the pubs in Hindley: The Hand & Banner, The Nelson and The Fingers. We were young kids, the same age but looked older, but it was more when I was 15. I came out of hospital and was taller; we all got more into going out together because we had all started working when we had all left school.

When I had not long been out of hospital, there was a place up at New Springs, where I lived, called the New Springs Legion. We'd heard this story about a drink called 'Toby'; it was a strong drink. So we put our suits on one Saturday night – me, Billy Cottam, Alan Dutton and Wilf Holland – and walked up the canal bank to New Springs Legion. I think I only had four pints. When we were coming home three of us fell in the canal; Wilf didn't fall in – he dived in.

We all finished up in the canal and eventually walked 'wom' from drinking this Toby. That was an experience; we heard stuff and just had to give it a go. It was good stuff. I don't think I ever drunk it again though. When we went in there, I can't remember anyone asking us our age or wherever else we went. Probably it was because we were dressed smartly and I had shot up in height. We just went in.

We would go out on the Friday and Saturday, on Friday because some of the lads could pull. On Saturday we went to a place in Hindley, before that we'd start off going to Nelson, the Hand & Barrow, the Fingers, the Balmoral. Straight across from the Balmoral was The Monaco, a dance hall which is still there now. We used to arrive there between half past eight and nine o'clock.

We stayed there for the rest of the night. There were no stamps on your hand to go out and come back in, just dancing, that was girl time. Sunday was rest day, park day, rugby tick-and-pass day, dinner and get ready for work on Monday. I went with my lifelong mates growing up, but I don't see them as often now; half of them are not here anymore. When I bump into them in Wigan when I've not seen them for years it's as if I saw them yesterday.

The Monaco was our introduction to girls that we didn't know, our favourite place and favourite haunt. Obviously I knew girls from growing up; more so from being 14 through going to our youth club at school. Ours was an all boys school, the girls school was back to back, but we had the same youth club. The lads and girls from Cardinal Newman and other schools came so we had a fantastic, mixed youth club.

That was on Wednesday nights and sometimes on Fridays when they had a special night on; sometimes they would have groups perform on the Fridays. All the lads and girls got to know each other at the Wednesday musical evenings, we would meet in the park, play records in the youth club and from that we did what we did. We wouldn't have a drink before we went to the youth club; we might call in at The Squirrel our way home.

We had a very close knit boy girl system, all my mates and the girls used to go out together. To this day there are at least five couples who met each other at 14, married and

27

are still together, so that was a really good close knit family. I know that Kenny Dumican married Jacqueline, Brian Warren married Irene, and Graham Foster married Linda. You wouldn't believe that they and others I can't recall are still together from being 14.

Other activities at the youth club, apart from music and dancing, were in the playground with the girls between the records. I think I lost my virginity aged 14 in Rose Bridge School. It was experimental, I never spoke about it. I put it down as a science project: I used to hate cutting frogs up; I loved experimenting with young women. Experimenting, you find out things for yourself, but in a nice way. We didn't think about our age. When I say lost my virginity, it was once on one occasion until a couple of years later when I met the love of my life.

We learned by talking and listening to everybody, 'Boydy' and the others who were older than us. Sometimes we would sneak around a corner and get our own real life blue movie, they wouldn't know we were watching them so there was a lot of peek a booing and being curious. We learned a lot from the older lads, but sometimes we got it wrong ourselves. I kissed girls and blah, blah blah, the real passionate thing was done with the one I've loved ever since I met her.

The day that changed my life was when I was 15. It was a Saturday night in the summer of 1964 in the Monaco with my mates, Alan Dutton, Billy Cottam. Wilf Paul was supposed to be with us, but he was on a blind date. We were stood at the top of the raised bar near to the steps with seats and tables below us near the dance.

We were standing at the top and Marjorie Wilson walked in with her boyfriend Sid and this girl with Wilf and they sat at the bottom. As soon as I saw her, I thought that she was absolutely gorgeous and knew at that instant that I wanted to take her home; I wanted to see her. It was love at first sight of Marjorie's cousin, Sheila. She was wearing a three quarter length lilac skirt with a white top, her red hair was flowing. Absolutely gorgeous and I had to get close to see her, luckily they sat at the table right underneath us. I could hear them talking all night, she had an odd glance at me, I couldn't take my eyes off her. I never stopped looking at her all night.

I mentioned about luck at that rugby league trial at school, anyway luck fortunately happened. We were all under age and the police came in. Luckily for me, the first thing she said when she saw the police uniforms was "I'm only 17, I'll get done if they come up to me and catch me." To me that was like a red rag to a bull, I shot down the steps and said "I know you're scared, I've just heard you and the bobbies will come past, when they come past give me a kiss and they'll not even look at you."

Anyway the bobbies came as she kissed me; the rest, as they say, is history. It was like something from a Rudolph Valentino film. When it happened that was it, I didn't give a monkey's about Wilf and we're still mates. Marjorie fell out with Sheila. She said "You were supposed to go home with Wilf." Sheila and Marjorie kissed and made up; Marjorie and I get on to this day.

That was the only kiss, we stayed there had a couple of drinks and I said "Are you ready, can I take you home?" We walked home from the Monaco all the way to where

28

Sheila lived in Price Avenue in the same village I came from. I found out that Sheila was nine months older than me, cradle snatcher.

From that time I don't think I ever missed a night seeing her, although I didn't ask her mum and dad if I could, those days had gone. I eventually met her parents who invited me in. I remember her dad Tommy's words when he saw the size of me and looked at Sheila "Now wench, that's a real Man, a real Man."

We became real close, our courting was we'd walk round and Sheila always used to carry a radio everywhere we went. We used to go on Fosters Playing Fields, walk along the canal, in the park; we just spent all our time together.

Sheila had an older sister, Mary, who was married, four younger brothers Tommy, Johnny, Malcolm and Terence. They were all alright about me, young Terence was only about 10 then, two years later he died with peritonitis. Tommy was a year younger than me, the youngest of all, Malcolm, died about seven years ago with cirrhosis of the liver.

Sheila's parents Mary and Tommy Garrity were lovely people. Tommy was a great bloke, he would do anything for anybody. Unfortunately, he was dyslexic with his reading, but clever – he could dismantle and mend watches, do anything with his hands, but reading and writing weren't there. Sheila's mum Mary, I later hated her for a long, long time, she was competition for me. For Sheila and it was always mam, mam, mam.

I told my mam and my sisters I was going out with Sheila and was seeing her most nights. On a night we were supposed to have a night off from each other, Sheila came up to mine. That first time she did she surprised all of us, Sheila was such a wonderful person that when my mam met her, she thought the world of Shelia. She always used to make sure my light blue jeans and white shirt were pressed. When I went picking Sheila up, I'd put my false teeth in, and the job was a good one. I had been with Sheila for about six months and once I hadn't got my teeth in. She was going on about these teeth and I ended up saying "if it's all about teeth", I threw them in a field and said, "Is it about me, not my teeth?"

Sheila didn't like sport, when she found out I was playing football or rugby she never came and watched. We used to go in the park. She would sit with the radio and one night I was so competitive that she nearly left me. While I was playing soccer with my mates, there was a lad who was a pain in the arse, a cracking lad, a friend of ours. He used to always pinch the ball off me and I used to go mad. On this night he took the ball off me again and fell over. I stamped on his head; Sheila saw it and said "I don't want to be with you anymore, if that's the sort of person you are." Anyway we finished up together.

Bill in action for Wigan in the 1969–70 season (Courtesy *Rugby League Journal*)

6. Marriage and back to rugby league

Sheila and I during our courting had talked about wanting a family and with her being in the 'family way', we decided together that was what we wanted, although the way I found out was not planned. I had got fed up with the way things were at home, my mam was getting older and she was a little bit poorly. My sister, our Bel, who brought me up, had got married and left home.

I just wanted to be with Sheila all the time, it wasn't a mistake we both wanted it. We had been courting for well over 12 months and we said months before she told me the news, 'Why don't we try and make a baby, we can be together and get married.' So we did, we planned it. We never told our parents that we planned it, not to this day did they know that. If they were all alive today they still wouldn't know and soon my sisters will know we planned it all those years ago.

Although, as I said earlier, Sheila didn't like sport I had continued playing football for the Ince Parish Church team with my mates. I played at centre forward and have been told that I still hold the Sunday School record of scoring 69 goals in a season. I was spotted playing for them and was asked if I would go for trials at Blackburn Rovers.

I had a couple of trials and met Johnny Carey, the first team manager of the football club then and a Mr Campbell. They asked me if I would be interested in signing for Blackburn Rovers. I was just becoming 17. I had gone to these trials on my own and after this one and the talk with them I said 'I've got to go and see my mam and have a chat with her about this.'

I came back from that trial excited; I was going to tell Sheila that I may be signing to play professional football. When I saw her she said that her mam and dad were waiting to give me the good news, that Sheila was pregnant. It wasn't a bombshell, we knew what we wanted together, but it was a bombshell at that time for the football side of my life. That ambition was well and truly out of the window.

It was her dad Tommy who told me. I didn't know what their reaction was going to be. Sheila had told her mum and dad the situation and I think what saddened Sheila at that time was that it saddened her mam.

We had not looked at it that way when we had planned it, we looked at how we felt about each other and what we wanted. Sheila was the only breadwinner and worker in the family and I think her mam was a bit upset that she would have to be leave home and the income wouldn't be coming in. The next problem was me telling my mam.

I was scared of my mam, and I made sure that Tommy and Sheila came round to our house with me to see my mam. I made him and Sheila go in first; I think I was hiding behind both of them. He knew my mam's name as Molly, even though she was called Mary.

He said, "Molly, I have some bad news". I don't know why he said 'bad news', to us it was good news. He said "Your Bill's got our Sheila pregnant." Well my mam darted, picked the poker up and chased me round living room with it shouting "I'll kill you". After the initial shock of being chased around the living room by my mam with a poker, she calmed down. My mam said that we would have to get married and Sheila's mum and dad realised that needed to happen and basically we had to sort that out.

Sheila and I got married on a Wednesday afternoon, 2 February 1966, at St Williams Catholic Church at Ince in Wigan. I just wore a suit and we got a lift off my brother-in-law in the back of his van. There were no windows in the van, we just sat in the back of his van, so romantic.

We made it on a Wednesday afternoon because we didn't expect many people there; we didn't have a big guest list, no money. We were both surprised because when we got to the church to be married it was packed. All our workmates from the factory had turned up, they'd had the day off and it was a cracking day.

At the night we had a little reception at the Park Hotel at Higher Ince. I'll never forget it; there were a couple of artists on. The worst I have ever heard in my life, two dancers, I thought they were absolutely diabolical. That night we didn't consummate the marriage, we'd already done that months earlier. It was a good night I think, I was obviously bladdered. Sheila was pregnant so she didn't drink. She was on orange juice and up all night. So it was a great wedding day.

We didn't tell the priest that Sheila was pregnant because she wasn't showing. I went to see the priest, Father Strawbridge, and had a couple of lessons in the vestry of how to try and become a Catholic, because I wasn't one.

All he wanted to talk about though was about two women who lived in the street, I don't know if he was giving them one or not. I said to Sheila "I'm not going to see that bloke anymore, or go to that place." I never went again, but they let us marry there.

Sheila was a church goer when we were courting, I'd wait outside church while she went to mass and confession and all that. There was no way that I was going to become a Catholic, I had nothing to confess. I wasn't interested in God and wasn't a Godly person.

They read the bands and said you can get married three weeks on Wednesday so we turned up on the Wednesday and were married. In the service when it came to does anyone in this church object to them getting married, I thought I know some cranks, workmates, friends but nobody shouted anything. The only thing I've said to Sheila many years ago, I wish I'd have objected. Only joking Sheila, we both wanted to get married.

They were good parents and in-laws, don't get me wrong and in the build-up and organising our wedding and everything as we were now working together I was living at hers. They had moved from Price Avenue to Kendal Road. However, when we first got married I had no closeness with Sheila's mam, at the beginning we hated each other. When Sheila's mum was dying of cancer I had a heck of closeness with her that I'd had never had with my mam.

When she died it had gone from heads to tails, when she was in hospital there was only me who could fluff her pillow up, or could sit her up. In the end we absolutely adored each other, when she passed, for 12 months I had a closeness that I didn't have with my own mam. Sadly, her dad Tommy died of a broken heart, Sheila lost them both in three months.

We decided that once we were married we live somewhere else, although you couldn't separate Sheila at times from her mum with a crowbar; they were joined at the hip. Although that was the case, we both wanted our own house and we moved into a house on Pickup Avenue, our first house, which we rented from Charlie Nelson.

It was just around the corner from her parents and brothers, so I couldn't get away from them. If Sheila wasn't at ours, she was at her mum's. I thought it would be good for babysitters with them just round the corner when our Carl was born. The bottom line was it kept Sheila happy, because at the end of the day that's what it was all about at the beginning, Sheila's happiness.

Carl was born on 20 August 1966. Three good things happened in 1966: our Carl was born, England won the World Cup and the marriage. He was born at our house as was Graham; our Kathleen was born in our place as well; by then we had moved up to Bell Green Lane.

That's how it was then at home, not at hospital, the man wasn't allowed in, the mother-in-law lived near us so I went there all the way through Sheila's labour. I'd been in just before she came to the end of it, but I couldn't be there for the birth, until the baby was born. I remember my mother-in-law saying "She's started off, go for the midwife". No car then, so I ran to the midwife's about a mile away. I remember the midwife saying Sheila was having some pains that had worsened, go and fetch the doctor, I went for him.

I remember someone saying her waters had broken. I jumped in then and said that "If you think I'm going for a plumber, you can naff off". As daft as it sounds, I knew that Sheila had given birth at the exact time she did.

I had that particular feeling; I think I was so close to Sheila. I knew he was just born; I ran home, I said "She has just had him hasn't she?" They let me in this time. Sheila had given birth to our Carl, beautiful child, blond hair, absolutely gorgeous. The midwife upset Sheila – she hates violence and war films. The midwife gave her our baby and said "Another little soldier for the Queen."

We had a beautiful little boy who was later paralysed through a mistake, he's disabled now; he was a beautiful kid. We named him Carl Ashurst after Carl Roden, who was my best mate through school and everything, a very close friend. He is one of three brothers Carl, Alan and Jack, who is a scout for Wigan Warriors.

Sheila was anti-sport when we got married. Sport was everything to me, but because of my love for Sheila I gave it up. I packed it in; apart from when those kids came knocking on the door at our house.

I was 17 years old and married. I had 12-year-old kids Jimmy Taylor, Georgie Taylor and Packy knocking on the door asking 'Is Bill coming out with the football?' So I went out playing with the kids on Ince Central School fields. I've spoken with Jimmy, who later coached at Wigan St Patricks, about it since. One day I was walking through Ince Park and Ince Parish Church football team, who I'd played for before, were playing. I knew some of the lads and joined in some of their training sessions. Then they asked me if I would like to start playing again.

We didn't have to go to church, or be forced to go, to be able to play for the team like we were when I went to school. Then we had to go on Ash Wednesday and different religious days; it was Church of England. We didn't mind going because the first time we went we devised a scam. When they came round with the big brass plate for the collection, we made sure we had a piece of chewy. We got a penny off the plate rather than put one in, so church wasn't too bad. We always had some toffee when we were going back. I don't know whether that will be mentioned when I pass on.

So I started playing football again. I had done the right thing in my eyes: I was working; we wanted a family, to get married and live in our own house. We had Carl and I packed in all sport during that time. We were married now, had to be, and both wanted to be. Sheila either accepted it or went back to her mam; she couldn't get any closer back to her mam. She was there 24/7 everyday anyway.

So Sheila accepted it and let me get on with it. She never came to watch though. Her excuse was – and has always been – and it's a good one: 'I didn't like seeing him get hurt'. Even today, all my grandchildren play rugby league, my own little ones have played the game. She only comes to the odd game; it always seems that she saw one of them get hurt when she comes. It was the same when I was playing.

I had heard that there were coaches and scouts watching games, but I hadn't been approached by anyone. I intended to carry on, and hoped that football would become a career because I'd had a great season.

Then one night I came home from work. We used to get the *Lancashire Evening Post*. As usual, I turned to the back page and read the sport, especially Wigan. What I read completely turned my career upside down. On the back page it reported a young lad, a mate of mine called William Cottam, had just signed for Wigan. He had joined them from Rose Bridge under-19s. I had known him all through school; we had played in the same rugby league team at senior school. He was one centre and I was the other. Don't get me wrong, he was a good player, but I knew that I was a lot better than him. I was stunned, shocked and read the article a few times. I felt dumbstruck. I looked at Sheila, showed it to her and, although she didn't like sport, I asked her to read it.

I said "Look at that, I'm playing for a football team at Ince Parish Church and he's just signed for Wigan. I was 10 times better than him at school. I'm going to play rugby league." I'd given up sport for over 12 months for my family. I decided at 18 years old, there and then, to sign for the Rose Bridge under-19s and return to rugby league.

I knew Billy (William); if he was good enough to play for Wigan then I was. He had not got the schoolboy representative honours that I had. I said to Sheila "Look, it's an ideal opportunity to test myself. If there's an opportunity that comes up that I can sign to play professional rugby league I want to try to do it. I lost the chance at Blackburn and I'm going to play for the under-19s at Rose Bridge to see if I can get a second chance at another sport."

No figures were mentioned as to how much he had signed for, but I knew that if anyone signed for a professional club they got some kind of remuneration. But it wasn't about money. I have never been a money player. Don't get me wrong, I've had a few quid out of rugby league; the bookies have had a few quid out of me. I was happily married and loving life, I just wanted to go and prove to myself that I could do something different.

I was glad really because I enjoyed it as much as my soccer; there were more of my schoolmates playing for that under-19 rugby league team than were playing for the Ince Parish football team. Sheila accepted that there were things in life that I wanted to do. I was still only a kid.

We had a fantastic football team at Ince Parish Church, a great team spirit and I promised the lads that I wouldn't leave until the end of our season. We won a Cup Final and I scored four goals. I left the team on good terms and we had a good night out.

We didn't have a coach or a manager, we did it ourselves. We used to train in the park, organise our own team and had a great set of lads. A few of them have died now, Billy Almond, Brian McCracken and Alan Hart. George Ashall has just had two big hip operations. We had 'Twinney'. We had a cracking team who enjoyed their sport and Sunday football.

So I went back to rugby league. We used to play on the Rose Bridge pitch, the old school pitch; we got changed at my old school, the secondary modern. There were a lot of players playing for that team who were in the same team as me at secondary school. Denis Boyd, the other Billy Ashurst, Carl Roden, Carl Riding, Roy Fraser, Norman Guest, Jimmy Moore, Gerry Cracken, and Jimmy Ellis.

We didn't have a coach as such, we had a great manager – a little bloke called Wally Blake. He'd been in the Boys Brigade all his life. He was our boss when I played football in the Boys Brigade when I was a kid at school; he was like a little sergeant major. We used to call him Sergeant Major Wally; he organised everything, but we did our own training even though he was always there.

We never had fitness training sessions like they do now with weight training. For us, it was turn up, have a game of tick-and-pass and a game of rugby among ourselves. Sort the team out for Saturday and that was it, go home. We did that twice a week and then played on a Saturday.

Wally was an avid manager and every game he was there, he would help us a little as well. I remember playing in a cup game for the under-19s and Wally was a touch judge. I got the ball at centre and was being pushed into touch. I ran in touch round him, came back on the pitch, he never put his flag up and I scored a try. It kicked off, there was brawling and fighting; he was unbelievable.

I didn't play many games for them before I got picked up by Wigan. My first game I think was against Stork, then GKN, Wigan St Pats, Bickershaw and Hope Rangers. Some great players have signed professional from teams like that. Billy 'Daz' Davies, who played for Swinton signed from Hope Rangers and Peter Rowe signed for Leigh from Leigh Miners.

We scored tries from everywhere as a team, I don't think there was a game where I didn't score a try for Rose Bridge. I mean, and I know it might sound big headed, I was a winner. In football I was a natural footballer. It's not easy to say that you were a natural footballer, but everything came spontaneously to me.

I'd played at school and from the age of 18 until the end of my career, half the time on the pitch I didn't know what I was going to do next. It was spontaneous and 90 per cent of the time it came off. I had played half a dozen games when we played a team called Adlington and beat them 134–0. I scored about three tries and kicked 14 goals; it was three points for a try and two for a goal then so you can see how many tries we scored.

I played in so many positions, swapping and changing. I played from one to 13 and it was after that game a wonderful little man from Wigan, their head scout Billy Cunliffe, came up to me. He said "I have been watching you, not just in this game; this is not a joke, but I have been watching you for the last two or three games, would you like to come for trials at Wigan?"

We never lost a game while I was with the team and I had the advantage of being a goalkicker as well. Whether that had any influence, because I was a decent kicker then, I don't know. He could have picked anybody up on that day I thought, but he had watched a couple of games before and had been impressed with what I had done.

My original reason for going to play for Rose Bridge under-19s was to impress someone to get to Wigan. But for that team and my teammates, it might never have happened for me. When I spoke to Billy after the game, it was from that moment that everything completely changed, my second chance had arrived.

Even then I did not have a clue what was going on or what to do although obviously I was delighted. When I got home I told Sheila that I was going to Wigan, Central Park. I had to go training on the next Monday. The 'A' team trained on Mondays and Wednesdays then. We were nowhere near the first team; they trained on Tuesdays and Thursdays.

I was very, very excited. Sheila was pleased for me, but not with the excitement that I felt; it was sport again, wasn't it? She is, and was, a fabulous wife. She just took everything in her stride, as when I gave her this news and just let me get on with it.

So, following Billy Cunliffe's instructions, I turned up at Central Park on the Monday night. It was training first and he told me I would have three trial games. The first time I went there I met one of the nicest men in rugby league that I ever met in my life, Johnny Lawrenson, who sadly passed away in March 2010, aged 88. He was the 'A' team coach with another great half-back who played for Wigan, Ted Toohey, who came from Barrow.

The training was completely different to tick-and-pass and a game of rugby that I had done at Rose Bridge. It was proper fitness training; the session was arranged properly, unopposed rugby. I'd never done unopposed rugby before, doing all the set pieces and proper sprint training on the cinder track at the Spion Kop, it was all completely different.

I had an advantage in that Bill Cottam was playing for Wigan, who had signed previously and was the reason for me returning to the game to try and get signed by the club. There was also Denis Boyd who had signed for them from Rose Bridge.

There were a few kids there who I had played against in the District teams when I played for Wigan, as well as a few old heads, such as Tommy Woosey, Len McIntyre – who died while we were writing this book – people like that. Len Mac, he was a great guy who taught me and all of us youngsters everything.

At that first training session I wanted to show that I was the best trainer – how times changed later in my career – that I was the man, even at tick-and-pass. Whatever I did I wanted to be a winner. I'm a shocking loser at darts, dominoes, whatever I'm a terrible loser. I'll throw a strop if I don't win a game of poker. I've just always had that winning mentality. Luckily, I was thrown in at the deep end after two training sessions and on the Friday I was picked to play in my first 'A' team game, away to Liverpool Stanley.

We played them at Knotty Ash, the old ground. I think I had a good game. I played at centre to a young lad called Phillip Eastham, a great winger. I think we scored more centre and wing tries in that season after I signed than what Boston and Ashton or anybody ever scored at Wigan in the 'A' team.

We had a superb centre-winger relationship and against Liverpool Stanley we won quite convincingly. I scored a couple of tries and kicked three goals. We had a really good 'A' team and won the 'A' team competition that year in dramatic circumstances. The following week, I was selected to play at home at Central Park, on a cold, muddy night, against Workington Town. It was the first of many interesting clashes against them.

To play a game on that sacred ground, Central Park, was fantastic. It was a dream I had had from watching my first game on television. I had gone from standing on the Spion Kop, when I used to watch other players playing on that pitch, to now supporters watching me play. The 'A' team used to get a good crowd then with 3,000 to 4,000 watching us.

Playing against Workington Town, little did I know that with still being a trialist, 'A.N. Other', that other clubs were waiting outside to talk to me. I didn't know, but Wigan did. Straight after that game I didn't go into the dressing room, the directors were waiting for me. Martin Ryan and Billy Woods were waiting at the end of the tunnel. From the pitch we bypassed the dressing room and they took me straight into the board room.

I had played a storming second game, which we won, and I scored one of the best tries they said they had seen at Central Park. I remember Workington kicked off, I caught the ball five yards off my own tryline and just stepped, stepped, stepped, and stepped all the way under the posts. I think I scored four tries that night and I think Phillip Eastham scored three as we won by 60 points.

With kit and boots on and up to my neck in mud, there I was straight through into the Wigan boardroom. It was an amazing room; I was afraid. I was only 18 and walked into that boardroom full of businessmen.

I'm a kid from Ince and I'm not sure whether there were 11 or 13 directors there, and they were all sitting around a big oval table. The chairman, Mr Broom, asked me to sit on a chair next to him and then they started talking to me.

He said "Listen lad, we have been very impressed with your two games. We have got good reports from Mr Cunliffe and we would like you to sign for this great club, Wigan." Well, I thought then that I knew I would get money; I was elated when I heard those words, and I was that nervous.

He said "What do you think?" and my immediate response was "If I do sign, how much will I get?" Mr Broom said "We have discussed it already and we will give you £1,000." I went "Phew, flipping heck, £1,000." My eyes must have gone tic-tack-toe; I could see the pound notes, £1,000. I said "I'll sign", straight away I said "I'll sign."

Mr Broom said "Hang on a minute son, this £1,000 – we won't give it you all at once." So I said "How will I get the £1,000 Mr Chairman?" When I was going in Johnny Lawrenson had said call him 'chairman'.

He said "We will give you £100 tonight, if you become good enough to play 12 first team games, we will give you £400 extra. If you're good enough to play for Lancashire we will give you £250, and if you are good enough to play for Great Britain we will give you another £250."

I wanted to sign. I said "Look," knowing it was only five pence to get into Wigan to watch the 'A' team, "If you get me that £100 in £1 notes now, I'll sign."

Within five or 10 minutes in the boardroom they put a contract in front of me and put £100 at the side of the contract. I don't know where they had got £100 from that quickly, but they did.

I didn't know till later on but was told that Saints, Warrington and Widnes were waiting to have a chat with me after the game. That was it though, I'd signed for Wigan. I wanted to sign for Wigan anyway; I'd always wanted to sign for the club since watching them on that black and white telly in 1958.

I had signed on the dotted line, a contract for life I had negotiated myself; no, not really – they made me an offer and without thinking, I agreed. But it was where I wanted to be. There were no agents, no-one to do the talking for us; players got what they could and £100 was a lot of money then, as were the other figures that were mentioned.

I've always been told, and it's so true, that average players make a fortune in this game because they go to different clubs right, left and centre. Good players don't make much because they have to stay where they are and that's the way it was then. The only way to make money was with backhanders.

I signed for Wigan that night and I had been in the boardroom that long, it must have been an hour. I went back to the dressing room to have a shower and go home and there was no hot water left. The big bath was empty, so I just put my clothes on and ran home. I was that excited.

A young kid aged 18 running all the way home. I only lived a couple of miles from Central Park and I ran inside the house. Sheila was there, she had got the little one ready for bed and I said "I have some news," and she said "What news?"

"I've just signed for Wigan, I'm a professional rugby league player and I've got £100 for signing, here you are. I playfully threw it at her and it flew all over the place.

To celebrate signing for my home town club, my dream, I said to Sheila "Get the tin bath out of the kitchen". We ran a tin bath and I had a bath in front of the coal fire. That was my celebration for signing for Wigan. I didn't go out; I stayed in and had a cup of coffee with Sheila and a tin bath in front of the fire. And they say romance is dead.

The elation, all my dreams coming true, it was the beginning of a career of ups-and-downs, highs-and-lows and tears and laughter. Not that humble, then the biggest laugh that night, I couldn't stop laughing, I couldn't wait to see Billy Cottam the day after and say 'Look Billy I'm a professional player too.'

Billy was pleased when I told him; we had been mates for years. He was really pleased, I would have loved him to make it as much as I did, but unfortunately Billy didn't. I also told my teammates at Rose Bridge under-19s.

I got drunk with them on that Saturday night. I used to work behind the bar at a local pub called The Squirrel Inn. I had been there for a couple of years. Bob and Lillian Mullineaux were the landlord and landlady, from West Street in Higher Ince. I don't think we spent a penny that night; they just paid for all my celebrations.

When I signed for Wigan, the biggest headline in the following *Wigan Evening Post* was "Wigan Sign Second Eric Ashton," that was a hell of a tribute, no pressure.

I had a full season in the 'A' team playing in the centre at number three. We had a good team and won the 'A' team league that season. We played Warrington in our last game of the season at Central Park and had to win to make sure we won the competition.

It was us or them. We were winning 49–0 and Len McIntyre, dropped a goal in the last minute. He said "I'm just making sure." We won 51–0 and I got my first medal with Wigan

I scored plenty of tries combining with Phillip Eastham, who was one of the most underrated players that I ever played with. Unfortunately for him, Wigan at that time had two good wingers, possibly three and then they bought Keri Jones. Phillip was only a young kid who was drafted in when injuries occurred, he never really got a proper chance, but in my opinion he was a great winger.

It was a great start for me in my first season, winning a trophy with Wigan. I was a professional rugby league player and had a young family as well. I worked at the pub Friday, Saturday and Sunday nights and had my job during the week.

Sheila wasn't working at this time and when we had Carl I wanted her to be a mother and housewife; Sheila has never worked since. Being a mother and a housewife was more important than going to work from eight till five at night. I'm not sexist, I have always been old fashioned, I was the breadwinner and Sheila was my wife and mother to our children.

She brought them up; she has been one of the best mums and wives that anyone could ever have. Later, I abused that with the fame and whatever came my way. I have been with other women later on, but sex was sex, there was no love with anyone apart from Sheila.

At the end of that first season, in the close season, the only time I played again was for Rose Bridge. They had a competition – and still do today in the Wigan area – called the Ken Gee Cup, after the great Wigan legend.

I was allowed by the club to guest for Rose Bridge, with Denis Boyd, in that competition. We won it. A lot of people don't think I signed for Wigan until after that competition, because I had a great time in the Ken Gee Cup.

I repeatedly tell them to this day I had and that's why I guested for Rose Bridge. I'll never forget the experience. We played the final at Central Park on the big pitch which I was used to. We played The Stork, a Wigan pub team and they had some good players such as Jimmy Roberts, Jimmy Akin and Lol Lowe.

I remember Jimmy Roberts kicked off and put it straight into touch, so I've got the ball on halfway at Central Park. John McDonald was refereeing. I said "I'll go for goal". John looked at me and said "F... off, you'll go for goal, you'll never reach it from here." I said "I'll go for goal."

I could hear the crowd in the background. There were about 7,000 on for the Ken Gee Cup Final – it's still played now, but in front of lot smaller numbers – saying 'What's he doing, what's he doing?' Anyway I put that ball high between those posts and we won 18–11. I kicked five goals that night. I walked into my local pub the same night, The Engineers Arms, where I used to drink.

There was this builder friend of mine, Jimmy Hilton, he came up to me and said "Here Bill, have a drink." I had never seen a £20 note and he gave it to me. I said "What's that for?" He said "Bill, I won a few bob on that goalkick; have a drink."

I think I was drunk for over a month on it. I didn't mention to Sheila about how I got the £20, this was my 'winning bonus'. Then it was only a pound for seven pints, some cigs and some chips, so that £20 lasted a long time.

At the end of the season was the highlight of my career. I was an 'A' team player and Billy Boston was my hero; he was everybody's hero. He had his benefit the year I signed for Wigan and he asked me to play centre to him for half a game in his testimonial match, even though I was playing for the 'A' team. My highlight was to pass a ball to him, even in a testimonial match. I was playing centre and had passed the ball outside to the greatest winger whoever played rugby league. At the end of the game I said "Billy, don't retire. I'll make you into a star, but listen to me!"

I was overawed when he asked me to play. I said "Why me?"

He said "Because you're a hell of a young talent and I want you in my testimonial game." I played in that game and we have been lifelong friends. He was the guest of honour at my dinner and I was one of the speakers at the launch of his biography in Wigan in 2009. The game itself was a laugh really; testimonials were not serious games. There were people like the pop star Georgie Fame playing, but to actually pass a ball to my hero was absolutely enormous.

In the close season, May to the end of July, the club didn't have us in to tell us to keep our weight down and we didn't do any training. I was told that I would get a telegram or post card when pre-training began. That was the way we used to know which team we were chosen for.

We used to get post cards on Thursday 'You have been selected for the 'A' team at Barrow' or 'You have been selected for the 'A' team at Central Park.' Later on, when I was on the fringes of the first team, if someone had pulled out then most of the time I would get a telegram saying I had been selected for a game. It didn't work like that though when

I made my first team debut; they came knocking on the door of a pub I was in after hours. It was hilarious really.

Pre-season training was six weeks of constant effort. Training was hard, really, really hard and we knew we had to do that part of it, the solid part of the fitness side. I didn't do anything in the summer, but Ted Toohey was a good trainer.

When I got in the first team, Eric was a great fitness trainer that first few weeks, but I knew that I had that many competitive games that I could manage with tick-and-pass, because there were so many games to keep us fit. We averaged about 40 games in the 'A' team; in the first team the most we played in one season was 53 or 54. Sometimes it was two or three times a week.

After that first season in the 'A' team, my goal was to get into the first team. I always trained hard until I felt that I was fit enough. I used to get bored with it then, but the first team was my aim.

On the attack for Wigan (Courtesy *Rugby League Journal*)

7. Not like this, like that

I began my second season, 1968–69, in the 'A' team. We were doing well because we had a good young side with some experienced players including Don Walker, 'Blakey', and Ray Price, who a young Welsh lad from union.

We had only played a handful of games and the call up came for me for the first team in fortunate circumstances. I'd trained for the 'A' team on the Monday and Wednesday. I got a post card on Thursday morning saying we were at home in the 'A' team equivalent of the Lancashire Cup on the Saturday.

As far as I knew I was playing for the 'A' team on the Saturday. On Friday nights when I was in the 'A' team, I used to have a drink at my local pub, the Engineers Arms. I don't know if it was good preparation for the game the next day, but I was with my mates.

The landlord was Don Thompson, a great bloke. If we didn't have any money we could always sub off Don. We would get drinks off him and pay him back when we had it. I was in there on a Friday night because I loved a game of cards. They used to have a good card school playing 'Nap', the game Napoleon. It was a good gambling card game, good money, so I could win a few bob and lose a few bob too. We always had a lock in on Friday and Saturday with Don, who shut the curtains and dimmed the lights. I remember it was 20 past, 25 five past one and there were two or three bangs on the door.

Well, as soon as there was a bang on the door, people thought it was the bobbies doing a raid. Everybody in the pub was flying everywhere, the back doors open, shouting 'I'm not getting done for after time'. People were under the tables, everywhere.

Anyway, Don opened the door and a few seconds later came to me and said "Bill, you'd better come to the door, you're wanted." I thought flipping heck, it's Sheila; I'm in trouble again. I got to the door and it was Wigan legend Martin Ryan. He was one of the directors at Wigan who I had met when I had signed for the club.

He said, "Bill, you'd best get home. I'll not tell anybody where you were. I've just been to your house; you're in the first team tomorrow. St Helens in the Lancashire Cup at Knowsley Road, somebody has cried off."

I thought, 'phew'. I didn't get chance to tell them in the pub; I just ran straight home because we lived 200 yards away, just across the road. I probably got there quicker than any time in my life up to then. Sheila was up and must have told Martin Ryan where I was. She always waited up when I'd gone out.

She always made sure I was alright. I'm a 'good drunk'; I just want to go to bed and sleep, never a 'trouble drunk'. Sheila would always say 'Do you want a butty before you go to bed?' That's how she has always been; so Sheila was awake.

I think that she was as excited as me. She could see the excitement in me when I told her I was playing for the Wigan first team in the Lancashire Cup against St Helens at Knowsley Road. She tried to disguise it, as she has probably for the last 48 years, but I knew when she was excited. I could tell that she was really happy when I told her.

I went to bed. I didn't sleep that night with excitement and nerves. I was going to make my first team debut. I never slept properly before big games, but that night I didn't get any sleep at all.

I got up later that morning, Saturday 7 September, for my debut and met up with the first team at Central Park at midday. We waited for the team bus to take us to Knowsley Road; I was terrified and absolutely bricking it. I went into our dressing room and just sat there rigid. I had watched them play as a fan. Later that day I became, as I found out recently, the 662nd player to make his debut for this great club.

I was scared of looking round, looking left or right. The players there, such as Doug Laughton, Dave Robinson, Danny Gardner, Colin Tyrer, Colin Clarke, David Hill, Cliff Hill, and Terry Fogerty. I was just a youngster, a kid who's only just come into the 'A' team and they are internationals, established first teamers.

I got on the bus and the first thing that Terry Fogerty, a great forward who sadly passed in 2013, said was "Come on young un, get on this card school here". The team bus had a card table, they were taking my money even before I got paid. I was playing cards with Clarkey, Bill Francis and Terry Fogerty. That calmed my nerves getting to Knowsley Road anyway.

It was the first team players' way of putting their arms round you and welcoming you to this environment to try and take your nerves away. They were trying to take my money as well, because that Fogerty was unbelievable, he never lost.

He would go to an away game and take £2 and 10 Park Drive cigarettes and would come back with 10 Park Drive cigarettes and £6 in his pocket. I don't know how he did it, but he took your money as well. He didn't do it for other reasons, but they were a great bunch of lads that day.

That first time getting off the bus was more civilised then than it is now among fans. As for the teams, it was still as intense then as it is today. I hated St Helens, one of my first memories as a Wigan fan was when they did Wigan at Wembley, that Tom van Vollenhoven try. I detested St Helens as a player. I started off in the game on the wing.

'Ashy' (Eric Ashton) was the player-coach and captain and there was no unopposed game plan before this game in the away dressing room. Whether they had said something in training I don't know; I had just been brought in at the last minute. Ashy never had an unopposed game plan until after the first season I was in the first team.

Then he brought it in. He did his team talk and was an absolutely fantastic coach. He would never rant or rave; he would pick particular people and say 'I want you to do this'. Everything was constructive, everything. I don't think, apart from at Wembley in 1970, I ever heard him tell off anybody. A brilliant player, captain and coach.

I was on the right wing and Bill Francis was right centre. That day Ashy didn't play, he just coached the team. He said to me: "Do your best, give it your best shot if you get opportunity take it, do your tackling." Although still nervous and in awe, I was quite happy with what he told me.

The Wigan team that day was Colin Tyrer, Bill Ashurst, Bill Francis, Peter Rowe, Steve Price, David Hill, Johnny Jackson, John Stephens, Colin Clarke, Danny Gardiner, Ronnie Webb, Geoff Lyon, Doug Laughton. Sub used: Keith Mills.

St Helens had a very good side and put one out that day although I didn't know their players as much as ours: Austin Rhodes, Frank Wilson, Tony Barrow, Billy Benyon, Les Jones, Alan Whittle, Tommy Bishop, John Warlow, Bill Sayer, Cliff Watson, Graham Rees, Eric Chisnall, Kel Coslett. Sub used: Joe Robinson. Many of these players I was to lock horns with over the years to come.

I can't explain how it felt wearing that Wigan number two first team shirt and walking out onto Knowsley Road in front of more than 13,000 fans. It was something else. It was packed, but I've never had any fear of crowds. For me, unless I hear funny quips or whatever, they don't exist. It's just about what happens on the park on the day.

Apart from Wigan then, the speccies were all at the back of the wall. At Wigan they had ringside seats. Fans used to have season tickets for them, a wooden form just off the touchline, all around inside the perimeter wall. That was the only time we had some communication with the speccies.

I remember in the winter there was a little old woman used to sit there on the 25 yard line at the Spion Kop End. We had Colin Tyrer, one of the best attacking full-backs I've seen or played with. He used to take 10 minutes to kick a goal and I'd take the touchline. I loved it because that woman in winter she'd say 'Have a drink Bill, while you're waiting.' There was more whisky in her flask than there was coffee, if we won by 50 points I was half pissed before full-time. That was the interaction we had with some of the crowd; she was brilliant.

Back to my debut, what I can say is how angry I was when we were losing 16–4 at half-time; they had scored four tries and two conversions to two penalties for us from Colin Tyrer. What made it worse was that I had only received two passes all the game and I was incensed that I was playing out of position. I have always been honest and straightforward. I remember barging up to Ashy in the dressing room at half-time saying 'You've got it wrong'. I was this kid just turned 20 years old telling this international legend of two Lions tours, Great Britain and Wigan captain and player-coach, that he had got it wrong.

He said "What do you mean I've got it wrong?"

I said "Look, I'm a centre, Bill (Francis) is a winger. You have got us in the wrong positions, put me in the centre and put him on the wing." Silence as I went and sat down, still angry, but I had got it off my chest.

None of the other players said anything while I said what I did to Ashy. To be honest, and I know it sounds daft, I wasn't bothered. I don't know why, but I've always had that winning mentality. Even then I could see that if I could change something to make it or me better I would. That's how it was then and I have always spoken up.

I've spoken to coaches where I believe they were wrong and I was right. Alright, I'm not a big head; there might be the odd occasion where I was wrong. Personally I don't think there has been one; I think I've always been right as a coach.

I spoke up for myself and Ashy could see that, although perhaps he wasn't expecting it. 'Who's this telling me how to do this?' He often told me later in life that he was shocked and impressed at the same time. He was shocked at the way I spoke to him as a young kid; but impressed with the confidence that I had in my own ability. It was that confidence that made him change me from the wing to centre.

As soon as I put my boots on, I wasn't bothered who was around me, who I was playing with, it was all about what I could do. I could make a difference and that's what I told Ashy at half-time that day. Anyway, Ashy said Bill Francis "Yeah, this is what we are doing" and had a chat with him. After they had spoken, I said to Bill "Look Bill, I'll give the opportunities and we'll make opportunities between us, but you couldn't make any opportunities for me because you are not a natural centre" and Bill accepted it.

I played with some great people – and Bill was one of them – during my career at Wigan. Bill played in three or four positions and I've done the same. Ashy picked us in different positions for different reasons; there were times I played stand-off, loose-forward, gone back to the centre and second-row. Ashy picked a team to do the job on the day.

He swapped us over and I had a great second half. We still lost, but by three points, 19–16. 'Bish' – Tommy Bishop – did us with an interception try which he did very often. The game was on television and I heard from my mates I got some wraps on television as well. Sadly, it was many years before the video recorder was invented, although then I wouldn't have been able to afford one then.

Afterwards I had to ask Ashy "When am I training? Still on Monday?" He said "No, from now you're in on Tuesday and Thursday," which meant I was training with the first team.

Ashy did everything himself, conditioner and coach. I was getting fitter and bigger as I came through the 'A' team into the first team, through natural growth. We didn't do weights. Training was mostly again up at Collinwood, behind where Tesco's is now.

We used to play tick-and-pass, then 20 minutes fitness, then we walked down to the cinder track at the side of the Spion Kop for 20 minutes sprinting. I had a bit of pace and was fairly fast. We all had a similar pace until we signed Stuart Wright and everybody felt like a tortoise beside him. Then we signed Keri Jones from Wales, who was an absolute flyer and enormous for a winger. I was privileged to play centre to him.

Then we would go back for another hour of tick-and-pass, that's how it was. We had games left, right and centre then, that kept our fitness right. Ashy was clearly in charge of the first team.

After that first match at St Helens I kept my place at centre for most of the season, and by the end of the campaign had made 27 first team appearances, scoring 15 tries and kicked a goal. I also won my first trophy with the club; we beat St Helens to win the BBC2 Floodlit Trophy. Bill Francis was our top try scorer with 40, mainly from the right wing.

8. Position change

After my opening season I certainly felt I was part of the team and couldn't really have asked for more. I got my knee right after missing the last few games of the season. I went through Ashy's pre-season fitness training for the first time which was tougher and more physical than I had experienced previously. At the end of it I was ready for the next nine months challenges to come.

The season began on Tuesday 12 August 1969 with a trip to the seaside to play Blackpool Borough. I started this and the next two games as a substitute on the bench with Terry Fogerty. The good thing, if there was a good thing, was that they had changed the rule on substitutes. A sub could come on any time during the game for the first time. Previously it was only for injured players, then for anything, but both were only up to and including half-time. This created problems in the second half if players picked injuries, however serious or minor, or things were not going right on the field. But the team was only allowed to pick two substitutes for each game.

We beat Blackpool 21–13, which was a harder game than usual against them. I came off the bench to replace Dave Hill. Next up was Salford at home in the opening round of Lancashire Cup which we won 25–9. This time I came on for the injured Colin Tyrer, who had already scored a try and kicked a goal. I went over for my opening try of the season and converted four goals. I'd already beaten my goalkicking record of one from the previous season.

Colin was a great kicker and was first choice kicker, I was becoming back-up kicker when Colin was injured or out of sorts. The following game was at home against Leigh. We won 24–8 and it was a lot harder than the score suggested. This time I came on to replace our hooker, Colin Clarke, but definitely not playing there.

I missed the next game, but in the BBC2 Floodlit Trophy, which we had won the previous season I started in the Preliminary Round first leg against Warrington at home. We won 22–6 and I went over for a try.

What sticks in my mind though was when I went over again, but this time not for a try. At Central Park the 'Dougie' side had a very low wall. The dugout was on that side. I brought Kevin O'Loughlin in on the inside on a short ball and Warrington's legendary winger, Brian Glover, thought I was going to hit him. Brian took me over the touchline and threw me, sending me over the wall. I finished up doing a somersault off the wall into the crowd, who caught me.

We took a healthy lead into the second game at Warrington which was always a hard game. We played them pre-season in the Locker Cup, which were always tasty games. We used to knock seven bells out of each other. I played in one of those games at Wigan and Joe Price broke two cheek bones in one game, both O'Loughlin brothers, Kevin and Keiron. He also did my cheek bone in another game against the Wire. I thought that Joe was noted for his elbow cheekbone jobs; he did quite a few that year.

47

I got on the scoresheet in a comfortable win over Barrow and was out injured for a few weeks before returning in a win at Widnes before beating Whitehaven in second round of the Lancashire Cup comfortably. I scored a try into the bargain as I did the following game at home to Batley.

I was in-and-out over the next few weeks. We progressed into the next round of the BBC2 Floodlit Trophy on aggregate, despite losing at Warrington. We also beat Hull in the first round which was to cause a shock to me in the next round.

In November there were again fireworks in our home loss to Warrington on the 5th, three days later, after returning for two games, I scored a try at centre in our win at Huyton. On Tuesday 11 November we were at home to Oldham in the BBC2 Floodlit Trophy second round. We had trained as usual leading up to the game and I expected to play at centre. I came to the ground that night; I was nearly always the first one there. I would arrive early, put my stuff in the dressing room and then walk up the tunnel to the groundsman's room and have a brew with him.

Ashy was also always early and this night, as I walked in the room, he was having a brew. He said "I'm thinking of moving you".

I said "Where?"

He said "Second-row."

I looked at him and said "Ashy, it's hard in the forwards."

He said "The way you can play football, you have got bigger and I think that the switch will make you a better player. I'm not putting you there to work as a prop."

When Ashy gave a team talk he always used to look at me and say "Go and enjoy yourself"; he knew that I could fit into any team plan he had. He continued "You'll enjoy yourself".

I said "I'll give it a shot." What could I lose? I always had respect for the great man's decisions and his record in playing and coaching. I went into, as Billy Boston called it, the pigs. He used to say to me "I would never go in the pigs in the thick of it; you'll never get me in the forwards."

There I was going out onto the pitch wearing the number 12 shirt for Wigan. I didn't know what to make of it. What would the fans think, having been used to me playing in the centre. I took to the position of second-row like a duck to water and I really, really enjoyed it. I didn't mind the physical stuff and had a good pack around me that night to learn from: John Stephens, Colin Clarke, Keith Ashcroft, Brian 'Ben' Hogan – my second-row partner – and Doug Laughton.

Later that season, we signed Dave Robinson from Swinton. He became my second-row partner. A lot of people have said that, together with Doug Laughton, we were the best back three to ever play for Wigan. Dave was not the biggest, but was one of the toughest second-rowers that I played with. I used to love him because he did my tackling. When I got established with him in the second-row we would go out onto the field; he would grab my shirt and say "I'll tackle, get them points."

Even to this day, when we meet at a reunion I say "You look alright Robbo".

He replies "I don't feel it".

I ask "Why?"

He replies "Because I did all your f...ing tackling." We had a good side that season and that great pack was built by Ashy and his coaching brain.

I remembered what our prop forward Danny Gardner, one of the toughest players I played with, had said to me in my first season. I'm glad he was on my side. He was an absolutely awesome number eight, absolutely scary. One particular game he looked at me nose-to-nose in the eye and said "Bill, you should not have just tackled him; he should have been laid in a riposte position with flowers on his chest."

I was more scared of Danny than anybody else. Nobody ever, ever got past me again, whatever way I could bring them down. Whether I knocked his head off or whatever, I was more scared of Danny, that's when I became a player that put something physical as well as skill into my game.

For the record, we beat Oldham 12–0 with my former 'A' team wing partner Phillip Eastham and fellow winger, new signing Stuart Wright, crossing for tries. So we had reached the semi-final.

It was as Ashy had said; it was different playing in the forwards and not the backs. He'd been there himself, albeit slightly further back at loose-forward. I was confident in my own ability; Ashy really was the only person that I took advice from. When I went on the pitch I made sure that I did what I wanted to do. We had good players in the pack, experienced people like Doug Laughton and later Robbie. They knew when I wanted the ball. They knew that if I asked them to run somewhere I would feed the ball to them; it wouldn't be a hospital pass – a Wigan Infirmary pass.

I had an awesome kicking game. Robbie always said "I've never ever seen somebody torpedo a kick so often and as pure as you did." We played with the old leather balls then and I would could make 50, 60 yards downfield with my kicking; no fear. It was the four-tackle era. I wasn't afraid of kicking on the first, second or third tackle if that saved our forwards some work in defence. That's the player I was as a second-row forward. My teammates were sure that when I called for a ball they knew that it was in the best interests of our team.

All the hard stuff; I couldn't give a monkey's if the props did that, I got on with it. When I knew something was on, that's when – as daft as it sounds – I got a bit more space in the middle. I was a blessed player; I was lucky. A lot of it was down to work rate and in that era I played in a tough pack. We would find out early on who in the opposition pack wanted to play and who didn't. We noted the players who didn't want to play. We would run at someone who didn't want to tackle, someone with a bit of fear in their eyes. There were some yellow bellies who played opposite us and that's what we would do.

I had the pace, size and was blessed with my short kicking game. I was noted for a little kick over the top. There wasn't a 'Bobby Seven' then as they have today. That's the scrum-half who covers the short kick. They often put the scrum-halves out wide in defence now because they reckon they can't tackle.

Then I was a vision player. If the full-back was deep I would put a five, six yard kick over the top and catch it – sometimes relying on the bounce. I was fortunate throughout my career that it bounced kindly for me more often than not, and I scored a few tries from them. The only person I can think that I see doing that now – and he's getting all the plaudits and is sometimes a bit petulant – is Sam Tomkins. He hasn't been made into a robot like many of the modern players.

Sam is a throwback, a brilliant player and the way he plays rugby league, he is a 1960s, 1970s player. He can play anywhere: full-back, centre or half-back. I love watching him play, he excites me when he has the ball in his hands. There are not many players in today's game that excite me. He has that short kick or chip over the top that I was known for, and has the confidence to go for it.

He's now gone to test himself in the NRL, the best competition in the world, with the New Zealand Warriors. He could have stayed here in his own comfort zone, but has gone to try to be the best-of-the-best. All the talk in England is about Zak Hardaker at Leeds Rhinos taking his place. But how many real challenges does he have in the season? Wigan Warriors, St Helens and possibly Warrington Wolves.

When I went back to Australia for the Penrith reunion in 2006, one of coaches there in the 1970s, Roger Cowan, said "We got this guy and he went on the pitch and put this short kick over and scored. I thought you lucky bastard, then he did it again, again, again and I realised it wasn't luck." That's the type of player I was and I scored a lot of tries like that for Wigan. With Sam's class I'm sure he'll score even more tries and wow the Australian and New Zealand media and supporters.

Four days later, on 15 November 1969, we went to Workington and lost by one point. My relationship with the Workington forwards really began. No disrespect to Oldham's pack, this was a different animal. Their pack had some grunt, and was an eye opener for me. Later on, I would clash with Bill Pattinson, one of two brothers and a legend there. He was a hard man from Workington and I was a hard man from Wigan. It was a very physical encounter I had to think on my feet for the whole 80 minutes.

Today's game is fast and physical in a clean way. Then we didn't get hurt when we had our hands on the ball, we got injured when we didn't have it with the toe-to-toe stuff. There was a lot of that, a lot involved, the referees would let us get away with a lot. Referees like Ronnie Jackson would see a smack and say 'give him one back and that's even'. There was a lot of leeway. It was not just about football skills, it was about the toughness again, we had to have some bottle.

On 22 November we played Blackpool Borough at Central Park and won. This is worthy of note because I scored my first try to join the real forwards union. It wasn't the hardest of games compared to the following week, a 29–13 loss at Castleford. As well as playing classy stuff, they were as hard as nails, as we found out later that season. It was an unusual game; all our tries were scored by the pack, including me.

I was out injured for a few weeks and missed out on a home draw and 15-9 win at St Helens in the BBC 2 Floodlit Trophy semi-finals. It meant we would play Leigh in the final at Central Park. I wanted to get fit to play in the final and the week before it I was back at Watersheddings to play Oldham and was back at centre. You never lose what you have always had. I had youngster John Whittle on my wing; I scored a try, kicked a couple of goals because Colin Tyrer was out and we won the game.

So, on Tuesday 16 December we faced Leigh in the BBC 2 Floodlit Trophy final. Our tails were up and we thought we would win and retain the trophy, especially as we were at home and had beaten them at Central Park earlier in the season. It was a close game, a no-holds-barred forward battle, and the kickers were on top. Welshman Stuart Ferguson, who Alex Murphy had signed from rugby union earlier that season, kicked three goals. Murph dropped a goal to make it 8–0, but Dave Hill's drop-goal put us back in the game.

Leigh defended heroically. We couldn't cross the whitewash and their flying winger – and Powder Hall sprint winner – Rod Tickle swooped in following a break from Murph. Bill Francis kicked a couple of goals to put us within a converted try to level the game. But Leigh tackled their hearts out to win the trophy. I don't like saying it as a Wiganer, but good luck to Leigh. They deserved to win it on the night and played really well. We were gutted, no one more so than me.

We should have played Widnes four days later, but the game at Central Park was called off due to a frozen pitch. We thought this was good because we could focus and concentrate on St Helens's visit on Boxing Day. My thoughts on them are clear ever since my debut and we had got the wood over them a couple of weeks earlier with a draw and then a win at their place in the Floodlit Trophy. So Christmas Day went, after a great time with Sheila and my family, and I was full of confidence, as usual, when I arrived at Central Park.

The rest of the team was as well as we walked out to start the match. We went from heroes to zeroes in front of 13,845 fans. The Wigan fans were stunned by the finish, as we were. I will never forget this game as long as I live, a born and bred Wiganer and playing for them that Boxing Day.

Back in the pack, I scored the first try without Saints even touching the ball. In a move planned by Ashy, Cliff Hill kicked off, a short kick off, and all the forwards chased it. John Stephens tapped it back to me as I bawled for the ball. I took it and like Moses parting the Red Sea I went through the St Helens defence to score under the posts. I felt like I was in heaven. It was my first ever try against them, after 15 seconds, the quickest try I ever scored. I believe it was the quickest ever scored at Central Park and in the history of the club, including at the DW Stadium, against St Helens. Cliff kicked the goal, 5–0. It was the only part of the game plan that worked that day; it didn't get any better than that for us.

From the conversion, Saints woke up and we got an absolute toasting. Talk about the Harlem Globetrotters, it was balls through the legs, balls over their head, their support play was phenomenal and we weren't at the races. It was one of the most embarrassing games I've ever played in. We got beaten for skill; we didn't even tackle as the 53–11 final scoreline suggests. We were already buried at half-time, when we trailed 25–5. They

51

carried on in the second half as they had in the first with an amazing exhibition of skills on show. After that first minute, their fans loved every one of the remaining 79.

We didn't get done physically because we didn't tackle. We went in after the game. The embarrassment, if there had been 18 golf holes, we would have jumped down them – every one of us, players, the coach and the staff – before the end of the game. In our dressing room, we could hear the celebrations coming from next door. Ashy came in and said "Phew, what can you say?" We shouted "Ash leave us, let us get on, don't come in" and fair play, he left.

We all ripped into each other after that game. We had never been in that position before, we called each other, and abused each other, but nobody took it personally. We didn't get into the bath for over an hour and 50 minutes as we ripped into each other good style. No fisticuffs, no damaging the dressing room, abuse flew out off from everybody. We certainly cleared the air with no stone left unturned; there was a lot of deep soul-searching. Whatever was said behind those closed doors will stay with me. We all went out together that night and got completely bladdered. What we did later in the season, whatever we said – the rights or wrongs, it certainly paid dividends.

To be quite honest, and I don't like saying it, Saints certainly put on a show that day after the 15 seconds try. Their half-backs, little Jeff Heaton and Frank Myler, that outstanding pack, Kel Coslett who also kicked 10 goals, Tony Karalius, Cliff Watson, Albert Hassall, Eric Chisnall, John Mantle and Billy Benyon. They just took us part and tore us to pieces all across the park from one to 15, head and shoulders above us. It was certainly a learning experience for me in the forwards which lives in the memory and still hurts today.

We worked really hard in training leading up to the next game and asked Ashy if we could have an extra session, to work on the offensive and defensive sides of our game. We threw everything into it, calling ourselves lazy bastards and cowards. Don't forget we all worked as well, so it was more hours at the club for that extra training session. I recollect us doing it without Ashy being there, we had good leaders anyway. Doug Laughton, our captain, was a great player and leader of the team, who later went on to be a fantastic coach, especially at Widnes. The toughness leaders were Colin Clarke and Keith Ashcroft who looked after the physical side, they just lifted us.

Sean O'Loughlin is the captain of Wigan today; I played with his uncle Kevin, who was not tall, but yet so tough. I was lucky I played a few games with Keiron, his dad, the following season and Sean is fortunate, he has the skill of his dad and toughness of his uncle. He has merged them together. I played with Kevin, who could beat four or five players and knock a post over before he put the ball down. I was just glad that I was playing with him rather than against him. He was tough as teak.

We were fired up after that Boxing Day defeat on 1 January when we travelled to Wilderspool for the New Year's Day clash with Warrington. Ashy had made a few changes to the team. The squad was ready for the game and those who played ripped into the Warrington for the whole game.

March 1970 Wigan team, ready to face St Helens (Courtesy *Rugby League Journal*)

We had lost at Wilderspool earlier in the season, but at half-time led 13–4 and won 25–8. The turnaround from the St Helens defeat to the win at Warrington was amazing and unexpected to those outside of our squad.

We thought we were back on song, but January was a bad month for us because we lost our next three games, two at home. The last one was home to Leeds. Dave Robinson made his debut for us. We then began our Challenge Cup run which will be covered later.

Our next league game was away to Rochdale Hornets 28 February, after our Valentine's Day clash with Huyton was postponed because of a frozen pitch. We won easily. It was a good away win though we didn't realise the significance of it at the time. We won at Swinton and beat Workington Town at home, when I scored. This took us to Good Friday; a trip to Knowsley Road to face St Helens on the back of our Boxing Day drubbing. We were on the back of a three league match winning run.

I don't know whether revenge was on the team's minds, it certainly was with me. There were only eight players in the side from that embarrassing defeat, including me. Saints lined up with the same starting XIII with Frank Barrow and Bobbie Wanbon on their substitute's bench.

Nothing needed to be said during training leading up to the game. It had all been said that Boxing Day. We walked into the cauldron in front of over 20,000 fans; both sides wanted bragging rights. In another tremendous, no-holds-barred game we led 11–9 at half-time, showed what we had learnt and won 23–16. I kicked a goal.

It was a warm feeling and one of satisfaction as we walked off to the cheers of our fans this time, compared with our last performance against the Saints. We had got in their faces, got stuck in and were so good that we didn't need to use our substitutes. We controlled the game through our half-backs.

We beat Salford to complete a happy Easter. I came off the bench when we beat Widnes, and scored a try and kicked a goal. I loved scoring against Widnes, they were a good side with players like George Nicholls, Mal Aspey and Ray French, who was still playing then in the second-row. We finished the league season with wins over Huyton and Swinton which saw us finish fourth in the table, a point behind St Helens with 23 wins from 34 four games.

We were at home to Whitehaven in the top-16 play-offs. They had finished 13th. We had battered them at home in the league, but lost at their place earlier in the season. They had only lost three times more than us. I missed the game because of a slight injury and they got a shock 20–20 draw at Central Park. We expected to win at home, and again at Whitehaven on a muddy night. I had always said that we could beat anybody on a dry day, but I remember the replay on a muddy Monday night two days later.

The reason it sticks in my mind is that it's the first time that I went to Whitehaven and got hit on the head with an umbrella by an old woman when I was walking off the pitch. This happened again for the next three seasons. We got changed in a house outside the ground and then walked through the ground, through the spectators and onto the pitch.

For the next three years she hit me on the head while I was walking through the crowd, not very hard, but she was funny. At first I was shocked, and I probably came out with a mouthful when it happened. But I just got on with it; I couldn't punch an old woman. If I had got involved in the crowd it would have just escalated, there was no other way to get to the changing rooms and I wouldn't have got there.

Anyway, the upside for her and the Whitehaven speccies, and the downside for us, was we lost a hard physical encounter 9–4; the only consolation was that I kicked what turned out to be my last goal of the season.

9. The 1970 Challenge Cup Final

The Challenge Cup, and the road to Wembley, began on Saturday 7 February. The first round saw a trip to Dewsbury, who had a good side at that time. 'Stevo' played, although I didn't know him then as I did later on in life. He was just another good player there, along with Alan Bates trying to stop us winning that cup game.

It was a tough game at Crown Flatt in front of a good crowd and we just edged through 11–6, I helped by going over for a try. We were drawn away again, this time to face Oldham at the Watersheddings; four seasons in 80 minutes. I remember going over for a try that day. It was on the last tackle and they knew what I was like, I could kick drop-goals. I set myself up for one and three or four Oldham players came flying in. I just showed the ball, went through where they had all come from and scored under the posts. We won 17–4; another tough game.

No cup luck in the third round draw; we were away again, two weeks later to Leigh at Hilton Park. It was an awesome game which we edged 6–4. We were up to our necks in mud, it had rained constantly for two days before the game; it was literally a mud bath.

Both defences were fantastic giving their all and both sides knocked seven bells out of each other, There were 18,500 in that day. The atmosphere was both fanatical and loud, cheering their sides on.

I had a picture of me and Robbo just out of a scrum; caked in mud, our faces can't be seen. It was similar to the famous photograph of a mud-soaked Norm Proven of St. George and Arthur Summons of Western Suburbs embracing after the 1963 Grand Final. The Provan-Summons Trophy is awarded to the winners of the Grand Final and was cast from that picture.

It was a war of attrition against Leigh; full on against our nearest neighbours, never any love lost when we played. They kicked two goals, I'm probably biased, but we scored the only tries in the game to go through and I thought we deserved it, two tries to nil. We knew it was going to be tough after losing to them at home just before Christmas in the BBC2 Floodlit Trophy Final in a close game. We knew what to expect, especially in these conditions.

There were two plusses in that win, revenge for that defeat in the Floodlit Trophy Final, and it was a cup game. We were on a big bonus to win; we knew whoever we played in the semi-final there wouldn't be a drop in the bonus. But the extra money in our pockets was secondary; we were playing the game we'd always wanted to play from growing up.

The bonuses we got were good and began against Dewsbury and then Oldham. We started off with a smaller bonus at Dewsbury. I remember one season after we played a good team; they tried to knock it down because of who we played. We all knew the bonus couldn't be less than the first round, every round it went a little bit higher.

On 21 March we met Hull KR in the semi-final at Headingley. In the other semi the holders, Castleford, were drawn to play St Helens at Swinton's Station Road. When we beat Leigh I thought our name was on the cup, having won on a sea of mud and played all our games away from home.

Like the game at Leigh, it rained all through the game, mud and muck, and we knew it was going to be tough because they had a good team, including Roger 'The Dodger' Millward, Pete 'Flash' Flanagan, Bob Coupland and Phil Lowe among others. The thing that stands out in my memory is the last two minutes.

We have got a scrum out on our 25 at the top dressing room end of the ground where the players used to come out. It was peeing down, and I'd gone to number six and from the scrum I kicked the ball, if it bounced once, twice into touch we got head and feed. Believe it or not, I kicked it straight from the scrum 70 yards, a heavy leather ball; it bounced and landed 10 yards off their try line. The game had gone for them with that kick.

I'll never forget it. Cliff Wallis, rain dripping off him, up to his neck in mud, and he just looked at me and went "You f...ing Lancashire bastard". I'll never forget that and the expression on Cliff's face. We just walked to the scrum, the whistle went and we won 19–8 after leading 6–3 at half-time. I'd meant to do it from the scrum and they had to chase back in those conditions before it went into touch, which I knew it would. So we could play out the clock.

I'm not a big head, it was just the way it was, like Dave Robinson and other people have said 'I've never seen someone put a torpedo up like him.' I know that the balls are different today, but the way I kicked the torpedo punt just sent it spiralling, making sure it shot forward. So once I adjusted the distance to two yards inside touch, I knew it would shoot out of play.

Even though I had switched playing positions that season, I still used to practice my kicking all the time. I would stay behind after training. There's an old saying that 'practice makes perfect'. That's rubbish, perfect practice makes perfect. I would position myself on different parts of the pitch, use tin cans at different places on the touchline as targets and practice kicking to those positions.

I always worked and worked at my kicking. It wasn't luck I developed it, I could turn and bounce the ball within a yard of the touchline. We had to bounce it in touch from the field of play and then we would get head and feed at the scrum. I worked on it and it came off big time in the closing minutes of that semi-final.

In Australia, I got a reputation of being one of the best kickers the game over there, long open field play. I remember making Easts' Russell Fairfax looking silly, it was not how, it was when; I had no fear factor. The sad thing in today's game there is too much fear factor; express it. They call them 40–20s now.

When the referee blew the whistle at full-time in the semi-final it was a fantastic, fantastic feeling. A thousand and one things flashed in my head; we had got to the Challenge Cup Final. I was going to Wembley to play in the game, achieving one of my dreams, wearing the cherry and white of Wigan. My dream had started when I saw Wigan at Wembley in 1958 on the black and white telly at my mam's.

The celebrations in my day were completely different to today. There was no running round; bouncing off each other, we just took it in a quiet manner, shaking hands with teammates, shaking hands with the opposition. Into the dressing room, all smiles, all laughs; the chairman had got us a couple of bottles of champagne to celebrate.

After the game, we had some players who wouldn't spend a flipping penny. We got bathed, changed and everything and went to the bar saying we were staying out for the night. Keith Ashcroft, who has now sadly passed away, bless him, said "First round". There were only five of us; he got the order in, got the drinks, came back and said "Listen Ashy, can you lend me 1/9d (8p)."

He'd not got enough for a round. Keith was a typical thrifty prop, but we did have a good night after that win. I couldn't sleep that night, anyway, knowing what I had achieved. The sad thing was though a few days later John Stephens broke his leg in a league game against Widnes and couldn't play in the final.

It was a very good pay day, winning the semi-final, including the bonuses. There was also the 'other bonus' at half-time when we only led by three points. Some extra financial incentive on the table at half-time, we were on £140 for winning. Think about that, what it was worth in 1970.[2]

The build up for the Challenge Cup Final at Wembley 1970 was fantastic. We would be playing the holders, Castleford, who had beaten St Helens 6–3 two weeks after our win. I had never experienced anything like it before; we were measured up for our Cup Final suits a couple of weeks before the final; royal blue suits, white shirt and blue tie.

In the week building up to the game, we trained on the Monday morning, stayed together afterwards and were taken for a meal at a posh place in Wigan. On Tuesday, we trained in the morning, played golf in Southport. John Stephens was with us on crutches walking round the course. I took one of his crutches and played a few shots with it.

We were playing for money. I was with Doug Laughton and Dave Robinson and drove my ball in the rough. I tried cheating a bit and put it on a tee by the time they had come across. They said "You cheating bastard, it's on a tee".

I laughed and said "It's not my fault it landed on there."

On the Wednesday we trained and then went swimming at the Wigan baths; then we travelled down to Wembley on the Thursday. We stayed at the hotel where the England football team used to stay and had a light training session after the long journey. We went to Wembley Stadium on Friday morning; looked at the dressing rooms and went onto the pitch. It was 'wow' and that was with the ground empty. That night Ashy took us to the pictures, a Clint Eastwood film; we were walking back to the hotel and came to a chippie.

I said "Let's call at the chippie, I'm starving." I was with Peter Rowe and Billy Francis. By the time we had got our chips and walking back the rest of the players were at the hotel. We walked in and Ashy was waiting: "Where do you think you've been?"

---

[2] Using historic standard of living, the value in 2013 was £1,889. Other indicators give a figure of up to £4,289.

We said "Just called at chippy."

He said "Yeah, did I tell you to call at the chippy? If I had wanted you to have chips I'd..." Peter Rowe was panicking, he went white.

He said "It wasn't me, it was him, it was him," pointing at me. Talk about a grass! "He did it, not me."

Ashy just looked at me, then the three of us and said "You may as well all go straight to your rooms and by the way, I've not selected the side for tomorrow yet." I don't think Peter Rowe slept that night. So he was very, very subtle Ashy; that was the way he coached. By the way, the chips were great. I don't know what the rest of the lads had.

That night I was sharing a room with Dave Robinson. I have never met a bigger insomniac in my life. He never slept, was up all night, walking up and down the room; he was so nervous. Robbo, this guy who played for his country and went on an Ashes tour, was so nervous.

We got up on cup final morning at nine o'clock and had breakfast about 10 o'clock. We didn't have a training session that morning. We went for a walk with Ashy in the hotel grounds. We came back to the hotel and went into a private room. Ashy announced the team. It felt like my first team debut announcement at Central Park. He read the names out, starting at full-back; I was in the team, took a deep breath and felt elated and good in myself. My chippie mates Peter Rowe and Billy Francis were also named in the starting line-up, which reflected Ashy's subtle psychology.

The team that Saturday 9 May was: Colin Tyrer, Keri Jones, Bill Francis, Peter Rowe, Kevin O'Loughlin, David Hill, Frank Parr, Keith Ashcroft, Bob Burdell, Brian Hogan, Bill Ashurst, Dave Robinson, Doug Laughton. Substitutes: Cliff Hill, Colin Clarke.

We put our suits on, got our kit together and began the coach drive to Wembley. It was phenomenal. I know it's changed now, but teams used to drive up right up Olympic Way through the thousands of speccies. For that final there were over 95,000 there. It was creepy; I'd heard about people saying that the hairs on the back of their neck stood up going up towards Wembley and going onto the pitch to play. Well, they did for me driving up to the stadium. It was an unbelievable feeling when the coach pulled up to the big doors of the stadium itself.

We went into the dressing room and I couldn't wait to get onto the pitch. In a matter of minutes all of us were on the pitch, in our suits, looking at the gathering crowd. I could feel and touch the atmosphere. It was a proud moment, a realisation of my 1958 dreams, but this was really happening here and now.

It was completely different to 24 hours earlier when we had visited an empty and quiet Wembley Stadium. I was so worked up; I think I shed tears walking out there. It's different from what it is today at the new Wembley. We couldn't hear the crowd until we emerged from the tunnel and walked out to the crowd and cauldron of Wembley. The absolute noise and pride that was within me in that cherry and white shirt; it was indescribable, walking to the centre of the field for the introductions and national anthem.

Wembley 1970: A clash with Malcolm Reilly (Courtesy *Rugby League Journal*)

I made us favourites. I would because I always thought that we could beat anyone. We had finished fourth in the league and had a three week rest after getting knocked out of the play-offs. Having said that, Castleford had finished second in the league and done the double over us. But with our end of season eight league and four cup matches winning run, could we make it lucky 13?

At half-back they had Alan Hardisty and Keith Hepworth; in the forwards Malcolm Reilly, Dennis Hartley and Bill Kirkbride, who were as tough as it gets. They were a great side known as 'Classy Cas.' Not on this day.

There are two reasons for the way the outcome was, and the way we lost. Luck left us, no ifs, buts or maybes; we can never change what happened. I mean if Colin Tyrer hadn't got 'done' the way he got 'done', I believe it was one of the most malicious hits ever. I did people in my life in the game, but in my opinion nothing as bad as what Keith Hepworth did to Colin that day.

The way I saw it, 'CT' collected a kick, passed a quick ball to Kevin O'Loughlin and literally jumped three feet in the air after an elbow-high, jaw-attacking tackle from

Hepworth. I think that he would have gone to prison if he had done that in the street, that's how bad it was.[3]

Colin was having a good game and was just unlucky not to score a try. If CT had stayed on for the full 80 minutes we would have taken them to pieces. We were creating width and space. Colin was coming into the line, he had kicked a goal in the opening minute and we were winning 2–0.

Castleford came back to lead 5–2 after a Mike Redfern penalty and an Alan Lowdnes try. I helped carry Colin off the field and I can't say what my feelings were when we walked him off in agony. The other sad thing was I was second choice kicker – or so I thought – for most of the season. The second reason we lost was that we got a penalty under the posts. I went for the ball and Doug Laughton bypassed me and gave it to Bill Francis. He had kicked 11 goals that season compared to my 14, but none since 1 January. I had kicked goals in six of the last nine matches as CT's understudy. I was blazing. "What are you f...ing doing?"

Doug said "Bill, he'll kick it."

I said "I'm second choice kicker."

He said "Bill, he'll kick the goal." He gave it him under the posts. He missed it and we stayed three points behind.

We even scored what we thought was a legitimate try by Keith Ashcroft, but the referee gave a forward pass. It was just one of those days we weren't meant to win. It was so disappointing. It just showed that sometimes your luck is out. When Ashcroft touched down it was under the sticks. Everything went for them; I thought they didn't out play us, we had more chances than them, but good luck to Cas. I never had any sour grapes with them as a team, just one person.

We kept getting penalties from the referee, Fred Lindop – who went down in my estimation after his wrong decision – and he seemed to lean to us, probably because he hadn't sent Hepworth off. I know Mick Redfern kicked some good penalties for Castleford, including his second half effort because his captain had confidence in him.

My captain didn't, we got penalty after penalty after penalty and he wouldn't let me kick for goal. I was so disappointed. I said "Look, let me kick for goal" and he said "We'll go for a try".

"Let me kick for goal".

"We'll go for a try," that was the answer I was given continuously by Doug when I asked when we got penalties. So I never got the chance to kick for goal that day. Ashy was not playing; he never sent a message or orders on from the touchline, 'Let him kick for

---

[3] Editor's note: Hepworth's tackle on Colin Tyrer remains one of the sport's great controversial moments, and over 40 years on, Bill is still understandably bitter about it. To be fair, it should be pointed out that Tyrer's injury was not as severe as first thought; he damaged his gums in the tackle, but did not break his jaw. Also, Keith Hepworth was not generally regarded as a dirty player. At this time, a player had never been sent off in the Challenge Cup Final; the first was Syd Hynes in 1971.

goal.' Ashy rarely did; he did his talk before the game and at half-time and Doug, as captain, made all the decisions on the park.

I didn't say a word to Ashy or question him about the goalkicking. I was so stunned, lost for words for once about that tackle. I never got an opportunity because Doug wouldn't let me. I don't know if he thought I was glory hunting, wanting to get my name on the scoresheet at Wembley. Why Doug made the decisions he made I'll never know.

I knew I could kick the kicks, and believed that we could win that final with my kicks. A few years earlier, in 1966, Len Killeen for Saints against Wigan, that final was won by kicks. At the end of the day, a team's kicker is an important part of the game.

We couldn't get at Hepworth because he didn't get tackled again. Every time he got the ball he passed it out quickly, giving the ball out to runners. I think the first Wigan player who would have got to him that day would have done him for what he did. I believe that he got rid of the ball knowing what would happen if he kept hold it. We planned the day after the game that we would have him the next time we played against him, when we played Castleford. Unfortunately, as far as I can remember, for a couple of years he often missed matches against us, especially at Central Park. Maybe he knew what was coming.

I remember when we came home the feeling the fans had towards him, the Wigan people and fans hated him even after he left Castleford. He was due to play against us after his move to Leeds in 1971, but didn't play.

All the players used to go to the Royal Oak pub then. Tommy Dickens had the pub then, we were all in and Tom had a big photo of the 'CT' incident just inside the door. One of the Leeds players walked in the Royal Oak and Hepworth walked in behind him, Tom just grabbed him by the scruff of the neck and said "See that, f... off" and wouldn't let him come in the pub. I'm sure he was hoping he would react, but he didn't.

The referee blew the whistle for full-time and we had lost 7–2. I couldn't console myself. It was the biggest day of my short career, but because of one person I couldn't shake hands. I didn't and I think one or two others didn't, although some did. I was so upset and disappointed; I was still only a kid don't forget, I remember breaking down in tears. Ashy came across and consoled me and a couple of my teammates did as well.

We had to walk up to the Royal Box for our medals, which was even more disappointing; we made that trudge up the steps. We had seen them already go up first, collect the Cup and begin their lap of honour. It was a matter of being given our medals and leaving the pitch. There was no lap of honour for the runners-up.

I got it between 4.30pm and 4.40pm and at 4.50pm I was crying in both my sisters' arms; our Jean and Agnes outside Wembley. Agnes did most of the consoling, it was the quickest shower that I had ever had. I felt that I just wanted to belong to someone. I wanted to be wrapped up; I was like a big baby, so disappointed. I had given my heart and soul. At the end of the day when it's not good enough you know; tears flood and I'm not ashamed of it. What made it worse was when I went back into the reception, leaving my sisters to make their way into London for the train.

Brian Batty, Jack Bentley, Eric Thompson and Jack McNamara all said my name was there for the Lance Todd Trophy. They didn't put me up; they put the wrong one. The press picked the man-of-the-match at Wembley. They said "You should have won the Lance Todd Trophy Bill, but they put up the wrong number 11." Castleford's Bill Kirkbride, their number 11 got it. That topped the day off. I wasn't allowed to kick goals, we lost, I missed out on the famous Lance Todd Trophy, so I had a great day. The greatest day of my life robbed from me. The sad thing that disappoints me, that may upset some players still alive today, is that I had teammates I felt on that day had not lived up to expectations.

We went to our reception at the Royal Garden Hotel, had a meal where everybody made their speeches and we had a special night. Colin Tyrer's jaw was wired up by then, after he gone to the hospital. He could only drink with a straw. I bought him a bottle of sherry. It cost me £3 at London prices which was nearly half my pay for losing that final.

I stayed for a while and then I and a couple of the single lads and went walking around Soho. We'd heard all about it, it was our first time in London; we had to go didn't we? I don't remember what time I got back, I know it was early morning. I only had an hour's kip before we set off to get back to Wigan for an open top bus parade.

We got a train from London to Wigan and this young woman was in one of the front compartments. A lot of the lads had used someone's name to try to 'pull' her. She kept asking their names and they gave the same answer and she said 'F… off, he's already been in. there's not two, three, four… of him'. We had a good laugh with her in between drinks.

We arrived at Wigan railway station and it took my breath away emotionally again. To welcome us home there were quite a lot of fans. We went straight to Wigan Town Hall and went onto the balcony to see and wave to the fans. The dignitaries, Ashy and Doug made speeches to the fans, but to me it was a great experience to see how many speccies were still behind us, still following us, backing us despite our loss. They were as disappointed as we were, there's no euphoria thing when you have not got a cup or silverware with you.

All I have is my memories and a loser's medal which I haven't got now. One year I was struggling with injuries, Christmas was coming and my kids hadn't much for Christmas. So I sold it for £500 to buy them some Christmas presents, so even that memory's gone.

Another disappointment around this time was that the Great Britain Lions squad for the Ashes series in Australia had been announced the previous month. Dave Robinson and Doug Laughton were in it, but I wasn't selected. The press and other people wondered why they had left me out. I was told from another party that the reason was that I had not had enough experience in the second row. My stats were better than those second rowers selected, everybody was saying that I would get in; I was in part of that Wigan back-row with Dave and Doug. That was a massive blow.

It was a disappointing end to a season where I had moved from centre to second-row and missed out on the Great Britain Ashes squad. But I'd played 40 games, scored 14 tries and kicked 14 goals. We'd finished fourth in the league and lost in the Challenge Cup Final. The disappointment didn't last forever; it was surprising what a couple of nights on 'Toby Light' did. I was as right as rain, looking forward to the next season, but had a rest first.

10. Record breakers

These days, in the modern game, coaches and players set goals. All I know was that in my day, I had aims which I had had from wanting to be a professional rugby player a few years earlier and sign for Wigan.

My aim as I began my third season in the team, 1970–71, was the same as always; that every time I crossed that whitewash, whatever the situation, whatever had happened, whatever will happen, was to prove myself. To prove myself people outside the club and within the rugby league hierarchy, but mostly to myself; I wanted to be the best forward in a pair of boots.

There's no getting away from it, I was still angry because of it the Great Britain Lions Ashes selection. No disrespect to the players that they had picked, good players – don't get me wrong, top players, but with the record I had that season, I still feel I should have gone on the tour. Whichever one of them I'd played against I had completely outplayed, for them to get in before me, putting it down to inexperience, was a gob smacker.

I wasn't interested in how they were doing until I heard and read that Malcolm Reilly had broken somebody's jaw. I heard that he was a plane and they were looking for him. Somebody said will Malcolm Reilly stand up, the whole squad stood up, I would have loved to have been part of that. Later on I had the privilege of showing the Australians what I could do, so I had the last laugh in the end.

The league season began on 21 August and we got off to a great start, given the opposition was Warrington at Wilderspool, which was never easy. We won impressively, 17–11. It was good to see Colin Tyrer returning to the side, having recovered from his injured jaw at Wembley, and kicking four goals.

We were on our travels again to the famous slope of Featherstone Rovers at Post Office Road in midweek. We built on the opening win to record a 29–11 victory and I opened my try account with a couple.

We won our next two, including a Lancashire Cup victory over Barrow where I kicked four goals, and I kept up my try scoring run with another double and one in the following league game. Then came another Yorkshire trip, to Castleford. We definitely were looking forward to that with what had happened at Wembley and went there with two things in mind. Winning was not the most important. 'CT' was in our team and when we arrived all we wanted to know was the Castleford line-up.

When we were told it in the dressing room by Ashy, we were well and truly disappointed. The scrum half's name began with an 'H', but it was Hargrave and not Hepworth wearing the shirt. We were even more determined that night. Both teams put on a show and we took great pleasure in nicking it 17–16. Colin kicked two goals; I kicked two as well, which showed our captain Doug and the fans what could have happened at Wembley. Little did I know there would be déjà vu later in the year.

I played in the opening 15 games of the season and did really well. I knew that there was a World Cup in England in October to the beginning of November and that there would be break in the league games. Until the beginning of that month, I had been in a team that had won every league game and Lancashire Cup tie. I scored nine tries and kicked 20 goals, not bad for a second-row forward. I was hoping that my – and the team's – performances had proved the point that I was good enough to get into the 19 man Great Britain squad.

Whatever I wanted to prove, it didn't to the selectors. I was overlooked for that World Cup. The only Wigan players in the squad, despite us being unbeaten all season, were Doug Laughton and Keri Jones. They used to say that the Great Britain side was an old boy's school and it was harder to get out than to get in, well with 13 out of 19 from the Ashes series win that summer it certainly proved that point. The rumours going round at that time was 'you vote for my guy and I'll vote for yours', all the old school tie stuff.

For the record, although I didn't take that much interest, it started on 21 October and ended with Great Britain being beaten in the final on 7 November by Australia, which showed what quick learners they were. It gave me a couple of weeks to get over some little bumps and bruises.

In those opening months I had shown my fitness, especially in two milestones for me and the club. In the Lancashire Cup, after our Friday win at Cas, two days later on Sunday 13 September we were at the Willows to play Salford in the second round. It was the first game our club had played on the good Lord's Day. Salford had a great side and we got a 12–12 draw after being 9–2 down at half-time.

Seven days later, we had the replay. The only slight problem was that we were playing Whitehaven at Central Park in a league game the day before. We won that game with something to spare. I shared the kicking duties with Colin and kicked four goals. The Lord's weather shone on us on the Sunday. It was a glorious, hot day and our biggest crowd that season so far turned up, just over 20,000.

Whether some were just curious or wanted to say 'I was there', I don't know, but I was named in the team by Ashy. He brought Colin Clarke in at hooker for Bob Burdell and Dave Hill replaced his brother Cliff at stand-off with Cliff going on the bench and playing later in the game. It was an inspired selection by Ashy because Dave scored two tries and Colin scored, along with me in a 32–6 win. I don't know what the full-time professional players and coaches would say about that now; some whinge about the Easter programme, playing twice in four days. For the players who played in both it was two winning pay days as it had been the previous weekend with our draw at Salford.

A few weeks later, we lost our first game of the season in the semi-final of the Lancashire Cup to our friends from over the hill, St Helens. There were over 23,000 at Central Park that day. We were 9–0 down at half-time and lost 23–0, a sign of things to come. It wasn't as bad as the previous Boxing Day defeat, but felt as bad. We were poor as a team, it was the first time since I had made my debut that the team had been nilled and I was so poor that day I was substituted. The only positive point, if there was one, is we lost to the eventual winners, but it was Saints.

After the World Cup, the league programme resumed and we kept on winning. The BBC2 Floodlit Trophy continued after we had won our opener against Keighley. We progressed to the semi-final where we again faced St Helens at Central Park. This time it was a cold December night.

It was my first game back after the Lancashire Cup semi-final loss, no pressure then. There were over 10,000 on that night and we were conscious of the last game, more so for me because it was the last time I had played. We were 7–5 down at the break. The second half was a slog and Colin's second goal meant a replay at Knowsley Road. It was shades of 12 months earlier when we had drawn at home with Saints at that stage.

The game had to be replayed the next weekend because the final was on the following Tuesday. There was no way they could change that date. The problem was that we had a home league game against Hull KR on the Saturday. We had to do what we did in September, play two games in two days. Spookily, this time the second one on Sunday 13 December; the club's first ever Sunday game was that Lancashire Cup tie on 13 September. Sunday had been good for us so far, a draw and a win.

We had in a tough game against Hull KR and kept our unbeaten league record with a 19–16 win. I played in both games. The fitness of the team showed as Ashy picked 11 of the 14 players, with a change on the substitutes' bench, for the Saints game.

At Knowsley Road speccies from both sides packed the ground with over 18,000 there. For a long time it was a penalty kicking contest between Kel Coslett, John Walsh, Colin Tyrer and me. Kel gave them a 4–0 lead before Colin cut it to two points; Kel gave them the same buffer again before we brought it back to 6–4 at half-time.

They got four points ahead again before Colin levelled the game up at 8–8. John's kick made it 10–8 before I again brought us back level. Then Saints scored the opening try to make it 13–10. Our heads didn't drop, we took the game to them and five minutes later we took the lead for the first time when our Jones, Keri scored a try. I kicked the goal to edge 15–13 ahead. As minutes ticked down, I thought it was ours, as it had been 12 months earlier, but with just five minutes left, Billy Benyon scored the winning try. He was a name to remember against us, but little did we know what was in store for us. Saints had done us again in a semi-final.

Our next game was on Boxing Day and it was against St Helens, this year at Knowsley Road. Although it was our fourth game against them this year, we all remembered what had happened 12 months earlier at Central Park. We hadn't lost a league game going into this game, had won 24 – including 16 this season and were flying top of the league. Saints hadn't lost at home in the league and were challenging us at the top of the table. They had played two games going into this match, including losing the BBC2 Floodlit Final Trophy at Leeds. For us, after a busy period of games, we had had a 13 days break – a luxury, but no winning pay leading up to Christmas.

In another great clash, we took control in the pack and led 10–2 at half-time. Colin Tyrer and I scored tries – I always loved scoring against them – and Colin kicked two conversions. In the second half, the battle carried on and a try cut our lead to five points, but I had the last word with a goal to win us the game. It was a fantastic feeling beating them, their first home defeat of the season and we had done it. We were still on that winning run – Merry Christmas.

Our last game of 1970 was a trip to Barrow two days later. Great. We won and I chipped in with a try and a goal. Our New Year's Day game against Warrington was snowed off, but after an 11 day break we were back and won the next two against Rochdale Hornets and Warrington. In the latter, Colin was injured so I took up the kicking duties successfully with two goals.

I remember our next game against Bradford Northern well at a welcoming Odsal Stadium. That day as well as playing them, I thought we played the referee as well. There was an almighty brawl, it kicked off good style, I don't know why or how it started. We won the brawl and the game.

But to get to the dressing rooms the players had to walk up the steps of the Odsal bowl. There was a hell of a lot of steps whether we had won or lost and we were packed in with the large crowd. We literally walked the gauntlet to bath and get changed. The speccies were not happy and as I was walking up the steps someone threw a punch at me and hit me on the side of the face.

Instinctively, I just turned round and hit the first person I saw. Believe it or not, I hit the bobby who was escorting us off the pitch and knocked his helmet in the crowd. I thought 'Oh no, what's going to happen here?' The copper came in the dressing room after and said he wasn't pressing any charges, it was just an instant reaction, and was okay. I thought I was going to get done for flattening a bobby.

We kept on winning. As players of most sports say these days, we just took the games as they came. A word they use today though is there was 'intensity' in our games and I hate that word. We just seemed to want to win more than before; especially after that humiliating defeat at home to St Helens.

These days, listen to every coach that's interviewed now: intense, intense. I was once speaking at a dinner with Mike Forshaw from Wigan and Bradford and every other word of his was 'intense'. I was sick of this and I said "Mike, I know what you mean now."

He replied "What do you mean?"

"The word 'intense'," I said.

"What Bill?" He said.

"I go camping every year and I'm always in tents mate, what's the difference?" I said.

He didn't like me taking the micky out of him, but it was a game of rugby league, we did our best. From the beginning of rugby league players did. They wanted to win more and be better than the opposition. We played the game to the full. 'Intense' my arse, it's a game of rugby league.

We played Batley in the first Round of the Challenge Cup at Mount Pleasant with its infamous slope. Batley in January wasn't very pleasant. Keri Jones was on the wing for us, a flyer and although he had played in the 1970 World Cup, nobody ever saw the best of that kid. He had terrible trouble with his hamstrings; he could beat anybody on a sixpence without turning with his pace.

I'll be honest; when he first came to Wigan I played centre to him so I knew how fast he was. I wasn't a tortoise, but he could give me 15 to 30 yards over 100 and beat me. We used to take the micky out of him; he would pull a hamstring or whatever. When he wasn't training, we would say to Ashy 'Don't tell me he's pulled a bootlace this time,' but he should have been up there with the best at the club in my opinion.

He was so fast. In this game he went flying down the slope along the touchline and stepped the full-back. The in-goal area was so small, three yards, and he was going so fast that he couldn't put the ball down and ran dead out of play. It wasn't as good as Sonny Bill Williams in the 2013 World Cup, but Keri had a good excuse with the slope and playing downhill. It didn't stop us going into the next round. The other winger, Stuart Wright, scored a try and I chipped in with a goal.

We won our next league games at home to Huddersfield and Barrow and on the evening of Friday 12 February had a nice long trip to Craven Park to play Hull KR. We had only beaten them by three points at home earlier in the season. They had beaten us twice in the league the previous year and run us close in the cup semi-final.

We knew we were in for a battle royal and that's how it turned out. The game had everything and was a great contest between the packs. We were level at 9–9 as the seconds and minutes ticked by, through a try from Doug Laughton, who was immense that night, plus a couple of goals from Colin Tyrer and one from me.

A draw, which would have been our first of the season, would have been a fair result. But nothing is ever fair, as we saw at Wembley. Hull KR wouldn't go away and for all our defensive strength and everyone playing for each other, our defence was split in the final minute. Their full-back, Ian Markham, scored the game-defining try for a 12–9 lead and when the extras were added there was just time to restart before the whistle was blown for time. The Hull KR players and fans were over the moon. For us, well it was an awful feeling, indescribable, the realisation that our unbeaten record had gone. We had been undefeated for nearly 12 months, winning 31 games and losing our 32nd. Heartbroken, disappointed and was even more disappointing was to lose the record to a Yorkshire team.

I hated Yorkshiremen to start off with, but to lose by a few points in the final minute... It showed the pride and determination that we had for each other that we wanted to keep the record going. The record itself was, and still is, the longest unbeaten record in the history of rugby league in both hemispheres. In my opinion it has never been given the credit it deserves. The only reason I can think it doesn't get the accolades is because it was done over two playing seasons, 1969–70 when we won our last eight and 1970–71 when we won our first 23 games.

I doubt it will ever be beaten, although Australia are currently unbeaten in 16 internationals. The 1982 Australian rugby league team were dubbed the Invincibles and are known as that, this record in my opinion will never be beaten and is not remembered, could we not be dubbed 'The Immortals' and the RFL make a big thing out of it. I'll ask everyone out there and the publishers and editors of the *Guinness Book of Records*: why is it not in there? Why have the RFL not promoted it? That Wigan team from more than 40 years ago deserves better.

The following weekend we went to Station Road to play Swinton in the Challenge Cup. Although not the team they were in the early 1960s, they still had some very good players. It was on a Sunday, the fourth time we had played on that day that season. It turned out to be our second loss on that day following on from the home defeat to St Helens.

We were favourites given our league form, even though we had lost the previous week. There were over 16,000 on that day. Whether they had gone for divine intervention or not I don't know, we lost 8–2. In the second half Colin Tyrer kicked a goal to cut the lead down to a try. That was as good as it got for us because their winger, Bob Fleahy, flew in at the corner. To lose in the Challenge Cup was disappointing, especially after the year before. We wanted to go back again and make up for Colin's injury.

We won six out of the next seven games coming up to the Easter weekend. This included a 10–8 win at Leeds which brought their 57 match-winning home record to an end. With what had happened to us, I knew how their players and fans would be feeling. The only loss was 15–3 away to Leigh where Murph was in charge. He had a good team which had won the Lancashire Cup and was to send Leeds to a shock Challenge Cup Final defeat. In that spell of games I kicked eight goals and scored a try from the three games that I played, including beating Leigh 20–7.

We went into the Good Friday home game against St Helens with an unbeaten home record and needed just one point to clinch first place over the chasing Saints, no pressure then. There were over 24,000 on at Central Park; a great atmosphere was building up ready to celebrate Wigan clinching top spot. At half-time we were trailing 7–6; Colin Tyrer had kicked three penalties for us.

We battled hard in the game to take a point that would see us finish first, but it was Saints who scored the only points of the second half when Billy Benyon did us again with drop-goal to win 9–6. They had done us again at home, but it was not as embarrassing as our previous home league game against them. They had done to us what we had done to them and ended our unbeaten home for the season.

On Easter Monday, we went over to The Willows to play Salford where we had drawn in the Lancashire Cup earlier in the season and had beaten them twice at home. We were confident we could come away with the point we required. How wrong we were. Salford's superstars turned us over 17–6. What a happy Easter that was.

We had lost back-to-back games; we now had to at least draw our last game, at home to Castleford to finish first. A defeat, and a win by Saints the next day, would see them leapfrog over us for the top spot on points difference. We were a bit nervous throughout the game, but managed the win we wanted, 16–4. So we had done the double over them and finished top, two points ahead of Saints who also won.

It was sweet to finish the season off beating Castleford, but could not make up for the Challenge Cup defeat at Wembley 12 months earlier. The only downside was that once again Keith Hepworth missed that game. I was elated that we had finished top of the table, especially after that great run in the first half of the season.

We began the play-offs with an opening game at home to Oldham, who had finished 16th. We hadn't played them during the season. We made hard work of it and Oldham played really well, we got through 12–7.

In the next round we were at home to Dewsbury, who had finished 11th. Once again, we hadn't played them. During that game I did one of the most awful things that I ever did in rugby league and that to this day I regret it. It was close at half-time, 16–12 to us. We came into the dressing room and the basic team talk was that they were a good side. They had a good scrum-half in Alan Bates. Ashy sat us down and said 'You take Alan Bates out of the game and you will win this easily'. I knew what he meant and said 'I'll do it'.

So that was the half-time team talk done. Nothing else was said. We went out for the second half and in the first three minutes I kicked a ball 40 yards downfield. I was running fast for the ball, everybody was looking the other way to where the ball was going. Not many saw what I did. The referee and linesmen didn't because they were also looking downfield. I hit Alan Bates with my elbow really late at the side of his jaw and broke his jaw, cheekbone and nose. They took him off. I had done what we thought Keith Hepworth had done to us.

It didn't kick off because the only people who had seen what I had done were the crowd and Alan. After they took Alan off we scored 20 points in the second half, including a try from me. I felt guilty about what I had done, especially after the incident with Hepworth. I would think that to some I was tarred with the same brush after what I had done to Alan. I went to the hospital to see him after the game and apologised. I don't think he has held a grudge because later I invited him and the team to Penrith.

One or two of their players, including Stevo, knew what I'd done. He said "I'll never forgive you for that." I wasn't bothered about his forgiveness. At the end of the day that's what it was. Nothing kicked off in the game because we would have taken them on in a fight and won that as well.

We were that type of team, we were not going to take a backward step. It was something that I shouldn't have done, but I did it. It was unfortunate for Alan, but for us that win got us into the final because we weren't afraid of anyone that we could meet in the semi-final.

If I hadn't had done it, somebody else would have, because we did everything that the coach told us and Ashy was one hell of a coach. His team talks were so much to the point, so relevant, he didn't rant or rave. He was a constructive coach. He was well before his time, looking at the teams that he had, and succeeded with, that is clear.

At times the game was evil when I played. He was going to cost us winning pay and a place in the semi-final. It was a case of taking him out and win the game, or leave him on and get turned over; so that's what happened.

We were on fire in the semi-final against fifth placed Wakefield Trinity the following week. We had already beaten them twice that season. They didn't help themselves when their stand-off, Jack Marston, was sent off after only eight minutes in the game by Eric Clay, who had already warned him. We had the game won at half-time and were 23–7 ahead. Our only worry was that Colin Tyrer was injured and had to leave the field. He had already kicked one goal. I was the second choice kicker as I had been all season, apart from when I was injured when Bill Francis took over.

We eventually won 49–15 and although I'm biased, we were very good that day. I believe even at XIII-a-side we would have won by the same score. We scored 11 tries and I kicked seven goals. My kicking radar was well and truly on as we reached the Championship Final where we would play St Helens. They had beaten Leeds a couple of days earlier.

We had a couple of weeks before the Championship Final. We had already played them five times and won one, lost three and drawn one. In the build up to the game, the question was whether Colin Tyrer would be fit because of his groin injury in the semi-final. We didn't think that Colin was going to play. I don't know whether he had a painkilling injection before the game. He definitely wasn't 100 per cent fit and his goalkicking in the final was way off target.

There were over 21,000 at Station Road that Saturday, 22 May, for the final game of a 10 month season. Our team was: Colin Tyrer, Kevin O'Loughlin, Bill Francis, Peter Rowe, Stuart Wright, David Hill, Warren Ayres, Brian Hogan, Colin Clarke, Geoff Fletcher, Bill Ashurst, Dave Robinson, Doug Laughton.

In the first half we played into a strong wind and took the game to St Helens. I made a superb pass to David Robinson early on, creating space and a big hole for him to go through and score to give us a 3–0 lead. Colin missed the conversion. We played some great rugby and were on top. I was playing well, confident with everything I was doing for the team and my kicking game was working.

However, Colin was having a really bad day, especially with the boot, and missed vital penalties. A totally fit Colin would have probably banged two, three or even all four over, but he didn't kick one. The groin injury was hampering his kicking. I begged Doug Laughton to let me kick for goal. "Look, I will bang them over. I kicked them from everywhere last weekend, so what's the difference this weekend?"

Doug said "He'll come good." He wouldn't give me the ball and let me kick for goal. The result shows that Colin didn't come good. If he had, then we would have comprehensively beaten St Helens. It felt like the Challenge Cup Final all over again.

Even though we were on top, we went in at half-time 6–3 down. Their captain, Kel Coslett, was having a good day with the boot and kicked three goals: a drop-goal and two penalties.

Although we were behind, we were confident that with the strong wind at our backs we could do it. We couldn't have got off to a better start. After a couple of minutes I took a pass and carved my way straight through Saints' defence and dived in between the posts to score a great try. It felt good. Colin kicked what turned out to be his only goal of the game and we led 8–6.

We had other kicking opportunities from penalties in the second half and with the wind behind us, got into some great positions to kick for goal. The penalties were mainly for scrum infringements, not like today, they were contested scrums: feet up, loose arm, throwing it in the second row (that's what the kids are coached to do these days), offside, collapsing the scrum. There were 16 infringements for which players could be penalised.

We had one of the best and most experienced hookers in the game, the great Colin Clarke who played for Great Britain. What he didn't know about hooking wasn't worth knowing in the era of contested scrums.

On the day, personally I was doing everything right and had a great game. I made a try, scored a try and kicked two drop-goals. I banged one over from the left-hand side of the posts, 20 yards out. The other was bang in the middle of the posts about 40 yards out, which gave us a 12–6 lead. It still wasn't good enough for me to take over the kicking duties and Colin continued to miss penalty kicks for goal.

It got even better going into the last 10 minutes. It got a bit fractious and John Mantle was sent off. I had tackled him and he put his hand down on the grass to get up to play the ball. He accidentally put his hand under my studs. I just stood on his hand and he was very angry with the pain I had accidently caused. He got up and lashed out with a kick.

He only caught me a love tap on my calf and I went down as if I had been shot. He didn't hurt me – he didn't catch me properly. I just went down because I knew the referee had seen the kick and he sent John off.

The anecdote from that for many years was John had a finger removed because it was stopping him playing because it was bent and damaged. Later on, when I became a Christian, I used to meet John at church sometimes. He always led me to believe he had his finger off because I had stood on it; then after about six or seven years he said "No, it wasn't your fault Bill."

So, I'd been praying for forgiveness for getting his finger taken off; been on a guilt trip for a few years and it wasn't my fault. He got the better of me than I did from the day I got him sent off, over the years he got his own back in good style.

With them down to 12 men, we had a six point lead and were in total command until four minutes from time. Saints swept the ball to the left for their winger, Bob Blackwood, to score in the corner. Kel Coslett did what we hadn't done in the second half and with a great touchline kick the ball sailed through the posts which reduced the margin to 12–11.

We were in the final minute. I'll never forget it as long as I live. We were in total control and had possession. Hold it for three tackles and either Colin or I could kick downfield with the wind behind us. Through a combination of our fault and the referee, the defining moment of the final came. We were bringing the ball away from our 25-yard line. Our winger, Kevin O'Loughlin, took the ball up and half beat the defender. He decided to try to get a pass out to David Hill. There was no need to, he shouldn't have passed, but he did and there was a knock on.

From the scrum, St Helens went through three tackles and on the last one – it was four tackles then – John Walsh attempted a drop-goal to win the match for them. He missed by 20 or 30 yards because he miskicked and sliced it wide out. Our winger, Stuart Wright, was in his own in-goal area and just had to defuse it. He let it bounce, but we knew that Billy Benyon was standing on our line when Saints went for the drop-goal.

As the ball bounced it just sat up, Billy took it and touched down. We thought it was a penalty for us, game won. However, the referee pointed to the spot and gave the try. We thought that the decision was disgusting. He was so far offside he looked as if he could have been playing full-back for us. We thought it was that obvious, blatant.

I was so upset at the referee's call; I nearly broke my ankle on the post as I ran up and kicked it. I ripped into Stuart Wright and into the referee. From our kick-off, the referee blew for full-time. It was over. We had been seconds away from winning 12–11 and being champions; instead we were runners-up, and had lost 16–12.

The only thing mentioned in the dressing room was the referee and what we thought was his disgraceful decision. I never spoke to Doug about why he didn't give me the goalkicking duties. A few years later I don't know whether there was anything in the back of my mind when I flattened him in Australia. We didn't speak for many years after that; he's okay now, we've put our differences aside.

After the game none of us asked him how he had given that decision; we had to accept it like every other decision that was made on the field during the game. He was the referee, there were a lot of referees who would socialise with us after the game, such as Ronnie Campbell, Fred Lindop, Billy Thompson and Ronnie Jackson. Some others didn't. We didn't give him any stick after the game; we couldn't do anything about it.

That's why, to be honest, I love watching the modern game. It's not because it's any better than when we played, but I love the technology. There is the chance to check for everything: offside, grounding and so on when a try is scored and there is a decision pretty quickly. I think it should be in all Super League games, today nobody can get robbed like we were.

I will say that even though Billy Benyon was offside and we were robbed of being crowned champions, I also blame Stuart Wright. This was his first final, but he should have caught the ball.

He played for Widnes against Warrington, in the John Player Trophy. Exactly the same thing happened, he let John Bevan score and cost Widnes the final. At Wembley, against Leeds, the same situation; he let the ball bounce and John Atkinson scored. What else can I say; I can't just put the blame on the referee and Billy Benyon, sorry Stuart.

That final was bitter sweet for me. It was so disappointing to lose in those circumstances in the last second. From heroes to zeroes; although personally I had a great game. I couldn't have done any more to win the game apart from taking over the goalkicking duties. I had already kicked 49 goals that season.

We were robbed, as I was of the Lance Todd Trophy 12 months earlier. This time, though, I was named man-of-the-match and received the Harry Sunderland Trophy. I believe I was the first for a long time to receive the award as a player on the losing side.

What would I have given to have been on the winning side and not won that award, created a try, scored a try and kicked two drop-goals. I was a bad loser at the time, but can look back fondly now at what I did in the game. I'd had a great game and I put it down to a bad captaincy decision.

I'm good friends with Bob Blackwood who I coached later at Runcorn. Bob always says "I couldn't believe it Bill, honestly, I was the winger this side of the wing and when John Walsh went for that drop-goal Billy was 10 yards in front of me on the opposite wing. We couldn't believe the try was given, but we took it." I'm sure we would have in the same circumstances; winners are grinners.

I remember that night I got so drunk; I was celebrating or drowning my sorrows at the same time, misery, moaning and degrading because we had lost and against St Helens. Celebrating because I had won the Harry Sunderland Trophy, very mixed emotions.

Now, as a Christian and after getting John Mantle sent off and their offside winning try and conversion it could be said that 'God works in mysterious circles'.

Summing up the season, as a team we were so near, yet so far. We were league leaders and lost the Championship Final in the closing seconds. Along the way, we had become record breakers and that, in my opinion, never be taken away from us.

Personally, I think I proved that I was one of the best forwards in the country. I had proved the decision makers wrong, but was still snubbed; I still couldn't get in the Great Britain side.

Scoring for Wigan against Leeds. (Courtesy *Wigan Observer*)

11. Player of the Year

After pre-season we opened our campaign on 5 August 1971 with the Lancashire Cup first round at Huyton. It was two seasons since we had been there. I remember pulling into their stadium, Alt Park, and nearly every pub and club was boarded up. I wondered where on earth we were visiting. It was a real eye-opener for me and the team, going from Central Park to Huyton, but fair play to them, they gave us a hard game. It was close, Les Chisnall was playing for them and they certainly went for it.

I got off to a great start and scored my first try of the season. Colin Tyrer was injured so I took over the goalkicking and kicked five in our 16–6 win. That was great; looking back it made me wonder why I didn't get a chance in our last game of the previous season.

We got a bye in the next round and a week off. We were into the semi-finals a week later; a trip to Station Road to play Swinton after they had beaten Salford. It was a quick return to the ground where we had lost the Championship Final in the last minute.

With their win over Salford, we knew that it wouldn't be easy and what a good side they were. Also, they had knocked us out of the Challenge Cup the previous season. It was another terrific, hard game. Our defence was superb; we kept them down to just a penalty and won 12–2. I kicked three goals. It was fantastic feeling that we were in our first final of the season and would play Widnes. They had beaten St Helens the previous night.

Before that, we started our league season at home to Leeds, full of confidence after two wins. Our form, especially in defence, continued as we won easily. I kicked six goals. What a good win it was showed because they became champions with only four defeats.

We hoped that we would go on a long unbeaten run, but we lost on our first trip over the Pennines, to Wakefield Trinity. I was among a few players who were injured and didn't play; we lost narrowly.

The Lancashire Cup Final was against Widnes on 28 August at Knowsley Road. I had recovered from injury to play. It was a cup that we really wanted to win; we hadn't won it for six years, and not won a trophy since December 1968, even though we had reached a few finals. After our last final it was ironic that we were playing at Knowsley Road. Everybody was up for it and Widnes had a good side then, Ray Dutton, Mal Aspey and Reg Bowden in the backs and in the forwards John Warlow, John Foran and George Nicholls. It was always tough against Widnes and this was no different. Also, it was a final.

I had a great tussle in the forwards against the Widnes pack. We eventually got on top for our backs to take the glory. Warren Ayres scored a try in every round of the cup; Phil Eastham and Bill Francis also scored. Colin Tyrer landed three goals as we won 15–8.

In such a short time I had played in all the finals I could play in then, sadly I had won two, lost two. I can always say I played in them, many quality players I played against in my career never played in a final. We had a good celebration that night and were paid £150 a man for winning the final; everyone was a winner.

With Super League and summer rugby, the season starts now in February. For everyone to get the barbeques out, the Lancashire Cup and other knockout cup competitions, except for the Challenge Cup, stopped as the sport changed seasons. From a Wigan viewpoint, they won the last ever Lancashire Cup, which now sits proudly in their trophy cabinet.

It was important to the players when I played. We didn't just play Lancashire clubs; the Cumbria clubs played in it; Workington Town, Barrow and Whitehaven. All the clubs competing got some good income when they played the top teams like us, St Helens, Warrington, Widnes and Leigh.

To end it was so sad, the records of those games show there were usually good crowds. Blackpool, Huyton and later Runcorn Highfield – who I later coached and played one game for – teams like that relied on the few grand that they got from the Lancashire Cup. Scrapping it was a kick in the teeth for those clubs.

We won two out of our next three league games. At Oldham I kicked seven goals, which probably helped my ultimate dream, to play for my country. We lost 6–5 at Widnes. That showed what a good performance it was when we won the Lancashire Cup. They had a good pack. It was always black and blue, every hooker when we played in those games was like one of those dogs in the back of a car window. The nodders, there were so many punches thrown through the second row; they were pass and duck games. In that match I got it wrong, took a bad one and only lasted 13 minutes. Brian 'Ben' Hogan replaced me from the bench.

We beat Bramley comfortably at home; it was the first time I had played against them. They had Jackie Austin playing for them, who was a prolific centre and try scorer. I also played in the return at Bramley. I played in a defeat at Dewsbury and at Barrow in the second leg of the BBC2 Floodlit Trophy on a Tuesday. Four days later I missed the match against Hull KR, which we won, because I was less than 24 hours from realising one of my dreams.

On 29 September I made my debut for Lancashire against Yorkshire. Lancashire had lost to Cumbria. We played Yorkshire at Leigh's Hilton Park. I did hope that I would be cheered rather than jeered because I wasn't wearing a Wigan jersey.

Amazingly, I was the only Wigan player in the team that night. The Lancashire side included Billy Benyon, Chris Hesketh, Tony Karalius and my former teammate John Stephens. In the Yorkshire side was Stevo, Roger Millward, Bob Irving and my opposite number Tony Halmshaw. A great friend, David Topliss, who sadly passed away in 2008, was a substitute.

I enjoyed the game, especially being able to hit Yorkshiremen. But they were superb that night and we lost 42–22. I did get some cheers at the beginning of the game, but by the end it was certainly boos and jeers. Roger Millward tore us to pieces with a try and four goals and 'Toppo' scored a try for them. I was upset for obvious reasons; we could hear that lot cheering and singing in their dressing room.

I missed the next game in Yorkshire which we lost, so it was a bad few days for me. I was back in action the following weekend when we played two home games in three days,

76

starting against Oldham. We won and I scored a try. On Sunday 10 October we played against the New Zealand tourists. They played their strongest side against us to prepare for the second test against Great Britain at Castleford the following Saturday.

I just wanted to be top dog, the best, to prove that to myself more than anything else, it was the way I played the game; boots on over the whitewash, I changed into a completely different person. I against the best at the time, because of this and other things that had happened a couple of weeks earlier which I will cover later, I had a point to prove again. Although we lost 24–10, it was no disgrace to lose. I certainly made my point and let everyone know how good my form was and what I could do. I went over for a try for good measure.

After the game I had a drink with the New Zealand prop Henry Tatana and we became friends. We had a good chat. When I later moved to Australia, Henry, another who has sadly passed away, was playing for Canterbury Bankstown before he moved to St George. He helped me a lot when I was settling down at Penrith.

I missed the next four games; we won three in the league, but lost in the BBC2 Floodlit Trophy at home to Widnes. I came back in November and played in another loss in Yorkshire although I scored. We then played in a new competition that the RFL brought in that season, the Players No.6 Trophy, which later became the Regal Trophy. That trophy is also in the Wigan trophy cabinet after they won the last competition before the change to summer rugby.

In the first round we were drawn away to Ace Amateurs from Hull, but they decided to play at Central Park because they would get a good pay day from the gate. We won 33–9 and I scored a first half hat-trick, my second for the club. I was disappointed that Ashy substituted me at half-time. He said he was resting me for the next game with this one already won. I'm sure I would have got another six or seven for a record. It wasn't to be; Ashy knew best. Fair play to Ace Amateurs, they gave everything on probably the biggest stage of their lives.

That win was the first of three games against teams from Hull. We made the long trip to The Boulevard next to play Hull. I used to love going there and to Hull KR's Craven Park. It was always a strong challenge. They never had bad sides, to go and win and to perform as I did that day was great. We won 20–8; I scored a try and our defence stood up to them really well.

Hull had the best fish in the world. After the game the first thing we did was go to a Hull chippy and get a three foot fish, it was gorgeous. So there were two reasons for enjoying the long trip to Hull.

The following Saturday we returned to Hull; this time to play Hull KR in the second round of the Players No.6 Trophy. Once again I thought about them beating us the year before to bring our winning run to an end. The second half was live on BBC television.

In a player's career there are times when everything comes off in a game; a perfect 10. I thought that game against Hull KR was one of my best ever performances for Wigan. We had a good side out that day, as they did, and in a great game we won 18–11. Everything I touched turned to gold. I won the game on my own; I scored all our 18 points with two tries and six goals. Everything clicked and worked to perfection.

Going into December, we beat Widnes. I continued in form and scored a try. Then we went to Headingley to play Leeds in the Players No.6 Trophy quarter-final. We went into the game knowing that we had thrashed them in the opening league game. However, they had come on since then and were having a great season. We had broken their long unbeaten home record last season, so we knew they would want to get one over us.

We played really well and drew 12–12. I tweaked my knee and had to come off. Four days later Leeds came to Central Park and won 12–5. I was really disappointed to miss the replay. We were undone by a good Leeds side.

I was back for the Bank Holiday Monday game against St Helens. Boxing Day was on the Sunday. There were still a lot of us at Wigan who played in the Boxing Day game two years before. We had beaten them since then and lost to them, but for me that loss still rankled. Another big crowd, on a wet, atrocious day when mud ruled the game, saw us get sweet revenge with an 8–3 victory. It was all about defending; both defences worked hard and there were many big hits by both sides. Both sides had tries disallowed. We led 2–0 at half-time. They scored the game's only try, but we stood firm to take the points and bragging rights with two more goals and a drop-goal. I had a good night that night.

The season was going really well for me and the team, although we both had some setbacks. On New Year's Day we lost 20–11 to Leeds. I scored a try against a side packed with Great Britain internationals.

After that, we went on our best run of the season and won eight of our next nine games, seven in the league, one in the Challenge Cup and a defeat in that competition. I remember the Castleford game in January. We always wanted to beat them every time, given what had happened at Wembley in 1970. We beat them 8–3 and I kicked three drop-goals. We ground out a hard-fought, no holds barred win. The headlines in the next day's sports pages were 'Bill drops in to sink Castleford'. Wheldon Road wasn't a place for the faint hearted and we always knew what to expect. Even though our 'friend' Hepworth had left, they still had some good, hard players there.

A couple of weeks later we played Salford in the Challenge Cup first Round at The Willows. It was very close. We were behind in the closing minute when I went under the posts for the winning try. I put a short chip over the top, re-gathered and bounced over the ground which was rock hard. In scoring, I hit my shoulder on the post and thought I'd cracked it.

After the game, two friends of mine who used to live in Salford, Jack and Elsie, took me to Salford Royal Hospital. I had X-rays and it was just bruising, which was a big relief. The following week Wigan were playing Dewsbury and I would continue my dreams elsewhere, still righting wrongs in my opinion. We came out of the hospital and straight to The Angel pub, which has been knocked down since then, across the way from the hospital. I stayed in Salford all night and got bladdered; it eased the pain until the following day. I didn't need morphine; just lager and Guinness & Black.

Ready to attack for Wigan (Courtesy *Wigan Observer*)

Every time I played at Salford I stayed out with Jack and Elsie. I got them free tickets for the games and others I played in. Sheila didn't go to many games and I knew this couple from when they lived in Wigan. They liked watching the games and we used to love it in Salford and Manchester. I never came back on the team bus when we played there; I always stayed with them.

I certainly remember the Challenge Cup defeat at Belle Vue to Wakefield Trinity a couple of weeks after we beat them in the league. Mick 'Moggi' Morgan was a great player for Wakefield. A makeshift loose-forward, he moved to hooker after Tony Handforth – for them – and Colin Clarke – for us – were sent off. It was contested scrums then, not like today, and we never had any possession after that. All we did for the rest of the game was tackle, tackle, tackle. Mick won most of the scrums. We lost 6–5. Bill Francis scored a try and I kicked a goal because Colin Tyrer was injured, but Geoff Wraith's try won the match for them. It was really close and they had to put their tackles in as well. They conned us, a great con job and it worked. We didn't have a back-up hooker when Colin was sent off.

We lost our unbeaten league run at home to Halifax. They were struggling and we had lost a close game earlier in the season at Thrum Hall. But, fair play, they did us again by three points. I played in the next two games which we won, but missed the last five league games of the season before the play-offs began.

Going into the final four games of the season, we had a chance of finishing second behind Leeds, who had been superb, but we blew it. We lost at St Helens in heavy rain on Good Friday and on Easter Monday star-studded Salford did us at Central Park. We beat Castleford at home and then won away to Hull KR to finish the season fourth on points difference ahead of Salford and three points behind St Helens.

In the opening game of the Championship play-offs we played Oldham at Central Park who had finished the season 13th. We had beaten them twice already, and I came on as a sub as we won 18–8. In the second round we were at home to Salford for the second time in four weeks. They beat us again, this time 21–9. Our season was abruptly over.

I finished the season as I had started it by kicking a goal. They had done to us what we had done to them earlier, won the league game and knocked them out of the Challenge Cup at The Willows.

At the end of the season I thought I had achieved everything I needed to prove those wrong from a couple of seasons earlier. I had played for my county and achieved my dream. I received, in my opinion, the ultimate prize; I won the Rugby League Players No.6 'Player of the Year' which was in its fifth year, the forerunner for the now newly named 'Steve Prescott Man of Steel'.

At the time there were 30 professional clubs playing rugby league and each club could vote for six players other than one of their own. I pinched myself when I was told that I had won it, I was first with 69 votes, Alex Murphy second with 44 votes and Kel Coslett third with 38 votes. I had always thought that I was the best at my position, but to be voted the best by all the clubs and players, well... I knew that Roger Millward had won it a few years earlier so I had joined some good company.

That year we got £6 from Players for being named man-of-the-match. I did very well that season and it all went into the players' kitty for the end of season 'do' in Blackpool. I've still got the base of the trophy at home; the kids broke the top. I went to take the trophy back intact and they said I could keep it, they didn't want it. It might be battered now, but I am still proud to have won the accolade of being the number one player that season.

12. Problems at Wigan

The close season came and went quickly. I was still working on building sites for Gerrards Building Company, keeping myself fit. Going back to training was different, but I soon got to where I was happy my fitness for the amount of games we played, not though perhaps in Ashy's eyes.

For the 1972–73 season, Wigan decided to play all their games on Friday nights, hoping after the game the fans would go next door to the Riverside Club and have a good night out. This certainly suited me. The club was also celebrating its centenary and had arranged to play Australia at Central Park after the World Cup in France. The six tackles that the sport now uses came in, but with a scrum after the last tackle. This meant more work on the field, but also more chance to create, score and have the ball in hand.

We started with the Locker Cup game against Warrington and the Sevens at Central Park. I had a niggling injury and missed the opening two homes games. We won the opener against Featherstone Rovers but lost to Stevo's Dewsbury. They later did the double over us and were crowned champions at the end of the season. Once again there wasn't going to be a long unbeaten run in the league.

Eager to play, my season began with a trip to the seaside on 26 August to play Blackpool Borough. Wigan legend Ces Mountford had just joined Blackpool as manager, but it didn't matter to us because we won 46–8, including my first try of the season. It was looking good. That was the start of a run of five games for me. In the each of them I kicked drop-goals for fun. We won the first three and then lost at Whitehaven and Warrington.

It was a great start for me with the Great Britain World Cup squad to be named in less than a fortnight. Jim Challinor, the coach of Great Britain and St Helens, had told me I would be in that squad. Then came a bolt from the blue that destroyed my hopes; from someone who never played the game and changed my career at the end of that season.

I broke my elbow in the defeat at Warrington, the week before we were going to play Wakefield Trinity in the Players No.6 Trophy at Central Park. People used to run onto my elbow in those days, you know what I mean, they were stupid and I had broken it. I turned up for training on the Tuesday and Thursday, and as much as I loved playing, I wasn't right to train, never mind play. Ashy said "If you're not fit, the board want to see you."

I replied "Ashy, you know I have broken my elbow. I can't play."

Ashy took me into the boardroom and I sat around the table. Four directors were there, Mr Bibby, Mr Woods, Mr Broom and I think Mr Gostelow. Mr Bibby asked why I could not play against Wakefield and I said "Mr Chairman, I've broken my elbow."

My impression was of a chairman who smoked cigars and drank whisky, but did not have a clue about rugby league. He said "Have a needle."

I replied "Look, if it was a muscle I've had many a needle to get through a game. It's a break in a place where the first point of injury is your elbow."

He replied that if he had his way, if I didn't play against Wakefield I would not play for the club again. That was like a red rag to a bull. I said "Listen then, Mr Chairman, if that's the way you want it, I don't want to play for Wigan again. Put me on the transfer list, I will not play for this club again." I walked out of the boardroom, got changed and went home. Within a couple of days the club publicly made it official that I was on the transfer list for a record £22,000. Also, I was suspended by the club, because the directors thought that I had refused to play against Wakefield Trinity.

He may have owned the club, but nobody owned me. I was always my own man and was adamant that I would never play for Wigan again. I wanted an apology from Mr Bibby and made that public to the press.

When the Great Britain World Cup squad was named on 4 October, I wasn't in it because I was suspended. I suppose the RFL had to back him as they did in those days. In reality players were like a piece of meat to the owners, who wanted us to put our health on the line. I have that much pain now, having put my body on the line for people like him; thank God times have changed. Today there is more concern about players' welfare and they have a say and opinion.

After nearly three weeks of meetings with this man and the Wigan directors, agreement was reached. I got an apology, was taken off the transfer list and the suspension lifted.

Although I was not right, I was brought into the Lancashire squad that to Castleford to play Yorkshire on 11 October. We lost 32–18, although with extra padding and strapping I did my best to show what I could do. Still out injured, I missed another five games until the elbow was right. The weekend I played again it was the World Cup Final, Great Britain against Australia in France. Not only had I missed the Wakefield game, I had missed nine games in all. I couldn't have made the Great Britain squad anyway, because of my injury; it was the principle of the original decision that led to me being suspended by Wigan.

It was a tremendous World Cup for Great Britain. I watched it on television screaming as Clive Sullivan stormed down the wing to score. I even screamed for Stevo to score. I love seeing Aussies cry, they can't take a joke. Clive made them cry that day; it was sweet. He was a great player who had pace and for a small guy had tremendous strength, a great side-step and swerve. Such a gentlemen, a great bloke and as I've said to his son Anthony many times, it was a pleasure knowing him, not just playing with or against him.

The day before that final I was picked for the Wigan 'A' team to test my fitness and see if my elbow had recovered. I was doing well in the game until a Barrow player ran high into a tackle I made. Two things happened, my elbow had passed its test with no pain and I got sent off in a game the 'A' team drew. Ashy couldn't believe it, but the next day I was in the first team that went to Barrow won comfortably. I was knackered after playing the whole 80 minutes after so long out.

On Friday 17 November was the Centenary Celebration Match against Australia at Central Park. What a great night, playing against the side Great Britain had beaten in the World Cup. It was chock-a-bloc; people climbed in over the 'Dougie' walls to see the game. Australia had a great side out that night including Arthur Beetson, John O'Neill, Bobby

Fulton, Mark Harris, Tommy Raudonikis, Bob O'Reilly, Elwyn Walters, Bob McCarthy and Ray Branighan. To even come close and draw with them was a great result. We played superbly on the night to recover from two interception tries; we even had a chance to win it with the last play.

Billy 'Daz' Davies, our stand-off, gave a soft interception to Bobby Fulton. Then the great Doug Laughton gave Fulton another interception on our '25' and he scored under the posts. He added a third. Trust a Brit from Warrington to stop a British side winning. Seriously, what a great player for Australia he was. Geoff Starling scored their other try and Ray Branighan kicked the goals

I had one of my best games ever in a Wigan shirt that evening; I tore the Aussies to pieces, and created tries for David Hill and Keiron O'Loughlin. Colin Tyrer kicked four goals and I added two drop-goals; the last one in the closing minutes to level it at 18–18. In the closing seconds we had the chance to win as we went downfield.

I'll never forget it. We were under the Australian posts, Jimmy Nulty was acting half-back and I was screaming 'Jimmy, drop-goal, we win'. He got the ball, scooted and decided to go for it himself and got tackled. There was no way he was going to get over the line. He went on his own and the final whistle went. I was set right behind him; two points – game over.

I was blazing. I picked him up by his neck and then put him down. That was the end of the game, 18–18. What a game. I would have got the keys of Wigan that night. I am sure I would have dropped the goal if the ball had come out to me, as it should have done.

I believe that Penrith said that from that performance against Australia they decided to sign me. The Australia coach was former Warrington legend Harry Bath. He knew Penrith were looking for players to sign, but didn't say anything to me. I think that Bath sent a message back to Penrith: 'Come and get this kid from Wigan, he is the best second-row I've seen in Pommie land.'

That night I had my first close encounter with a true rugby league legend, Artie Beetson. He was a powerhouse in the Australian pack. Artie was such a character, literally a gentle giant, but on the park he was fast, strong, had every aspect of the game and his pace for a big man was phenomenal. As a ballplayer he was sublime. Years before I admired Wigan and Great Britain forward Brian McTigue, but Artie Beetson... You could put a pack of cards around him and he would still get the pass away, a superb footballer.

Many years later they had a series in Australia called *Warhorse* and Artie was a true Warhorse. I was shocked to hear the news when he passed away in December 2011, aged just 66. He had only just gone back home to Australia because he had been over here for the Four Nations.

I spoke to Artie at a hotel in Leeds after the Four Nations Final between Australia and England. He had brought a touring party over and I was fortunate to spend 15 minutes in his company. He still had that charisma, we were both a lot older, but we had a good chinwag. To have known him and played against him is something I will remember and cherish. Arthur 'Artie' Beetson is probably the best player I played against. He was the complete player for a forward. I would not say the toughest, but as a complete player the best I ever played against.

Back with Wigan, we won two league games, but then blew it in the second round of the BBC2 Floodlit Trophy. We lost at home to Leigh after leading at half-time. I wasn't happy; we should have held on and made the semi-finals but it wasn't to be. Leigh went on to win the final.

We then lost at home to Widnes before going on our best run of the season, winning five of our next six league games and drawing at St Helens on Boxing Day. During that run we also just got the better of Leeds at Central Park, who had thrashed us by a record score in October. We lost at Whitehaven and then won our next four, including two wins in the Challenge Cup.

We travelled to Headingley to play Leeds, who were the cup holders, in the first round. After that record loss we were big underdogs. This was the £400 game. I had been poorly all week and couldn't train. The club gave me some tablets and I was told to go home and go to bed. On Friday morning Martin Ryan came to my house, a different situation from when he found me in the pub for my debut. He asked "Are you playing tomorrow?"

The game was on television. I said, "I'm bad, I'm poorly, I can't play."

He asked "How much will it cost us?"

I said "I'll play for £400."

Martin replied "No problem. I'll sort it with the board and we'll pick you up at the top of the street tomorrow."

The team bus came to the top of my street. We went to Leeds, played the game and I kicked four goals. We won 25–11. I came back home, they gave me a brown envelope, dropped me back at the top of the street and I went back indoors and went back to bed. That was on top of winning pay and another good bonus for winning at Leeds. As a team it was a very good day; a great performance from the team and me.

In the second round we were at home to St Helens, who had lost to Leeds in the final in 1972. There were over 27,000 on Central Park. We well and truly toasted St Helens 15–2. The highlight though – and I gave him stick earlier on in this book – was Stuart Wright, who went the length of the field to make sure we went through, to the joy of our supporters. The players were on a good bonus that day and quite right too. We had now knocked both of last year's finalists.

There was no love ever lost beating St Helens. Now all these Australians come over and play, but they will never really know or feel what it like to play in a derby. Unless you're a born-and-bred Wiganer or St Helener you don't know what it's about. Bill Shankly once said 'It's more important than life itself'. To win the derby game was everything, especially for the fans. As a Wigan lad, when we toasted them we always had a good night afterwards. Whoever we played in the season and whoever we beat, we had to win the Saints games.

In the Challenge Cup third round we were drawn to play Bradford Northern at Odsal, but the week before we had play there in the league. Going into that game we knew that the RFL had made what I thought was one of their dafter decisions. They decided all of a sudden how the league would change after the final two months of the season

I wouldn't call it the St Valentine's Day massacre, but on 16 February the RFL decided at an Extraordinary General Meeting that at the end of the season the league would split into two divisions. The top 16 teams would be in the First Division and the unlucky bottom 14 clubs would be in the Second Division. After our league win just before that decision we were okay, but not anything like the previous season, we had 29 points having won 14 and drawn one of our 29 games.

I believe Ashy's decision for the league game against Bradford cost us the cup game the following week. He rested a large number of the first team squad and chose players from the 'A' team. He left six of us out: me, Stuart Wright, David Hill, Jimmy Nulty, Colin Clarke and Doug Laughton. Ashy was confident we could win the league game with the team he chose and didn't want any injuries for the cup game. If we had fielded a full team for the league game and won, I think we would have gone to play the cup game with our tails up.

Well, it didn't work out. Bradford Northern were really up for the league game and needed the points to try and get into the top 16. In the first half, Colin Tyrer was sent off for a high tackle on one of their substitutes and we were ahead. But in the final minute a mistake cost us the game and the points. Despite that loss we were 12th in the league with eight games left.

The six of us came in and Ashy made six positional changes. only Colin Tyrer and Alan Bence stayed where they were. It was a tough physical game and from the start we could tell they were really up for it after their win the week before. Bradford played very well that day. We were level at half-time, 7–7. I had gone over for a try.

It got even tougher for us in the second half. We gave a penalty away; 9-7 and we got a penalty under the posts. The referee warned both sides 'That's it, there's no more.' Colin missed the goal which would have put us level again. Then Colin Clarke got sent off, they kicked another penalty. We were down to 12 men and crashed out of the cup. I was so upset – we had beaten Leeds and Saints. I thought our name was on the cup; the defeat was like losing a cup final.

I missed our next game against Leigh. We lost and dropped to 13th in the table. I played in the next four games, starting at Dewsbury. They were on fire and we lost 25–14. We had dropped to 16th and next up was Rochdale Hornets at the Athletic Ground. They were 17th, so it was a battle for 16th place in the league. We were rubbish that day, worse than in the record loss at Leeds earlier in the season. We were battered 22–8 after being 15–3 down at half-time. Rochdale, who finished the season 11th, moved up a place and all of a sudden we were in a relegation position.

We had to win at home to Swinton, who were also fighting to be in the First Division. The first half was as bad as at Rochdale and we were 7–0 behind at half-time. Ashy said some sharp words; somehow we won 10–9 and were back in 16th place. Next was a home game with Warrington. They showed their class and at half-time we were 13–0 down. We improved, but lost and were now 17th. There were three league games left in six days going into the Easter week; two against Salford and the derby against St Helens. They were both battling to catch Warrington.

Salford came to Central Park with all their stars, but what a difference a week made. We realised that our great club, from thinking we were going to Wembley, was going to be relegated, thanks to the RFL, if we didn't start winning. I don't know how we did it, but we won 23–6. That win saw us leapfrog Halifax for 16th.

I picked up an injury and missed the St Helens game, which we had to win at all costs, at Central Park on Good Friday. With over 13,000 on, we led 4–2 in the first half, in a fierce game which both sides needed to win for different reasons. In the second half two vital tries and a conversion saw us home 12–2.

We had edged up the table a couple of places as we went to The Willows to play Salford. This time they won; we dropped down again, but finished in that crucial 16th position over York on points difference. It was thanks to our great defence throughout what for the club and me was an eventful season. What a relief, it would have been a disaster if we had been relegated.

I came back for the Championship play-off game at Wilderspool against Warrington who had finished the season as league leaders under Alex Murphy. Apart from losing 30–15 I remember the game for three reasons. I finished the season as I'd begun it, kicking a goal; it was my final game for Wigan at that time and I flattened Murph. I'd waited five years to do what I did to him that day. The game was gone for us, going into the last 10 minutes. I knew we couldn't come back. I saw the ideal opportunity when Alex went blindside with his head up. I just hit him with my elbow, shoulder, knees and as he was going down finished it with a head butt. I was getting my own back for an incident many years earlier. I hated those who used their feet. I didn't kick him.

I wasn't wearing my boots on my knees. Billy Thompson was the referee. He came over to me and I said "I know Bill, I'm going". He didn't need to point to the dressing room. I remember Kevin Ashcroft came running towards me. Billy Thompson shouted "Stop in your tracks, Kevin." Kevin shouted "Why?"

Billy shouted "Kev, there's room at the side of him and you'll end up next to him."

I just walked off Wilderspool to boos and venom from the Warrington fans and that was it. I smiled as I saw them carry Murph off on a stretcher. He wasn't winking this time.

I'd had an up-and-down season, a great time playing wise, a superb time off the field and happy times generally. But it was coming to the end with people like the chairman and what he had done earlier in the season. I couldn't forgive him, even though I was injured I felt I would have been picked for the Great Britain World Cup squad and that they would have had players on standby if I hadn't recovered, which I didn't at the end of the day.

I had a fantastic five years at Wigan. I was revered by the crowd which meant more than anything. When there are 26,000 speccies and most were shouting 'King Bill, King Bill Ashurst', then a lot of people thought a lot about me. I had some wonderful teammates, good times off the pitch and loved every minute of it. One thing's for sure, Wigan certainly got their money's worth from my £100 worth of flesh.

13. Great Britain

I had enjoyed two fabulous seasons for Wigan, but somehow couldn't break into the Great Britain side. At the end of 1969–70, people were telling me to pack my bags for Australia. I didn't and we won the Ashes.

In 1970–71 I began superbly and hoped to get into the Great Britain World Cup squad for a home World Cup. Again I didn't get a call up. As that season continued, both Wigan and my form got better. In February and March 1971, we had a two test series against France, starting with the away game.

I was told by everyone again that I would be in the squad, but there was more disappointment when I wasn't selected again. The team went to France for the first game and lost 16–7. They lost because the forwards hadn't gained the upper hand so I thought I might be chosen for the March return match. Again, there was no call up; Great Britain got revenge, and won the second test 24–2.

As the 1971–72 season began, I thought just keep my head down and prove to everyone that I am the best second-row in the country because the Kiwis were coming over for a three test series. If it happened, so be it; if not just get on with it.

My form was good again and the press rumour mill began. My name was mentioned and that's how players found out what was happening then. The team was named in the newspapers. The RFL sent a letter to the player's club, and one to the player. It said that you had been selected for the Great Britain squad and when to turn up for training.

When the letter came, I had no idea what it was going to look like; but it had a Leeds postmark. I excitedly opened it and quickly read what it said. I took a deep breath and slowly read it several times. I was selected to train and play for Great Britain against New Zealand. That's what stuck in my mind; I just stared at the letter feeing warm, proud, fantastic; to know I had been picked was a dream after watching that Cup Final on television in 1958.

All I had wanted to do was play for Wigan and Great Britain. I had played for Wigan and now I was going to train and play for my country. I was achieving the pinnacle of any sport, for me in rugby league, putting on that white with red and blue 'v' shirt. It was a tremendous achievement for me.

The Great Britain coach was Jim Challinor. He was a great bloke who used to play for Warrington, and a great coach. So at 3pm on Saturday 25 September 1971 I walked behind the coach and some of my teammates, wearing a Great Britain shirt, onto the field at The Willows to face New Zealand in the first test. The team that historic day for me was: Derek Whitehead, Les Jones, Billy Benyon, Chris Hesketh, Clive Sullivan, Roger Millward, Steve Nash, John Warlow, Tony Karalius, David Jeanes, Bill Ashurst, Mike Coulman, John Mantle. Subs: Derek Edwards, Vince Farrar.

There was emotion in my debut for my country. I stood singing the national anthem with tears rolling down my face. I wore my heart on my sleeve. If there had been close up cameras like now, I would have flooded the camera. It was such a proud, proud moment for me. We were introduced to Lord Derby and stood and watched the New Zealanders perform the Haka. The game kicked off in front of a small crowd of 3,764. That didn't matter, I was playing for my country and the game mattered to me.

We got off to a great start, attacked New Zealand and scored our first try in the early minutes when Billy Benyon finished off a move involving Tony Karalius and our captain, Roger Millward. I started off really well with some good touches and drives and hard tackling. My debut got even better when I ran at the New Zealand defence, chipped over and caught the kick to score. Derek Whitehead converted. I was in dreamland as we were 8–0 ahead. I had tried some individual skill like I did every week for Wigan and it came off.

New Zealand replied with a superb try from Dennis Williams. He beat a couple of tackles, side-stepped and ducked his way to a try. They converted it and a penalty by Henry Tatana made it 8–7. We had a game on our hands; I began going for bigger drives and bigger hits.

Chris Hesketh, playing on his home ground, scored a superb try for us with Derek adding the extras before the Kiwis' John Whittaker scored after a brilliant 50 yard burst from Bernie Lowther. The kick made it 13–12 to us at half-time. The speed of the game was something else.

Phillip Orchard scored a try for the Kiwis; he bounced defenders out of the way and it deserved to win the game. Two points behind, we drove forward, but couldn't get over the line. The New Zealand defence was on its game and in the closing minutes Robert Orchard scored the final try for them. So we lost by a converted try, five points.

We were down in the dressing rooms after the loss, but I had had a good game. I couldn't have done any more. I believe I was the Great Britain man-of-the-match. I thought: 'this is the start of something big for Bill Ashurst.' How wrong I was.

When the squad for the second test was announced and I had not received a letter through the post, I was gutted. I didn't see that coming at all. Nothing had been said after the game, I just got pats on the back. I had scored a 'trade mark' Bill Ashurst try, and was the only forward to score from either side. I was one of seven players dropped and five others switched positions. After the first test I had to hand my kit in. I didn't get a cap because players had to play two games for Great Britain to be awarded a cap then. The others dropped were Derek Whitehead, Les Jones, Steve Nash, John Warlow, David Jeanes, and Vince Farrar.

There must have been somebody from Wales watching that game thinking 'How on earth has he been dropped?' A few days later, I got a telephone call from Wales rugby league. Did I qualify for Wales? Would I go and play for them? I didn't know, but they knew that I qualified through my grandparents who came from Pontypridd. Wales weren't a bad side in rugby league; they had some good players, but I was English through-and-through. There was no way I could play for Wales. It's like asking an Australian or New Zealander to play for England or Great Britain, but we do that now, don't we?

When I played for Wakefield Trinity at Wembley in 1979, we watched that Great Britain versus New Zealand test the night before. Our coach, Billy Kirkbride said 'How on earth did you get dropped from that game?' I replied 'It must have been politics Bill. Somebody didn't vote for me, they voted for someone else.'

The weekend before the second test I played for Wigan against the New Zealanders and again showed what I was capable of, both to them and the Great Britain selectors. I scored one of our tries in a 24–10 defeat.

New Zealand won the second test at Castleford 17–14; so they won a series in Britain for the first time in 63 years. We won the third test at Leeds 12–3, but New Zealand had done the job the game before. Don't take anything away from New Zealand, they had a good side.

In January 1972, I received some great news. I got another letter through the post telling me that I had been selected to train and play for Great Britain in the first test of the series against France, in Toulouse on Sunday 6 February. It was unexpected; I couldn't wait to get a second chance. My form at Wigan had been great, but because I had been dropped after the first test against New Zealand I thought that I had blown the chance of a second appearance.

We met up in Manchester for the game. We didn't have a uniform. I remember Tony Karalius came a little bit late and he had a light blue suit on. Jim Challinor looked at everyone else and said "What on earth are you wearing?" We all burst out laughing.

There was no Great Britain suit, trousers, tie or blazer for representing our country. They gave us a badge and we had to put it onto our own blazers. But we had to buy our own navy blue blazer first. If we wanted slacks, we bought our own grey slacks. We were playing for our country and it cost us money.

We stayed in a Manchester hotel overnight and the next day got a chartered flight to Toulouse. I had never flown before and didn't know what to expect. It was a different experience. There were jokes about winding the elastic on the propellers and when we were up in the air 'Yes, my son'; 'Yes my son, that's how high you go to heaven.' As we took off all the lads were singing 'Our father on earth in heaven.' It was fun. Another experience was sitting next to hard man Tony Karalius. He was terrified; I had more nail marks in my hand than any injury I got.

When we arrived in Toulouse and I got my hand back, we went to our hotel where we were given our rooms. The RFL had us sharing rooms. I had no problem with that, at the end of the day we were all part of the team. My roommate was Tony Karalius, enough said.

The day of the game came and we went to the Stade Municipal ground. We were all aware of what we were up against and it was not just the French team. I had heard stories from my Wigan teammates who had played there about what they had had to put up with. Great Britain hadn't won there for four years.

It was interesting how the team had changed from my debut only five months earlier: Paul Charlton, Clive Sullivan, John Holmes, Billy Benyon, John Atkinson, Ken Kelly, Steve

Nash, Mike Harrison, Tony Karalius, David Jeanes, William Ashurst, Phil Lowe, George Nicholls. Substitutes: Alan Smith, Bob Irving. Steve Nash and David Jeanes, who had been dropped like me, were in this team. Only Billy Benyon, Tony Karalius and our skipper, Clive Sullivan, also played that day.

I said earlier how proud I was as the whole team sang the national anthem at Salford in front of a small crowd. In Toulouse it was different. There were 11,508 French fans plus 15 French players and three officials baying for blood and wanting us to lose. So when we sang, we were a band of brothers. The hairs stood up on the back of my neck. We now knew what we were up against.

We kicked off with the wind behind us and got hit with a whirlwind from France. In next to no time they were leading 7–0 and I thought 'oh no'. We were not getting the little decisions, so took the game to them. I joined the line in a fantastic passing move which saw Clive Sullivan score in the corner. John Atkinson kicked the goal and we were just two points behind, which looked good. But then France got a drop-goal which only counted for one point. To my amazement I saw the referee jumping for joy as he confirmed it had gone between the posts. So it was 8–5 to France at half-time.

It was a tough game and we faced a hard pack of forwards, especially because nearly every decision went for them. We had to be more physical and do more defending. We had to keep our eyes open because there was a lot of off-the-ball stuff. I thought that the referee and touch judges let them get away with it.

The supporters created a great atmosphere of hatred, great for those wearing a French shirt. Playing into the wind, we had it all to do, but early on we drew level when a great move involving Steve Nash, Tony Karalius and Mike Harrison put Billy Benyon over. It was clear why they had an unbeaten home run against us. The only surprise was that the touch judge did not hit the referee over the head with his flag for giving our second try.

France got another drop-goal, but for some reason this time the referee just had a big smile on his face. With six minutes left, he gave us a token penalty 35 yards out near the touchline with a really cold wind, which had got stronger, blowing into our faces. The late, great John Holmes slowly composed himself and hit the ball. We watched in amazement and chased the kick just in case. But it sailed between the posts and we led 10–9.

We all knew what was going to happen now and it certainly did. It was the longest six minutes and injury time I ever played. We didn't know where so much injury time came from; the game had been hard and tough, but there were not that many stoppages. Every decision went to them and late on the referee gave them what I thought was a joke of a penalty for offside. They had been given a scrum on our 25 yard line. As the ball came out, they kicked it forward to chase. It went straight to Ken Kelly who scooted away for the winning try, or so we thought. He gave France a penalty for offside. We argued with the referee, but it was a waste of time. We thought that he had decided that France were going to win. Don't ask me how they missed the kick and eventually the referee had to blow for time. There was a God wearing a white shirt with a red and blue V.

I was full of emotion. We had beaten 11,526 French supporters, players and officials. The feeling of elation was completely different from my debut, I now felt like an international player. Surely I wouldn't be dropped after that win. I shook hands with all the French players. One of the French forwards came up and said 'Swap shirts, swap shirts', which I did. I thought that's what we did, especially when we had won. Later, when I picked up my wage packet it said £25 less shirt £5. So I had gained a France shirt, won the game, but lost £5.

After the game that evening, it was strange. We had all played as Great Britain for Great Britain; lads from Lancashire, Cumbria and Yorkshire. But at night there was still a Lancashire–Yorkshire separation. We had a drinks kitty. Paul Charlton had it and he and the Cumbria lads had gone off. I was sitting on a chair, leaning back against the wall, with my feet on the table with the Lancashire lads. We were having a beer when the Yorkshire lads came in. One of them said "Where's the kitty?"

I said "I don't know where the kitty is, Paul Charlton had it."

He said "You've got the kitty."

"No I haven't," I replied.

He pushed my chair away and I fell over, I picked my chair up and – bearing in mind I'd just played with him in the pack and we'd beat France in the afternoon – I threw my chair at him. I was shouting "You Yorkshire bastard, I'll …"

Then Tony Karalius jumped up: "We'll fight the lot of you Yorkshire bastards."

There was me, Tony Karalius, Ken Kelly, and George Nicholls shouting "We'll fight the lot of you Yorkshire bastards." It was unbelievable.

We just went mad, Tony and I; ready for a fight four hours after our win. Fortunately, Paul Charlton came back. I don't know what would have happened otherwise, but it wouldn't have been nice.

We had a great role model that weekend in Jack Wilkinson, who used to play for Wakefield Trinity and was on the trip. We were in The Concorde Hotel, because the Concorde was built in Toulouse. There's a big river at the back of the hotel and Jack took over running the bar, so he was a fabulous role model.

We wrecked beds. I remember we wrecked Clive Sullivan's bed, and he came and told me to get him a new bed. I denied wrecking it. He had my false teeth in his hand; I'd left them in his room. I'd have got him a bed from anywhere; anyway Tony and I ransacked Phil Lowe's room and took his bed, so Clive would be okay. Justice really, after what had happened earlier.

At the beginning of March, I received another selection letter to say I would be training and playing in the second test against France on Sunday 12 March at Odsal. It would be the first time a rugby league test match was played on a Sunday in England. I was really confident of playing well for Great Britain in a home game after our great win in Toulouse.

A few days before the match I was sent my Great Britain cap through the post after my second appearance for my country. I was so proud, but didn't think I would receive it through the post. The funny thing was they'd taken a fiver off me for the shirt and paid five pence to post the cap.

We trained during the week and after the final session the team was announced. We were told what time and where to meet. There were only two changes from the team that had won in Toulouse, Mike Stephenson came in for the injured Tony Karalius, and John Walsh replaced Alan Smith on the substitutes' bench.

On the day of the game, I was in Higher Ince Legion at 11am having a game of snooker with a mate. This was great preparation for me because I was only drinking orange. I remember my mate Terry saying "I can't believe this, you're playing snooker with me and you're playing for Great Britain at three o'clock."

We had to meet up at the Odsal Stadium at 1.30pm. My friend Peter Carroll took me and a couple of close friends and we got there about 1pm. The M62 motorway was built by then, so we went on it to Bradford and took our time. Peter dropped me outside the big house at the top at Bradford Hill and I met up with Jim Challinor and the squad.

There were 7,313 supporters at Bradford that day and as in my two previous tests I took great pride in wearing the shirt and singing the national anthem. I would never get tired of doing that. That afternoon we were simply superb from start to finish. We hammered France and definitely didn't need any help from the referee. By the time I crashed over for my first try, which was the team's third, on the half hour we led 13–2 which became 16–2 at half-time.

In the second half we opened the scoring immediately when John Holmes strode through a static, dejected French defence. France scored their opening try of the game when the game was over because we led 29–2. We gave the fans great value for money as we showed off our skills to the full, especially as an attacking force. Although they got another converted try, we just blew them away. We toyed with them throughout and I managed to score a superb second try, leaving the French players trailing in my wake.

Including me, 10 different players scored Great Britain's 11 tries in a 45–12 win. I believe that this is still a record today. The other nine scorers were Paul Charlton, Clive Sullivan, John Holmes, Billy Benyon, John Atkinson, Mike Stephenson, David Jeanes, Phil Lowe, and substitute John Walsh. John Holmes only kicked six goals, or we would have topped 50 points. After the game we shook hands with the French players, but didn't see them after the game.

It was our last game before the 1972 World Cup in France at the beginning of the 1972–73 season. I had a great game producing another man-of-the-match display; I was the best forward out there. Leading from the front I scored two tries, created three more and showed brilliant handling, tackling and my tactical kicking was supreme.

France had no answer to me; I knew it, France knew it and my team knew it. The Great Britain selectors knew as did our coach Jim Challinor who told me he would see me at the World Cup. I was elated and after how I had performed that day, I didn't swap my shirt a second time. I kept it and later gave it to charity, this time we didn't get charged.

The celebrations were completely different. We went to the dressing room, had a shower, changed, had our butties and went our separate ways. No reception, nothing – just sandwiches. I met up again with Pete and my mates and went home. We had our own celebrations; it was a very good late night.

That was rugby league then, that was approach of the people who were running the sport, not like it is today. Now there are so many receptions, so many VIPs. As a guest, I've been to a few which have been fantastic, but then it was just 'thank you very much, see you later, you'll get your wages on Thursday through the post'. That was it. At the end of the day, whether we got £25, £5 or £500 we had that Great Britain shirt on and that's what mattered.

That win against France was my last hurrah for my country; not a bad record: played three, won two, scored three tries. I went to play for Penrith and that prevented me going further in my international career because Great Britain then had decided they would only select players playing at home for home internationals and Great Britain Lions tours, not like today.

It was disappointing, but not just for me. I believe that the record books show that at that time there was a better Great Britain team playing in Australia than the Lions that toured Australia in 1974. I'm sure that if that team of British players playing in Australia had played either the Australians or the Great Britain touring side of 1974 they would have won both games.

There were some tremendous British players playing in Australia; Great Britain would have had a great side. They included Malcolm Reilly, Brian Lockwood, Doug Laughton, myself, Stevo, Gary Stevens and Phil Lowe among others playing over there. I think a side with those players would have beaten either of the 1974 teams.

Bill with the Players No.6 Player of the Year trophy at the awards evening
at the Lord Daresbury Hotel in Warrington.

14. Cold soup and a hot welcome

The 1972–73 season had come to an end and I had given my all to Wigan. Niggling at the back of my mind was what Mr Bibby had done. I had helped Wigan stay in the First Division by the skin of their teeth. In my 'signed for life' contract I had now received all the money I was offered when I turned professional and joined them. The close season had started, but I couldn't get Mr Bibby out of my head. The other thing I had hanging over me was the suspension for taking Murph out in our final game of the season which would see me miss a few games.

Anyway, one evening in June I was sat watching television with Sheila when there was a knock on the door. I was gobsmacked when I opened it. Standing on the doorstep were Tommy Bishop and Cliff Watson. I had played against Tommy before he went to Australia. As for Cliff, we nearly got sent off together for fighting in a John Player Trophy Final, but Brian 'Ben' Hogan came between us and got sent off instead.

We went inside and they began talking to me: "Bill, we have had reports of your performances, we think that you are the best second-row in the world and would love you to come to play for Cronulla." I had read that Roger Millward was on his way to Cronulla as well, so I said "I am interested".

At that time Sheila and I were again having an on-and-off rocky relationship because of the way I lived. Twice we had nearly got divorced and had tried to reconcile. So, before we knew it, there was a chance of going to Australia. We decided that whatever had happened we would start again for the third time.

I said "I know that you have got money, what are you looking at? What will I get? What will the situation be if I came to Australia?"

They replied "Bill, we can't give you more than the capping system." There was a cap in Australia at the time and it was $2,000 a year. "We will give you the playing money and will get you a house and a job."

I said "Give me a bit of time to speak to Sheila."

It didn't take long. Tommy and Cliff stayed in the front room and had a cup of coffee; Sheila and I went into the kitchen. We said to each other that whatever had happened, we'd give something a chance if it came up. I said "Look, it's an opportunity, let's go." I wanted to get away from her mam, so it was ideal. I said to them "I'll come, I'll come".

They said they would sort out the contracts which would take a few weeks. I said "All right, great." I shook hands with Tommy and Cliff on that.

Well, believe it or not, a few days later I had a visit from two people from Penrith Panthers. Wally Ward, who was either the chairman or vice-chairman, and a director, an even better bloke called Bruce 'Wello' Wellerson. I told them I was going to Cronulla. They asked what Cronulla were offering, so I told them the cap, a job and a house.

They said "We know for a fact that the cap's being lifted this year, so we can bang it up straight away at the end of the season. We can only give you the $2,000 now. We'll get you a house and a job, a swimming pool, and a new car every year. Also, we will give you £500 spending money while you're waiting to get the immigration papers sorted out."

So I thought about it and said "Give me a few minutes with Sheila." Penrith Panthers would contact Australia House do the immigration process from their side. So I went into the kitchen again with Sheila as we had when Tommy Bishop and Cliff Watson had called a few days earlier.

I said to her "Pretend we are talking, but I'll tell you what – I can't drive and I can't swim, but I know where we are going." Sheila agreed with me to give it a go at Penrith. So I shook hands with 'Wello' and Wally Ward and verbally agreed to go to Penrith. They said they would sort everything out with Wigan.

I had agreed to move to Penrith, so they decided to stay. They said they would contact me in a few days and would draw the contract up. They were staying at a new hotel in Leeds, the Dragonara, and said they would bring me over to finalise and sign the contract.

My friend Peter Carroll was a taxi driver. Earlier that year he had taken me and my mates to Bradford when I'd played in the second test at Odsal. I knew that we could get a few bob in Peter's pocket if he took me in his taxi and they looked after him. I also took Kathleen, who was then aged three, with us and we drove to the hotel in Leeds

Wally and Bruce met us at the reception. They said we would have lunch and discuss the final details and the contract. So we were in this new hotel, you can imagine how posh it was for a lad from Higher Ince in Wigan. I looked at the menu and thought 'I'll have a starter, a main course and a sweet', because they were paying.

I looked at the starters and thought this soup looks good; I've never tried it before. It was called Vichyssoise. I said to the waiter "I'll have some Vichyssoise, mate."

He said "Thank you" in a posh voice. A short time later, he came back with prawn cocktails for Wally and Bruce.

Peter struck lucky – he said later "I didn't risk anything" – and just had a mixed grill and no starter. At that time he was 27 stone, so probably was thinking about his figure.

Anyway, the waiter brought my soup and I tried it. It was absolutely freezing. Honestly, I should have ordered ice cream. The waiter was walking away and I shouted "Hey mate" in my broad Wigan accent. He came back to our table and said "Yes sir".

I said "Can you go and warm this soup up? It's freezing."

He said "Certainly sir. But, by the way, did one not know that it was a cold soup?"

Did I heck! I said "Take it back and warm it up," so he warmed it up, brought it back and it was okay. I think I felt six inches tall in front of the two Australians who just cracked up laughing. It was quite funny at the time. Peter was laughing and his 27 stone nearly slid under the table. I bet they thought 'What are we buying here?'

When we had all stopped laughing and eaten I left Kathleen with Peter in the hotel lounge and went up with Wally and Bruce to the room where they were staying. We had another good talk and made sure they would sort everything out as previously agreed, including dealing with Wigan and Mr Bibby. I didn't want to deal with him, with the feelings I had for him. I signed the contract on the dotted line for a world record fee that they sorted out with Wigan; they were both happy as I was. I was leaving Wigan and going to play in Australia.

After I had signed the contract I was even happier. Moments later I got a surprise, they gave me £500 cash which wasn't in the contract. They said "That will tide you over until you get your immigration papers through, then you can get new gear when you're coming over. With everything signed, sealed and delivered we rejoined Peter – who they looked after – and Kathleen. After shaking hands again, we left for home full, stupid and a lot better off. There was just a small problem I needed to sort out.

I had agreed within a few days of each other by shaking hands to join Cronulla and Penrith Panthers. I had now signed for Penrith; there was no turning back. I thought about what I was going to say and decided to be blunt and to the point, nothing new there then. Tommy Bishop had left me his telephone number because he was in St Helens having a holiday as well as seeing me. I rang him and said "Look, I've changed my mind. I'm going to Penrith not Cronulla."

He wasn't best pleased. In 2006, I went to the Penrith Panthers Legends Ceremony While I was there I went to an Australian Reunion. I was talking to Artie Beetson, Bob O'Reilly and John O'Neill. Then I got a little tap on the back of the head. I turned around and it was 'Bish'. He said "You bastard."

I said "Why Bish?"

He said "That year you didn't come to Cronulla, we got into the Grand Final against Manly and lost. We would have won it if you had come to Cronulla." That was the last time I spoke to Bish. Even Australian Brits can't take a joke. I was blamed for a game I didn't even play in.[4] I just burst out laughing and had another drink.

Once the transfer had been agreed, Wigan were happy to receive their world record fee. They let me keep training at the club to keep fit. Graham Starkie, their new coach, and the Wigan lads at the first team training sessions, had no problems with it. When I left they wished me all the best. I still had a great rapport with those lads when I went to Australia and that continued when I came back from Australia.

With Penrith's help we sorted out all the immigration papers. It took a bit of time to get right, going through all the correct channels. We all had smallpox injections which people had to have when they went to Australia then and were just waiting for the flight to be arranged. On Monday 3 December 1973, Sheila and I and our three children, Carl, Graham and Kathleen, flew out to Australia for my new club, our new life and adventure.

When we left it was in the middle of a bad winter, with two feet of snow on the ground when we left Wigan. Penrith had given us that £500 at Leeds when I met them. We used it to get clothes for us all. I was the thickest person at school; I bought winter clothes to travel in. I didn't know it was their summer.

---

[4] Tommy Bishop's memory was wrong on this occasion; his Cronulla team lost to Manly in 1973, a year before Bill arrived in Australia.

After a mega long flight, we arrived at Sydney Airport knackered, but excited. As soon as the plane doors opened we started walking down the boarding steps onto the tarmac. The unbelievable heat hit me. I had a big overcoat on, a bri-nylon shirt, flared tweed trousers and winkle pickers. It was 120 degrees humidity. I looked like an idiot with sweat pouring off me; like a king-sized drowned rat.

I had come to Australia, a rugby league player for a world record transfer fee so the Australian press, television and radio were at the airport waiting for me to arrive. Penrith were waiting to pick us up. What on earth would they think seeing me like this?

My first impression of an Australian was when I was walking through Customs. I had this little Australian bloke looking at me and then my passport in immigration. The first words I heard on Australian soil were unbelievable: "Have we got a criminal record, Sir?"

My reply was "Why? Is it still compulsory?" That was my introduction to a proper Australian. He let me and the family through, it was funny though. Welcome to Australia Bill. We went into the arrivals area and I did a couple of interviews. One was for Rex Mossop, one of the main Channel 9 television guys. Another was for a Sydney radio station.

We were met at the airport by one of the club's secretaries, Liz, a wonderful young woman. Blonde and beautiful she was too. Penrith wanted to get me to the club; everybody was waiting there to meet me. They had their own press and media people and supporters at the club.

The reception was unbelievable. The Penrith club was packed and we met everyone from the chairman of the club down. It was a media circus that I had never encountered before. I was just a normal bloke from Ince in Wigan; a nobody, and all of a sudden I was thrown into a George Best scenario. I loved it. Sheila loved it and the headlines in the papers the next day, because they now knew her name, were 'Bill's Sheila loves Australia' with a photograph of us.

After a hectic time at the club, Liz drove us to the new home they had arranged for us in the bush. I walked in the living room and said "I don't like that wallpaper". It was real green frogs all the way up the walls, plastic frogs all over the place. The house hadn't been lived in for a while; I thought "What are we doing here?"

They got all that sorted and we stayed there, within a four mile radius there were three or four homes including ours. There was a swimming pool. In a hectic two weeks after arriving, I had seven days continuous driving lessons and got my licence at the end of the week. The following week I had a chocolate brown Ford Falcon automatic, a big rocket, a top car. I couldn't drive at home; over there I passed in seven days.

Penrith weren't daft in sorting me out with a car; it saved them a fortune in taxi fares because I lived so far away from the club. It was six miles from home to the club's training centre. Before I finished the driving lessons I used a taxi.

While all this had been happening I had my first training session with my new teammates and new coach. My first coach at Penrith for me was one of the most underrated and best ones that I ever played for. Ashy, I've always said, was the best coach. But in my first season we had Roy Masters; he was awesome. He came from a schoolboy rugby league background.[5]

My first training session was unbelievable. They took us to Glenbrook National Park. I wasn't the best of trainers. I've always been lazy really and I heard stories about spiders: look out for the spiders, look out for the snakes. We had to do a run through the park. I've never been so scared in my life. I was looking on the floor and in the trees for spiders. We were running past kangaroos and I've never ran as fast in my life. I thought I'd got to avoid snake and spider bites. We got to the end of it with me unbitten. Then there was the humidity. We went to a pond, Jelly Beam Pool and all jumped in. I couldn't escape. I came out covered in leeches; they were pulling black leeches off us all over the place. That was my first training session at Penrith.

It was a long run; it seemed to take all day that first training session. For the next session we had a guy from America, Bob Tapper. I remember that second session vividly; I couldn't drive home – I was so exhausted. We had done so many runs and so many laps and I heard his voice say "Right lads". I thought "That's my first in the ground session over."

I was slowly walking to the changing rooms for a shower when he came over and said "Where are you going?"

I said "You've just said 'right lads'".

He said "Listen to the end Bill. That's your warm up lads, now we'll start." I was shattered, done in. I couldn't get up or walk. The secretary had to drive my car home. I was absolutely knackered. This type of training was a culture shock to me and my system. It was twice a week; but a very intense twice a week.

I knew then, as at Wigan, the first six to eight weeks training sessions were always the important ones for me. Once I had got my modicum of fitness I played the games. That used to keep me fit along with other stuff like playing squash. I just wanted the ball in my hands. I got bored; I just wanted the ball in my hands. There were times when I got bored with training; I would muck about at the back and have a laugh and a joke with players in the squad at Penrith. I used to get away with it at Wigan, not here.

---

[5] The Penrith system at this time was a coaching panel of Masters, Barry Harris and Tom Wilson, headed by Jack Clare. Harris later became first team coach. In reality, Masters was the first team coach and is now recognised as such.

A pensive look during Bill's time at Penrith (Courtesy *Rugby League Week*)

15. Starting at Penrith

Even in Australia I used to get bored with training as I had in Wigan. Once at Penrith in the build up to my first season I was really bored with training. I was mucking about at the back having a laugh and a joke with the players. Bob Tapper shouted "Bill".

I shouted "What?"

He shouted "If you don't want to do it, f... off." Next lap, then I was in the changing rooms, showered, in the car and home. I think it was 12.30 that night the telephone rang. It was Roger Cowan the Penrith head manager. He was an absolutely top bloke and had pulled the club up to where it was himself.

He said "Bill, meeting at Penrith tomorrow. You've breached your contract."

I went "What?"

He said "You didn't finish training. You breached your contract."

I said "Fair enough, not a problem. What time?"

He said "One o'clock." I got up the following morning, rang the newspapers, the *Sydney Sun* and *Sydney Herald*, and said "I think Penrith are selling my contract. I've breached my contract; see if there are any clubs interested in buying my contract." That was at 8am on the day of the meeting at Penrith. Whether the media had rung clubs or not I don't know, but I knew how it worked in Australia and how it worked when I was at Wigan.

The other 11 clubs had rung me before I went into that meeting, saying that they would buy my contract. I had no problem with that and went into the meeting. I sat in the boardroom and it was explained to me I was there because of breaching my contract by not finishing the training session the previous day. They asked "Why did you not finish training last night Bill?"

I said "Where's Bob Tapper?"

I was told "He's working."

I said "Well, this meeting is not going ahead until Bob Tapper gets here."

They asked "Why?"

I replied "Get Bob Tapper to this meeting."

They said "It will take a couple of hours, he works in Sydney."

I said "I don't care, get Bob Tapper here."

They sent for Bob Tapper and had to give me lunch. I had a great lunch; oysters, king prawns, the lot. The club were paying. Bob eventually came went into the boardroom, I followed him in and we began again. They said "You wanted Bob Tapper. Why didn't you finish your training session?"

I looked at them and Bob Tapper and said "I did as I was told."

Roger looked at me and said "What do you mean you did what you were told?"

I said "Bob, I've asked you to come here for a reason. Tell them what you shouted to me last night."

Bob said "You were messing about."

I said "Tell them what you said to me last night."

Bob said "I said 'If you don't want to do it, f… off.'"

I said "There you are Mr Chairman. I didn't want to do it, so I f…ed off." They just cracked up laughing; they were sitting down and laughing. They said "Bill, on your bike, see you later." That was the end of the breach of contract meeting. Ashurst 1 Australia 0.

I was settling at Penrith, but all I'd had was being shouted at and called a Pommie bastard and all that. I was fed up with it. It was the players in the squad taking the piss. One day I was doing some shopping at Penrith Market with Sheila. I saw this plain yellow tee-shirt, 'print anything you want' it said. I bought it and remember the expression on the face of the guy when I handed it to him. He said "What do you want printing on it mate?" in his Aussie accent.

I said "Print on it 'I hate Aussie bastards'." He looked at me with his eyes nearly popping out and said "What?'"

I repeated it "I hate Aussie bastards."

He still looked at me, didn't ask me again and printed what I wanted in big, bold, jet black letters on the front of it. I went to training with it on, and told my teammates "Look, I don't need to call you one, just read it if you're intelligent enough." From that day on, I wore it in training and when I walked into the club. I only had it on for a few days. I think I got the message across: "Stop calling me a Pommie bastard, whatever you say to me I can give you twice as much back." Sheila used it afterwards to clean the house.

I picked up the Aussie accent, which was funny. Not long after I arrived, the capping ban was lifted and I signed a new contract. Life was good. One day Sheila and I were walking to the Penrith club. There was a guy mowing his garden and in an instant we just caught each other's eye. I said to Sheila "Listen": "Gooday mate, how're you going, is it rosy?" in a loud Australian accent. The bloke looked at me and said "F… off you Aussie." Sheila said I had picked up the accent well. How unlucky was that? It must have been somebody from the other side of Golborne.

Penrith had been as good as their word when Wally, Bruce and I signed the contract earlier in the year: a house, swimming pool, car, money, spending money, a better contract and they found me a job. We immediately renegotiated my contract when the salary cap was lifted. The jump was from $2,000 a year to $12,500 a year, which was massive. I've never been a money person, it was a perk for playing. The money I wasted and frittered away; of that $12,500 I probably kept $6,000.

Half went to the Australian tab (betting), bookies, some went on drink at the boozers, so I got respect from all the people in the bars. Respect is given and taken, in the second season some went on the women ('Sheilas'), of Penrith. I got the respect from them probably because I was shagging half of them.

When we finished the games we had a drink; it was part of the game's culture then. The players from both sides were in the bar and had a drink together, went to a club and we respected each other. I've never been an idiot. I've got into one or two scrapes as wayward people sometimes do, but at the end of the day I had settled down, got respect and given it back. That was me and my lifestyle. I've never valued money, it's just come and gone. That's why now I've not got ha' pennies to rub together, but I'm happy; I've lived the life.

I began working at Simmons Sports Shop, which was one of the biggest Australian sports companies then. I left because I didn't enjoy that type of work. The club got me a job managing a gymnasium and squash courts which really kept me fit. Often players wouldn't turn up for their squash court or just one would turn up, so I'd play squash for an hour or two. I would then make time to use the sauna and showers afterwards, which was superb. I had everything to keep fit at my fingertips. Stupid me; I didn't like training, but even though this was a fitness thing it never entered my head. All that running about just kept me at a good level of fitness.

Before we arrived at Penrith, another Brit had come to the club. Mike 'Stevo' Stephenson got there before me, so he had acclimatised and established himself by the time I turned up. He had gone there from Dewsbury. I'd played against him; he was a good player, one heck of a hooker. His support play was superb, his defence good; an awesome defensive hooker. In my view, the sad thing was that I thought that he didn't take his team ethos off the field at Penrith.

He just did his own thing. I don't remember him buying many drinks. Stevo was Stevo, I mean, good luck to the guy; I have no animosity towards him. A lot of people have come up with stories about me and Stevo; we didn't get on, we didn't like each other, a clash of egos, we put a face on looking to get on because we were Brits in the same team.

It's like if someone falls out with their wife, but when friends come round they both put a face on for the sake of them; then finish it off when they have gone. That's how Stevo and I were at Penrith. We played together, two good players in a good team and I was pleased that the coach gave me more control.

I could get more ball than Stevo, who was under orders to give me the ball when I wanted it. I still controlled the game whether Stevo played or not. During my time at Penrith we weren't the best of friends. I didn't live in his pocket and he didn't live in mine. We lived quite far apart, about seven or eight miles. I lived on one side of the ground and he lived on the other in Castle Ray.

We played at Brookvale against the Manly Sea Eagles. They had Malcolm Reilly from Castleford and Phil Lowe from Hull KR in their side. The Sydney rugby league press played the clash up. Who would be the best second row; me or Phil Lowe? Being the modest person I was I said "We'll find out on Friday, won't we?" I said "I'll beat him in the fight and in the game."

So from that it built up in the papers. Anyway, Phil didn't get involved. Malcolm's probably one of the hardest players I've ever played against. I got sent off that night, but not before Malcolm and I knocked seven bells out of each other. Anyway, someone had to go and it was me for a head butt. So a trip to Sydney to the New South Wales League Disciplinary Committee to see the judiciary followed. They gave me a three game ban. Malcolm was sent off as well.

When I went back to Australia for the Penrith legends event in 2006, I met Malcolm and we had a night out at the Newcastle Trots racing. We got leathered together, and left the racing at four in the morning.

We had friendlies against some country sides and three lined up in the pre-season build up against Souths, Balmain and Newtown. I decided I wanted to make a mark to these Aussies before the season began after I had made my point to my teammates with the yellow tee shirt. I certainly did that: three friendlies, three sending offs. This included a game against Balmain.

One of the friendlies was at Gosford. I took the family with me for the weekend and we stayed at Keith Elwell's place. He had heard that this guy was going to do this and that and I made a point of finding out who he was. I innocently sat next to him in the stand and introduced myself as that Pom and I knew what he was going to do to that Pom. I whispered in his ear "Come anywhere near me in the game and I will bury you or they'll be cremating you at five o'clock." I never saw the guy during or after the game.

In another friendly it was a tough game – like when I played in the Locker Cup, there was no such thing as a friendly. This guy ran at me with his elbow out. I'd just passed the ball and I thought 'he's going to do me'. I got it in first, put my elbow up and hit him. He went straight down and his face was open. The referee said to him "Get up, he missed". I thought the ref needed bifocals. That was how the game was played then, an evil game. I enjoyed it, especially as long as I got mine in.

I got sent off in the friendly against Souths. I think it was my first game against a New South Wales League club, a proper club. I'd already been caught once so I had to get mine in, which I did. Off we both went. I'd rather have won with football, but whatever it took; I was that type of player. It was a sad game, I love it now, no racism and all that.

In our day, there was so much volatility and racism, it was unbelievable. Whatever it took me to get the better of someone I did, as in the game against Balmain. I bumped into Denis Monteith, we had a tussle, I head butted him and off I went again.

Whoever I was playing against, whether it was calling names – which we all did – the physical stuff, or anything else, no one was going to be better than me. I suppose it was all psychological; it's called sledging today, it was abuse then. I wasn't bothered about what the Aussies said to me. The only way they could scare me was to sign my mother-in-law; if they had done that, then they would have won.

When I put my boots on I became a completely different character: an animal, a footballer and a genius. Many people put me on a pedestal – although I don't – and have said I was a genius and an animal at the same time, whichever turned up on the day. That's how it was with me. I was a world record signing, a Pom, from their point of view, especially in the forwards where the game is won or lost, I would be the first target. Late tackles did me; as a footballer if somebody tried to take me out and didn't catch me properly, then it was in with the head butt. If you miss me, I'm not going to miss you. From memory I got sent off three times in league games in three seasons. Once for head butting which I've mentioned, twice in the second season for punching and a high tackle; I was an 'angel' in the third season.

I thought that I had a great first year at the club; it was a matter of the players and club building around me. I was a dominant person and a leader. Our coach, Roy Masters, realised this after three games and gave me full control. The previous season they had been awful, bottom of the table, and had a record 70–7 defeat to Manly.

I made my New South Wales RL debut for the Penrith Panthers on Saturday 30 March 1974. I was the 100th player to represent the club, an unexpected honour. It was against Eastern Suburbs and I was as confident at the start of the game as I was when I started a game for Wigan. But the game took my breath away. It was faster and a bit of a shock to the system compared to the friendlies.

We lost 31–6, our heaviest loss of the season. Easts were coached by the legendary Jack Gibson. It was the first of four successive defeats. The second was to South Sydney on my home debut at Penrith Park. I scored my first two tries for the club, but that was no consolation for me or the team in a heavy defeat. I scored the tries with little kicks over the top, which was my trade mark then and for many years, as Roger Cowan recalled when I went to the Panthers 40th anniversary celebration in 2006. I missed the next game, a defeat against Canterbury Bulldogs, but was back for a narrow loss away to St George. It was not what I had been expecting from the opening four games, especially after the hard graft I had put in.

A funny thing happened in my third game of the season. I'll never forget it and the reaction of the Australian rugby league media. It rained all day, like the 1968 'water splash final'; wet puddles everywhere. Rod 'Rocket' Reddy was playing for St George, Graham 'Changa' Langlands was at full-back and Billy Smith at half-back; they were a good team.

I put a high kick up and Langlands caught it and fell on the floor. I slid into him through the puddles from 10 yards and on impact could hear the sound of three cracked ribs. It was music to my ears; crack, crack, they went. He had to go off. The headlines in the newspapers were 'Pom purposely puts full-back out of the test series'. That year the British Lions were coming to try and regain the Ashes after the 2–1 loss at home in 1973. I thought, 'You idiots'. That day was a great confidence boost; even more Aussies hated me now after I had crunched one of their main men. Oh woe is me.

Stevo and I were the club's big close season signings, but I had been told there were already some good experienced players with some great youngsters ready to step up. What they didn't tell me was that I would be introduced to a hypnotist. I thought it was hilarious. The club believed in it and thought it worked on the young players, but the older ones just took the piss out of him.

They brought this guy in to improve the young players and develop their confidence, what I did find useful was a relaxation tape. 'Relax from your toes to your hair, imagine you are in the most beautiful of places, the clouds the clouds are taking you.' I'm falling asleep as I tell you about this, I'm sure it was a fabulous relaxation tape. I asked him once to make Sheila into a chicken, but he wouldn't cluckin listen to me.

105

During that season I got to know Tim Sheens, the current Australia head coach whose side won the 2013 World Cup superbly. It was easy apart from their opening 25 minutes against England, who came third in a three horse race. From our time at Penrith we became very good friends and I would like to thank him for writing the foreword for this book. His side are on a fantastic run and seem to be unbeatable at the moment.

Back then, 40 years ago, Tim was a young prop and part of the Penrith side. He became a cornerstone of the club for years to come before going on to coach them. That Penrith team was a good side with Reggie Walton at full-back, Graham Moran, Ross Gigg who sadly passed away in 2014 and another great friend, Terry Quinn. Then we had the other Moran; the Morans were great players, Graham and John 'Crazy' Moran, his brother. Graham was one of the best players I ever played with and was named in the Penrith Panthers Legends team. We had one of the hardest props I've ever played with, Terry 'Dollar' Geary.

He absolutely loved the dollar, wouldn't spend it, kept every dollar, hence the nickname. Tim Sheen was number 10. Then we had a tackling second-row who I thought was great. The best two second-rows I played with defensive-wise and toughness-wise was David Robinson at Wigan and this kid at Penrith, Denis Tutty, what a second rower.

Later on, we had a young kid at loose-forward, Barry Le Brocq. He was a good young player in a youthful team. Another great young kid was Wayne Brain, who did me a big favour in his day job in the police. If he would have been at any other club, he would have been the regular first team hooker. The cherry on the top was me, but the team was directed by a top coach in Roy Masters, a genius who was ahead of his time.

I'll never forget 'Dollar', he was hard, but also so dry and funny. We had a young kid who came in from the reserves. The game was at Penrith Park. Dollar used to always get changed near the toilet. The youngster went to the toilet before the game, no toilet roll there. So he grabbed Dollar's playing shirt and wiped his arse on it.

I have never played in a first half of so much laughter in my life. All through the game, one of the kids would say 'Dollar, I've put the shit on these men today; Dollar crap on these players' and Dollar couldn't understand them. But when we came in at half-time we had all been laughing and our opponents couldn't understand what was going on. We all knew apart from Dollar.

He went mad at half-time when he realised what had happened. Playing in the second-row packing down behind Dollar needed a health warning. He'd tucked his shirt in. After the game he chased the youngster around the dressing room. It was very funny.

He was so dry it was unbelievable. He was ostentatious and serious all the time, a tough, tough nut. He was superb as a player, character and good friend.

Our next game was against Cronulla and our coach was by now aware of what I could do. I was a leader, although Stevo didn't agree with my assessment. After the opening four games, Roy Masters gave me full control, a roaming role, but with a condition that I put the defensive work in.

I knew that whatever happened I would get stick from former St Helens man Tommy Bishop, who'd tried to sign me before Penrith came in with a better deal. Knowing what was going to come before and after, I was focussed to play well and help the team. We got going, outclassed Cronulla and edged it 28–24 with a good performance. I was walking on air again; I scored a try, and the result must have annoyed Tommy big time. The boys knew how to celebrate after that win. We had waited a few weeks, but it was worth it. Our supporters had seen us win at last.

We were ready for anybody now. A second home game followed against Balmain. We carried on with the same attacking rugby and beat them convincingly. The star of the show was Glenn West who went over for four belters. Now either Roy Masters was a genius, a bastard or master of the mind games because Glenn wasn't even as good as his last game; he was in the reserve grade the following week.

I missed the next three games, which included the Amco Cup, which we lost. I was back for the Round 10 game, a trip to Wests. This began a run of eight games in the side, but we had yet to win on our travels. Another really good team performance saw us win 26–20. The star man again for us was Glenn West; he lowered his standards and had to settle for a hat-trick.

We then beat Newtown at Penrith. At the halfway point of the season, after a rocky start, we were ninth with four wins from 11 games; four points off the play-offs.

The next game was the big one. Easts had toasted us in the opening game, had only lost once, were unbeaten in seven games and league leaders by four points. I wanted to show Jack Gibson the real Bill Ashurst and what the team could do. There were 7,000 there on 16 June, it was packed and the atmosphere electric. I knew it was going to be special.

For me it was one of those games when everything turned to gold. If it sounds that I'm being big headed, I was truly magnificent and unstoppable. Creatively, I showed all my tricks, supreme footwork off either foot, penetrating kicking game, driving, tackling, creating mayhem and panic every time I had the ball to hand. We outplayed and outfought them to win 19–9. Saving the best till last, I went over for a try and slotted over a drop-goal for good measure. I was playing on another level after that, no disrespect to Wigan. Australia were learning quickly after their Ashes and World Cup Final defeats at the beginning of the 1970s.

Could we kick on from that magnificent result? We lost our next two games; at Redfern Oval to South Sydney by three points – Stevo scored one of our tries – then at home to high flying Canterbury by the same margin in front of nearly 9,000 fans. Henry Tatana, who I had met when Wigan played Australia, scored their winner. So near yet so far.

We won the next two games. Over 9,000 were at our place when an amazing individual performance – not by me – by Peter Langmack with a club record amazing five tries in our 22–21 win over St George. Words can't describe it. For the record for Australian readers, Changa's ribs had recovered and he scored one of their tries.

In Round 16 we went to play Cronulla. I got great pleasure from a 14–11 win and a double over them. David Waite scored for them and again Tommy Bishop wasn't happy.

We had won five out of seven, close to seven from seven and there was a great feeling around the club. I played in four of the last six games and we only managed to win twice. It was a frustrating, rather than disappointing, end to my opening season.

I played in the win over Parramatta on Sunday 4 August. The significance of that win for me was that I scored my first hat-trick for the club and in Australia in my first season. I doubt many Poms have done that, especially second-row forwards. I was elated, though it didn't beat the win against Easts.

That season was also the first year of the Amco Cup, a midweek knock-out competition and we reached the final. Unfortunately, I didn't play in the final or semi-final because I had torn my hamstring, and couldn't get fit in time. The team put in a great performance, but lost the final 6–2 to New South Wales Country side Western Division.

One of the things about this new competition was that they had a fantastic prize for the man-of-the-match and I enjoyed showing my skills when the cameras were there. Colour television was gradually coming in and the winner received a colour telly.

The only Amco Cup game I played that season was the quarter-final on 31 July. We played the Northern Division at Leichardt Oval. It was the first time supporters in Australia saw my round-the-corner kicking technique. At the time I was the second choice kicker, because we had a good kicker in Reggie Walton, but he had picked up an injury and missed this game. The supporters had seen how I could kick a drop-goal.

The goalkicking technique prior to mine was a full-on, Len Killeen type toe-ender, used successfully later by the great Mal Meninga among others. I was just hoping to be the first one to kick in this style, a bit innovative in Australia. My kicking technique was from my soccer days. It was easier for me; I could get more power and distance kicking side-foot than I could with a toe.

I dazzled on television that night as we thrashed Northern Division 31–11. I played with a swagger in my step and my kicking game was outstanding. Every positional kick went where I wanted it to go. I was in the right place at the right time and went over for two tries. When I took my first conversion there was a sort of hush in the ground. I took my time, weighed it up and bang – a perfect connection right between the posts. There was a roar of approval; it was the first of five goals that night. There was only one place that colour telly was going.

That same season saw the Great Britain Lions come to Australia for an Ashes tour. They lost the series, but before the intensity of the tour began I got Penrith to put on a massive welcome for them. I invited them to a game, the boys came to a party and they had a great day. Jim Challinor was still the Great Britain coach; it was the first tour for John Gray, Alan Bates and Stevie Nash. But, there was a better Great Britain side playing in Australia then the squad that toured. British players playing in Australia included Mal Reilly, Brian Lockwood, Doug Laughton, Roger Millward, Gary Stevens, Phil Lowe, Stevo and me. The rules were then that if a player was playing in Australia they weren't selected for Great Britain. That was the chance we had taken. At the end of the day we were better paid and lived in a better climate than playing at home.

It was an great honour to play for Great Britain three times, for my country, but now I was proving myself, playing against the best players in the world for three years, not just a couple of months on tour. I always maintained to the kids I coached: if you don't want to be the best, don't play. Stay at home and play Xbox, don't bother putting your boots on.

When the Lions played Australia at the Sydney Cricket Ground, I made a few quid. They had a goalkicking competition. All the club goalkickers were there and there was $2,000 on offer to win the competition. We had to kick one from one side, then the other and finally from the middle. There was me, Henry Tatana and a young kid from Souths in the final at half-time. We'd each kicked two apiece. Henry and I were sitting in the Great Britain dressing room watching the first half of the match. We agreed that if either of us won we would get a grand a piece. So I kicked two, Henry kicked one and when the time came for the kid from South Sydney, who was last to go, only a young 18 year old, we were saying so much to him that his kicks ended up missing. So Henry and I ended up with a grand apiece just for kicking two goals.

On another night at Harold Park greyhound track they selected an Australian, Great Britain and Guest Select four by 100 metres relay sprinting team. Phil Lowe was in my team with another two players. It was just $1,000 for running 100 metres around a greyhound track. On the back of Great Britain Lions I won two grand in seven days, what a great way to earn money.

It had been a good season for Penrith. We had come ninth, four places better than the previous year. I was looking forward to our end of the season trip, which certainly wasn't to Blackpool. We were going to New Zealand and Fiji and all we had to find was our spending money. The club was fantastic, and took the first team, second team and under-23s. They paid for all the lads. We cruised from Sydney around New Zealand and on to Fiji for another five days. We flew back from Fiji back to Sydney, what a trip.

What goes on a tour stays on a tour. There were bets as to who could pull the most women, who could drink the most beer and so on. It was a close and great trip, but we nearly lost one youngster.

I remember two of the players panicking. I joined them looking all over this big ocean liner. We eventually found him at the back of the ship, legless. He was trying to get the rope that was used to tie up the ship, and was standing up and shouting: "Leave me alone, I'm going water skiing". If we hadn't found him, I'm sure he would have gone over the top. He was well and truly gone. The rest of the trip, well...

When I got back, it was the close season so Sheila and I decided to go home with the kids to see our families and have a good catch up. We all loved the lifestyle in Penrith. The weather was to die for. We got on well with most people and had made some good friends. The kids loved it and had settled in well. I sometimes had a few drinks too many, that was my only sin although there had been temptations. Sheila and I were closer than ever. In hindsight, coming home was one of the worst decisions I made.

As soon I knew we were coming back, I had spoken to Penrith and they were happy with that knowing that I would be back for pre-season training. I also told them I had some irons in the fire while back home. They were happy with that as long as I kept them in the picture. I'd been contacted by Phil Worthington at Warrington where Murph was coaching and he asked if I would come and guest for Warrington.

The Australian season had just finished as the English season started. We only began pre-season in February. Warrington offered me £500, my air fare and everything else. In the talks I asked the club: "Can I bring a young centre with me called Glenn West?" He had been our top try scorer that season. I thought the experience would do him the world of good, he was a good prospect. Warrington said "No", so I ended up coming back to Britain just with the family.

So I came home back to my mam's and went training with Warrington twice. At the club was one of the best young trainers at that time; one of the best I ever trained under – Tommy Grainey. He was also a good coach, and was assistant to Murph. I met Murph in a different setting than when I took him out when he was playing for Warrington in my last game for Wigan, but at that time I didn't like the guy.

I finished up doing two training sessions, told Phil Worthington I was homesick, and didn't want to stay. I asked if they wanted their money back. He said "We can't do anything with home sickness, keep the £500, that's it." We all came back to Australia; I could only tell the same old stories to my family for so long. It was one of the worst decisions I ever made in my rugby league career. That was a great Warrington side who played in the Challenge Cup Final. I did just the two weeks training at the club, what did I know? I think that a player has to get on with someone, especially the coach, if it's to work. After that meeting I never thought I would work with the guy again.

17. Family visitors

Off the field events in our second season in Australia as a family brought an unexpected surprise for me. This created a different sort of rollercoaster ride for me, although it didn't start like that. It wasn't as dramatic and sensational as that on the field, but it led to me making an about turn.

Looking back, when I think about things, it was my own fault really. When we had all gone back to Wigan after my first year, we all had a great time. I invited my mam over and I think Sheila invited her mum and dad over as well.

My mam came first, stayed with us and enjoyed herself. While she was there, she came to watch a couple of games I played in. It was a big adventure for her. Sheila rarely came. My mam came to support me and cheer for me while I was on the field in the thick of it, or so I thought.

I'll never forget it, Sunday 11 May 1975, Mothers' Day. We were at home to Norths. I was getting ready for the game. I thought the club were looking after my mam and keeping her out of mischief. During the game, we were getting well beaten. I wasn't enjoying staring at our fifth loss running when one of the biggest brawls I've ever been involved kicked off. I've been in a few in my time, everyone was into this: players, speccies, dogs and cats were fighting. It seemed to go on for ages, it was a belter.

As soon as it all stopped, the referee said "Ashurst off". I said some choice words to him and he repeated "Ashurst off". I was walking off, and my mam passed me walking the other way. As I turned around to ask what she was doing on the pitch, she hit the referee with her handbag. The stewards carried her off. When the referee came off at the end of the game, she cracked him again. It was all over the papers: 'Mummy comes to son's rescue on Mothers' Day'. I got a one match ban for the sending off; I banned my mam from going to another game. I never took her again. The referee didn't mention her in his report and didn't take it further. She could have got a criminal record, so fair play to him.

When she had gone home, Sheila said "Well, you got your mum over, I'm bringing mine over." But in her case it was buy one, get two free: her mum, dad and brother came. But my mum stayed for three months; they never went back. Part of our reasons for coming to Australia was to start again and get away from her mother. Now she was back. They stayed until Sheila later went back home with the kids.

When my mam came, it was on a visitor's three month visa. She could have a look round and it was good for her health. When Sheila said her mum was coming, I thought it was for the same time and after throwing a party before, and after, she had left, I could live with that. When they all arrived, it was a shock. When I was told that they were not going back it was an even bigger shock. I didn't know Sheila was that deep, when she set her mind to something, although later on I did because of my going-ons.

I didn't know that Sheila had sponsored them thanks to my 'Golden Try' and the $6,000 cash equivalent for the Alfa Romeo I had won. They emigrated to Australia and got a house 300 yards from us. They were closer to me in Australia than they were in Wigan. Sheila and her mam – I always came off second best. Sheila and I had done everything together, we'd been everywhere together with the kids since we had been in Australia.

I had not been a dickhead while I was at Penrith, but as soon as her mum arrived permanently I had to think about it. I never looked at other women while Sheila's mum wasn't there, there was no competition and I know it sounds pathetic, but it's true. It was me, Sheila and the kids, then they came and Sheila was always with her mum, always at ours or Sheila at hers.

I thought 'f... it, I'm going back to doing what I was doing before: women, drinking and gambling in between playing, training and work.' I thought I might as well go for a drink, then I would get into the drinking and there were girls throwing themselves at me. I went down that path again after vowing to make a fresh start when we came over to Australia. I got involved with one or two women.

One night, I must have been drinking. I drank a lot then, although I never drank two days before a game. I trained hard at the last training session and then the booze was off limits. I would go out and have an orange, a game of snooker, a game of darts and go to the club. Drinking didn't exist in my game preparation because I couldn't relax at home before a game. I always went out the night before a game, back home for around 10.30pm and settle down for the game the next day. That was my routine when I played for Wigan. Now I was back into the women scenario.

Anyway, I went out a couple of nights before to a club for a game of snooker with Peter Langmack. All of a sudden this woman turned up and said "Where are we going?"

I said "What do you mean?"

She said "Well, you told me to meet you here at eight o'clock."

I thought 'Oh no, I'm just having a game of snooker.'

The next thing was another woman turned up and said "Where were you? You told me to be here for eight o'clock."

Then another turned up, so there were three of them. Peter and I took the back door and just shot off. I had made arrangements to meet three of them at the same time, but I must have been that bladdered I couldn't remember doing it. I finished up with none of them that night, because I was with Peter and his moustache.

Young Malcolm, who was 17, got a great job working for the parish council driving diggers. He was a great young lad and I had no qualms about him, we did some boozing together. His dad, Tommy, got a job; Sheila's mum was occasionally alright for babysitting.

Malcolm was a good kid and one night he came out with us after I'd been training and we stayed out. It was a hot, hot evening and we were driving home when all of a sudden the alternator went and all the electrics cut out in my car. I said that we would have to run it. I was fit then, but young Malcolm wasn't. We got out of the car, I stripped off to my underpants and threw everything in the car. We started jogging the two-and-a-half to three miles home. We were on the way and I could hear these noises getting louder. I thought 'snakes on the road' and started running faster and faster. I finished up shouting "See you later, Malcolm". I got home and had a shower.

Malcolm got back and was absolutely knackered. We got some jump leads and he drove us back to the car. When we got there, there were loads of police. Fortunately, our reserve hooker at Penrith, Wayne Brain, was a policeman and said "Bill, is this your car?"

I said "Yeah".

He said "Listen mate, they're looking for bodies around here. They have looked in this abandoned car with all these clothes in, you better f... off mate." So we started the car and shot off home. I got away with it through Wayne being a copper.

In the close season I was back to work and spending the winter with Sheila, the kids, mother-in-law, father-in-law and her brother in between my extra duties. Don't get me wrong, occasionally I had a good time with her mum, but those were only odd occasions and we spent a lot of time together. We did barbeques up in the Blue Mountains, Bondi Beach, and Wollongong. But really we didn't get on.

What I did in Wigan, and in Australia after Sheila's parents arrived, I've always regretted. It was just sex, I have never loved another person like I love Sheila, so forgiving, caring and at that time I didn't realise what I had. I remember going out one night with Sheila, we went to a top club, there was a famous band on and when we walked in they stopped the band playing. They shone spotlights on me and Sheila. I thought Tom Jones or someone like that was coming in behind us.

I was a young lad from Wigan and didn't knock back a freebie; everything was thrown at me and I lived that life. I was involved in gambling and apart from when I was training or playing I drank night and day. I used to arrive home at one or two in the morning. I hardly saw my kids.

When I was younger I remember going home drunk and one of my kids, our Carl, being really poorly, on the verge of dying. I was drunk and said I'll take him to hospital, big man take him to hospital. I prayed in the back of the ambulance. I didn't know how to pray: 'God make him better I won't have another drink, I won't shag another woman, I won't have another cig, I won't have another bet.' Three days later, Carl was better. I was back again doing what I had done before. What a dickhead I was.

At the end of our second season in Australia, Sheila, I and two of our children, Carl and Graham, came home for a holiday to see our families. We stayed for four weeks. We stayed with Sheila's sister. She's a great person, her Mary, and we had a good time. Our other two children stayed in Australia with Sheila's family. We had had our other son in Australia by then, young Billy. Kathleen stayed there as well.

While I was at home this time, I wasn't approached by any clubs and didn't contact any either to see if they could poach me during the close season, especially after my poor decision 12 months earlier.

Preparing to kick for goal for Penrith (Courtesy *Rugby League Week*)

Looking to offload for Penrith (Courtesy *Rugby League Week*)

114

17. The greatest game of my life

My second season in Australia, 1975, was one hell of a rollercoaster, both on-and-off the field. It finished with me getting an unexpected honour and playing the greatest game of my life.

The start was mediocre and I picked up a couple of injuries as well. I had done my knee ligaments, which was why I hadn't played in the Amco Cup Final the previous year. When I came back I had a special trainer, Brian, who was a football coach. I did a lot of training on my own to build the muscle up. I also had trouble with varicose veins, so I'd had an operation on my left leg and missed all the club's pre-season training.

When I returned there had been a change of coach. The club got rid of Roy Masters as first team coach, who was one of the best ever in my opinion, who did the dignified thing and stepped down to coach the Under-23s. Roy saw out his contract before leaving Penrith for better and bigger things. Stevo was offered and took the coaching job. There was a feeling among the players that the club had got rid of Roy and that it was in Stevo's contract that he would get a chance at coaching. There had been rumours going around before the end of my first season when we did well. I thought to myself at the time be careful for what you wish for.

It didn't really work out in my opinion. I believe that the worst thing they ever did was get rid of Roy, we would have won a Grand Final sooner rather than later. We did get off to a better start than the previous year, and won two of our first three games. Our season began on Saturday 23 March with a trip to Cronulla. In a really tight contest we edged it by two points; I kicked four goals. It was my third successive victory over Cronulla.

We seemed to get stage fright in our opening home game of the season against Manly in front of over 13,000 fans and were well and truly taken to the cleaners by a very good side. The only positive point for me was that I dropped a goal early in the game when we were in contention.

Wests were our next visitors to Penrith and Stevo's tactical planning saw us win 20–11. Our player-coach went over for two tries and I kicked four goals. We then went on a terrible run, losing our next nine games, including the final three under Stevo's command, which I played in.

Round four took us to South Sydney. Eric Simms scored all their points with two tries and four goals to beat us. I chipped in with three goals, we deserved more from that game. We then had a trip to Canterbury Bankstown and weren't at the races at all. I put the conversion over for our try; we were heavily beaten 27–5.

The last thing we wanted then was to face Jack Gibson's champions Easts at Penrith. I missed the game, but over 11,000 fans came. No matter what I thought of Stevo throughout his tenure, I still always wanted to win. However, Easts showed why they were so successful and won comfortably. Ron Coote and Ian Schubert destroyed us that day as Stevo's reign came to an end.

I've touched on the relationship with Stevo, but whatever our thoughts were about each other, it was okay on the pitch. I rarely spoke to him; the only words I would say were 'My ball'. We didn't mix off the pitch.

At the end of the day he was a very good hooker. I would not knock what he did on the pitch; he played for his country and Penrith because he was a good hooker. He got a coaching job at the club that second season because people thought maybe he was a good coach, but it didn't work out, these things happen. I like Stevo for what he was as a player. As a person I think he is different now, I've met him a few times. When I became a Christian I went to him and apologised for every wrong thing I'd said to him and everything I'd done against him. I asked if he would forgive me; we get on well now.

I had hoped that Roy Masters would come back to guide us out of what were becoming stormy waters. Whether he was asked or not, I don't know because they appointed Barry Harris to move up from reserves coach to first grade. He was a good bloke. I don't know whether he was anti-Pom, or just anti-me or not, but he did have a go at me on occasions that season. He dropped me a few times, including for his first game in charge, at Parramatta. I was in the reserves who played before the first grade game.

I didn't want to play in the reserve grade. I just walked around, not putting any effort in. We were losing by four points with three minutes to go. Dennis Coffey came up to me and said "Bill, do something mate. We need winning pay. You might get it in your contract, but we need winning pay."

What do you do in those circumstances? I knew I was too good to be playing for the reserves, but when someone makes a passionate request like that there's not much I could say. I got my head on and scored two tries, kicked a goal and we won.

Coffey has always said: "The way he [Bill Ashurst] could turn it on was out of this world. Within three minutes he had won us a game, three minutes of genius and he had got us winning pay." In those days they selected the subs for first grade from the reserve side. I wasn't going to be a replacement, it was hot out there, red hot and I'd strolled in the park and won the game for us in 80 minutes.

Barry came over to me and said "You're backing up in first grade."

I said "Am I f... my ankle's knackered." I'd done my full 80 in the forwards. I wasn't playing back-to-back games.

The following Wednesday I was back in the team for the Amco Cup first round against South Brisbane. I was sitting with our chairman, Barry Walsh. Before the game, as I was getting changed, I said "Barry, do you want to buy a colour telly?"

He said "What do you mean?"

I said "I'm going to win that colour telly tonight."

He said "How much do you want?"

I said "$1,000 for it." Eventually, after nagging and mythering for two hours just before the game kicked off, he agreed. I had worn him down and out; he said "Alright". We played the game, I was man-of-the-match and won the colour telly. Barry was probably one of the first people in Penrith to have a colour telly and I had $1,000 in my bank account.

While playing in that competition I won three colour televisions. The third was after our second round win over Illawarra, who like the South Brisbane were a country division side. I took control of the game and made sure we progressed. That was as good as it got because we then lost away to St George in a game I missed because of injury.

They also had a competition within the Amco Cup, the Golden Try. This was for the best try of the competition; whoever scored or set it up won an Alfa Romeo car. I won the car as well. I got the ball in my own 20 against the Brothers in the opening round. In the opening attacking set I threw more dummies than they have in a chemist's shop, chipped over, re-gathered the ball and burst through. As I came to their full-back on his 20 yard line I stepped him, left him flat-footed and gave the ball to our winger for a walk in try.

Instead of receiving the car, I took the $6,000 cash equivalent. It was the worst thing I ever did really. Sheila put it in the bank and we know what happened from there.

Barry Harris once pulled me to one side. He was trying to make a point and said "You're not doing enough tackling. If you don't improve your tackling, I'm going to put you in the reserve grade again." The next weekend, before the game, I told the lads "I'm going to be doing all the tackling tonight, don't look for me with that ball please."

I only got two passes in the game and I kicked from them. I made 49 tackles and we lost. The side had no general, no footballer in control, they were like chickens with no heads and we lost heavily. I walked into the dressing room after the game knackered; more so than usual. Barry came straight to me and said "Bill".

I said "What?"

He said "Whatever I said before, forget tackling mate, just do what you do for me."

I thought that will do for me because I never tackled when they ran at me. I had established that I was going to do my own thing. I was that type of player. I couldn't set into a team coach's pattern because I was spontaneous; I didn't know what I was going to do next. Thank God, I was given a gift, it just came naturally and that was the way I played. I did what I had to do, but deep down Barry wasn't a bad coach. God bless him, he died of cancer a few years later. Whoever the coach was, I played my own game anyway. And off the field things were as crazy as ever.

After our Amco Cup win, the whole team and club were buzzing. After my man-of-the-match performance we were looking forward to the visit of North Sydney to Penrith. They were also having a poor season and were only ahead of us on points' difference. Would this be the one after four defeats or was the cup win a false dawn? It was the latter as we lost badly. However, the game will be remembered for an entirely different reason; my mum's intervention as I described earlier.

The losing run continued. I was kicking occasional goals in those defeats and although I was always a confident person, even I was beginning to wonder when we were going to get a result. Going into Round 13 against Cronulla another loss would give us a perfect 10 defeats. We had been propping the league up for the last four weeks. I had never been in a losing side against Cronulla in my time at Penrith.

No-one can ever tell how or why fortunes change; how a team can go from champs to chumps or heroes to zeroes and that's what happened against Cronulla. The fans had responded to our slump, going from a crowd of over 13,000 in our opening game to only just over 5,000 for this one. We were on fire that day from the first to the 80th minute and turned them over 40–15.

We hit them with eight try blitz and eight successful kicks from me. Although they scored three tries we were a try and defence juggernaut that day. We also collected a $1,600 Wills Try Award for our eight try haul. We were back on the horse; about time. We cheered, had a drink and could kick on. It was a lucky 13 for us.

We beat Illawarra in the Amco Cup and then came a trip to Wests who were in the play-off spots. We were looking for our first double. In a terrific game we won at Lidcombe. I kicked two goals from four attempts. Souths came to Penrith and our three match winning run saw the crowd grow to more than 11,000. This was a belting game; we really showed our character, guts and determination. It was Bill Ashurst against Eric Simms. My try and three goals edged Simms who could only manage a try and two goals; we won 9–7.

Canterbury Bankstown were also riding high in the play-off places. We won at home again, 23–8, which showed how resilient our defence had become and how lethal our attack was. I was certainly on the ball with my kicking game in open play and showed flair with the ball in hand. I scored a try and kicked four goals.

But then came a trip to Manly who were second in the table behind Easts. We didn't fear anyone, but Graham Eadie took us to the cleaners with two tries and eight goals. We scored a couple of tries. I kicked a goal and was going okay until I had a misunderstanding with their little scrum-half. I put a short kick over and he caught it, just beating me to the ball. I 'coat-hangered' him. He was out for the count and carried off; I walked off to another trip to the Sydney Disciplinary Committee.

They laughed after they asked "What happened Bill? Give your own description."

I said "Well sir, I had put this little kick in and I thought I could see him juggling with the ball, so I thought I'll knock it up and catch it at the other side."

They just went 'F... off' and gave me a three game ban. It was only the second time I was sent off that season. I started to settle down and hadn't got as much stick as before. The players and clubs knew I could look after myself and there wasn't a lot of off-the-ball stuff on me. It was still obviously full on aggression, the sledging never changed; it was a settling down period.

After that defeat our season petered out. Going into our last game, we had lost three out of four matches. To avoid taking the wooden spoon for the first time in two years, we needed to beat St George who were guaranteed third place in the league and a play-off place whatever the result. We were at home and our destiny was down to us, South Sydney were a point behind us and had to travel to Manly who had already secured second place. Given how we had fallen away a crowd of 8,303 was outstanding.

Stevo had been player-coach and captain. He had been replaced by Zac Olejarnik when he had to return to the United Kingdom for personal reasons. He came back to reclaim the armband. That's how we all thought it was going to be when we got to the ground for the game. We prepared, went for the warm up and came back in the sheds. Fifteen minutes before kick-off Barry Harris dropped a bombshell. He told the team that I would captain the side for this game.

I was gobsmacked at his announcement. I had no idea and from the reaction of my teammates neither did they. It was hardly the best preparation for the game. Inside I felt really proud when it was announced. It was the first time I had ever captained a side, I knew I had led by example and led teams around the field. I had never had an armband and the responsibility that goes with it. Even if it was only for one game; and even though we didn't get on, I couldn't imagine what Stevo felt about it and if he had been aware of this change. The decision had nothing to do with me.

It is said that the role and responsibility of captaincy can put added pressure on a player to perform and how they play. With 16 minutes left, I had aged 10 years. We had been playing with 12 men after only 30 minutes because Terry Geary went for an early bath. He had decided before kick-off that he was going to take Henry Tatana out with a high hit and that if he was going to get sent off Tatana would come with him on a stretcher. Well part of his cunning plan worked... Terry went for an early bath and Tatana stayed on the pitch. He was laughing as Terry walked off.

To add insult to injury, Tatana scored a try and kicked five goals. They were leading 19–0. We were doing okay, I was trying to get the boys round the pitch barking at them, shouting at them to get them going, but St George were playing some great stuff. The side had class all through the team through captain-coach Graeme Langlands and their great general Billy Smith. They were in cruise control, guiding them around the park.

Our species had seen enough and were going in their droves. As things were steadily going downhill, Stevo, who had played well for us, and me, was spark out unconscious on the ground after a scrum. All I had seen was a fist come through the middle into the front row. A lot of people thought it was me who did him because I didn't like him. I wouldn't hit a teammate, especially when we were that many points down with just less than the final quarter to play. At that moment I thought 'This is good. First game as captain, beaten nil points, what a way to be remembered, for all the wrong reasons.'

So the last throws of the dice, down to our last 12 men and no-one with Stevo's experience to get us the ball in the contested scrums, great. As Stevo was being treated I got all the team together and told them we could either lie down and lose quietly or give it a final dig to at least get some points on the board and lose with dignity and pride. Maybe we could still win; I didn't think so, although I've always been confident of my own ability. They agreed so when we restarted I wondered what their response would be.

Gary Allsop scored and I put one over from the touchline; 19–5 – a consolation score. Then he scored again out wide; another conversion, 19–10. By this time Changa had taken his tackling machine Peter Fitzgerald off. I could see the players looking at each other.

119

Their body language had changed, what confidence they had was visibly growing as the seconds ticked by.

Youngster Barry Le Brocq burst on the ball to score near to the posts and my kick brought us to within four points. I was looking at the St George players, some of their heads were down, some were shaking their heads and the body language said 'what are we doing?' The crowd that was left sensed something and got behind us with the volume rising. I told the lads "Let's go for it, let's believe we can do it." I got the ball and drove down field, just mowing through St George players and got tackled. We then moved it out wide and Tim Sheens scored near the touchline to make it 19–18 for St George.

The crowd and the team went wild. There were only a couple of minutes left as we nearly smothered Tim, but I realised we were still a point behind. Although the St George players were down there was a slight smile on some of their faces which made me think that they thought I was going to miss the kick and they could nick it. I placed the ball on the touchline. The crowd had gone quiet. The tension was unbearable as I tried to compose myself.

This was one of those moments when you realise why you play the game. I had always been a born winner. I knew what these next few seconds would mean to everyone at the club. I took a couple of steps back a couple to the side, deep breaths, looked at the posts for a final time, head down, focussed on where I was going to strike the ball. I did the same as I always did in practice and when playing it was like riding a bike. I walked up and struck the ball, boom, it was that feeling like when Carl Froch landed that punch at Wembley on George Groves... I turned around and went back towards the halfway line into my own half smiling. I knew it was going over and we were ahead 20–19. As the roar of the crowd grew I knew it had gone through the posts. My team came and patted me on the back. All I could shout at them was "Concentrate, concentrate" although I didn't think St George could come back.

Unbelievably, in the last minute we got our fifth try when Ross Gigg went in under the posts and my golden boot made it five out of five. We won 25–19. I was walking on air. Fans came streaming onto the field, pats on the back everywhere for all the players. I've spoken before of those few occasions when a player is in the zone and everything they touch turns to gold. Both the team and I were in the mega zone, if there is such a thing. The team had died, gone to heaven, and come back to perform a modern miracle of rugby league. Words can't describe how I felt and that was before I thought about being a winning captain and winning my first game in the role. That game is in the folklore of Penrith and the pity of it is that there is no film record of such a sensational rugby league match. I played the greatest game of my life and I've played in some great ones in my career. By the way, Souths got hammered by Manly.

18. So near yet so far

When I returned back to Penrith from a break at home to see Sheila's sister and family, there wasn't the turmoil of 12 months earlier. Barry Harris was still in charge. Roy Masters with his contract completed sadly moved on, a big mistake by the club. This year, 1976, was the 10th anniversary of the club joining the New South Wales Rugby League

I had been having trouble with varicose veins. I had a big operation to get rid of a few and it took quite a while to get fit in the build up to the beginning of the season. Two club officials had gone to America to see what they could learn to improve the club.

One of the things they did was appoint a full-time trainer and conditioner. He worked on getting me fit again for pre-season. He was a real good fitness trainer and it didn't take me long to get fit. That was the first and only major operation I had in Australia.

I was probably the fittest I had ever been after these one-on-one sessions. It broke up the boredom of doing tedious work training all together. I absolutely loved it; we didn't just do rugby league exercises. We did many different exercises; such as goalkeeper training.

In the close season the club signed a great prop forward from Parramatta, Bob O'Reilly. He'd proved himself and toured three times with Australia. His nickname was 'The Bear'. I had a whiff in the breeze about how much he was getting, so I pulled the Penrith board and said "I want you to sell my contract, I'm not happy anymore."

They said "Why? For what reason?"

I said "I know what's he's [O'Reilly] is getting and I want one more dollar than him."

I wasn't having that fat bloke earning more money than me at Penrith, so they ummed and arred and it finished up with me receiving one dollar more than him. It eventually became $7,001 more. It jumped up to 18, 19 grand then, I was on a heck of a lot of money.[6]

I've been fortunate. I didn't put myself on a pedestal, that's for other people do. I went back to Penrith in 2006. The chairman who negotiates contracts said "I won't lie to you Bill; you would be on $2,000,000 a year if you was playing now."

I thought I was lazy, but Bob was lazier than me and liked a drink. We went on runs in pre-season training and he found all the hiding places, all the ducking and diving, so I made sure I ran with him. We hid under benches, behind trees and wait for the first dozen coming. We would jump in among them and only do half a mile, while the rest had done a mega run. We got on well, but lazy.

The club had also signed England and Great Britain international Dave 'Toppo' Topliss from Wakefield Trinity, who I later got to know very well. He was a wonderful player and a great number six who had a bad time at Penrith. The coach didn't like him, he never got on well with the coach and there is only one winner then, the coach. I felt really sorry for him,

---

[6] In 1976, £1 was worth $1.47 (Australian Dollars)

but sadly there was nothing I could do about it. He had dropped me to the reserves the previous season. Dave missed more games than he played, he should have played more.

Toppo's biggest problem was that Barry Harris had brought a lad in, Kenny Wilson. He was not a bad player and was a good goalkicker. But he was not in Toppo's class as far as I'm concerned, but Kenny used to get the nod regularly ahead of Toppo.

Also in pre-season there was a change of kit, although we still had the nickname 'The Chocolate Soldiers' which in years to come would just relate to 'The Panthers' or now sometimes to the 'Penny Panthers.' There were no more chocolate striped shirts. The kit was a chocolate bottom part of the shirt with a white top and red, white and blue sleeves, white shorts and socks with a red stripe down the side of the shorts and a red band at the top of the shorts.

Barry Harris then announced that Stevo was going to captain the side for the 1976 season. I did think I would retain it, but it didn't bother me. When I was on the field in the action playing I was always shouting to the players what, where, how and when I wanted the ball when I saw or envisaged a gap being made. If I was only as good as my last game as captain, then what a game to lead the team, the win against St George.

The season began on Sunday 21 March 1976, with a home game in front of just over 6,000 fans. I thought that was disappointing, given what we had delivered in the final home game of the previous season. We were at home to Norths and I had a run of six appearances at the start of the season.

We thrashed them 43–9, which turned out to be the biggest win of the season and in my time at the club. Everything we did that day come off as we went over for nine tries, including two from me. What a confidence boost; we were top of the table after Round 1.

Then we went to play the champions, Easts, at the Sports Ground. I wanted to show how good I was; I went over for another try and the hosts showed why they were the champions by winning a close game.

Next up were Wests in Penrith. Nearly 12,000 fans turned up and saw a great game. I made bursts throughout the game and waiting for runners to latch onto the offloads and final passes. I gave John King three beautiful balls for him to score a hat-trick. A draw was a fair result; we stayed unbeaten at home and had the last play-off spot.

Sadly, we couldn't carry that form into the Amco Cup and crashed out to Brothers at Lang Park; I scored a try, but it wasn't to be. Then we entertained Newton at Penrith and again produced another great performance. My kicking game and distribution came to the fore again; we won 22–17 and outscored them six tries to two. My rich vein of try-scoring continued. I scored one with my traditional chip over the defence and for the second powered through a gap to score.

This was the club's best start for many years. We were third after the opening four games, a point behind Balmain and three behind unbeaten Manly. My form was superb; I made a contribution in all the league and cup games and had already scored seven tries and a drop-goal.

However, the next 10 games were disappointing because we only won twice. The frustrating thing was a couple of close back-to-back defeats. We had a very close, hard and aggressive side and our biggest defeat of the season was by only 14 points. I played in the opening two losses and scored a try against Souths. Our heaviest loss of the season was 18–4 at Balmain, which took them to the top of the table.

Further defeats to Cronulla and Manly saw us drop out of the top five play-off positions. I was still injured when we returned to winning ways against Canterbury Bankstown. It was our first clean sheet of the season and the only time when I was at the club that we managed that. It was an outstanding effort with great spirit, defence and attacking options.

I came back the following week against St George and we beat them again. I was in fine form and kept it up with another try. I had now scored nine tries in 11 league and cup games. Those two wins saw us return into play-off contention in fourth place.

I missed narrow defeats against Parramatta and Cronulla. We played superbly in both games and came away with nothing. The losing run continued with a narrow defeat away to Norths followed by a seven point home loss to Easts. I was leading the side around the field and the manner and closeness of all four matches was frustrating.

It meant that we needed to put a really good winning run together to have any chance of making the top five. That third position after Round four seemed a million miles away. The difference between success and failure is a fine line. The team's spirit was still there despite those four losses. It was probably the best team spirit and team I'd played in; we did everything together, drank together, played hard together on and off the park and it made a great team spirit.

I was going through my idiot phase with Sheila's family being there. After training sessions we would go to the Red Cow for a drink and then slip into a club. We did that for the first five days of the week together. None of us drank two days before a game, but did we play hard before we went dry.

I was living the life; we did the gang bangers, together in a van outside the training ground. Gang bangers were what it sounds like, another name for the 'ladies of the night', prostitutes. With some other words in Australia meaning a different thing to those in Britain, I had to watch what I said.

For example, the word 'bun', we all know what a 'bun' is don't we? When I was working in the sports shop when I first arrived, this lady had asked for an exercise bike to be delivered, so I took it. Darrell, a workmate at the shop, said "Be hospitable when you've delivered it and made sure everything is okay. Ask for a bun and a cup of tea."

The next thing was I got a slap across the face. I said "What's that for?"

She said "Do you realise that you have just asked me for a gang bang?"

I said "Have I, flipping heck." That was one of my problems with the Australian language barriers when I first arrived there.

In my first season, it was funny. I didn't know what about the language differences and that expressions we used at home meant something else in Australia. I would go into a shop in Australia ask for a packet of Durex, they would give a roll of Sellotape.

123

I knew what a 'root' was at home; a cigarette or rooting about in a drawer. A 'root' in Australia means sex with a girl. Before I knew this I kept saying 'Stop rooting about' and people kept saying 'Hey, mind your language'. I wondered what on earth I was saying, it took a while for me to get used to the language and meanings of words in Australia.

Enough rooting about after those four losses, we needed to get back to winning ways and travelled to play Wests who were in the play-off places having won nine out of 15 games. We put in a master class that day as I marshalled the troops around the park. Our defence was superb, and restricted them to a penalty. In our second biggest win of the season away from home we won 25–2. I kicked two goals and Kenny Wilson got three.

The following week we travelled to Newtown and had another terrific game against them. We won and outscored them two tries to one and five goals to three. I kicked three goals. Those wins had moved us up to eighth, but we were five points away from the play-offs. We needed to kick on to have any hope

Crucially we had two very close losses next; 23–17 to Souths at Penrith when I chipped in with a couple of goals, and a second home loss, 12–5 to Balmain. A youthful Phil Gould made his debut for Penrith and kicked a goal.

What a stellar playing and coaching career Phil has had. He is general manager of the Penrith Panthers who at the time of writing were top of the NRL. He was recently recognised in the Queen's Birthday honours and appointed a Member of the Order of Australia (AM) for services to rugby league. He was a young whippersnapper as a kid and we could tell even then there was something about him.

Those defeats meant that we could not reach the play-offs even if we won our last four games. We were all gutted: players, coaches and fans. Next up was Manly, the league leaders who had been there for most of the season. Until then I had never played in a side which had beaten them.

There were only 6,260 there and I don't blame the fans for staying away after four defeats, although they had been close ones. This was no different and for the first time this season we had the luck and rub of the green. In a superb game from the start to the end this game had everything and I wanted to put on a show against the best in the league.

My kicking game was on; I directed the side around the park and they responded to my calls and orders. All the team were heroes that day. Four tries and two crucial goals saw us home after a magnificent defensive effort.

We nicked the game 16–15 and when the whistle went for full-time we moved up to eighth. I knew how Manly felt after our 16–15 loss at Cronulla and 12–10 loss at Parramatta. I wanted to feel sorry for them, but I couldn't. We had beaten the best side in the league who went on to become the champions after winning the Grand Final. We were all walking on air and had a bloody good drink that night; quite right too.

In Round 20 we travelled to Belmore Sports ground to face Canterbury Bankstown who were a place off the play-offs on points difference. We were up for it after our win and they wanted to make the play-offs. It was another cracking, hard encounter. We put on a great defensive effort and came away with another close win. I scored one of our tries and Ken Wilson kicked five crucial goals so we remained eighth.

The penultimate round was a trip to play St George who were third. We had already beaten two sides in the play-off places already and went there full of confidence. Again we played really well and threw the lot at them. Our defence played its part in another close game, but we just missed out by three points. I suppose revenge was sweet for them for what we had done 12 months earlier. Stevo scored a try, Ken Wilson kicked two goals and I scored a try after a powerful run and stepping their defence. It was my 11th of the season and my last try for the club.

Sunday 22 August saw the final match of the season, and my last game for the club. It was against Parramatta. There were 15,342 at Penrith's ground, the biggest home gate that I played in front of in three years and the biggest for any game I played in Australia.

Penrith against Parramatta was like Wigan against St Helens. The rivalry in those games was really intense. They had had the wood over us in my time, four – one in those three seasons. The one we won was in my first season, 29–21 at Penrith Park. We hadn't signed Bob Reilly from Parramatta at that time. I made him look like a clown that day, scoring three tries, my first and only hat-trick for Penrith.

This game was all set up. Parramatta had had a great season and been in the play-off positions for most of the season. They were safe in second spot and their points difference meant that even if they lost they wouldn't drop down. We were still eighth. The atmosphere was fantastic and I had one of those games when I was involved in everything, running, kicking and I got a great response from the whole team who to a man were great. No-one was going to go off the pitch at the end of the game wondering what if... they put everything they had to give in attack and defence.

The problem was so did Parramatta. There were some good belts; after all it was a derby and the final chance to get out any pent up feelings. We agonisingly lost 11–10 after we had outscored them two tries to one. They had completed the double over us and were second in the league; they got to the Grand Final that year and lost to Manly.

We were gutted. That loss meant we dropped down a position to ninth. We had experienced lows and highs, the low of that second one point defeat.

It is often said that the table never lies, teams finish where they should finish; but sometimes it can be so cruel. Although we finished 10 points off the play-offs, we were a better team than that. Competitive, we suffered close defeats many times; our biggest loss all season was by 14 points. We had done well as we celebrated our 10th season in the New South Wales RL.

What a way to bow out of the game in Australia. I'm not being big headed, but the games I played in Australia I found it much easier than in England. Don't get me wrong, there were some good, young, tough footballers in Australia; but my type of rugby baffled me, never mind them.

They were always susceptible to the short kick over the top, which was my trade mark. It's seldom used now in the modern game. I wasn't intimidated by what they said and what they did; I played my own game and was fortunate that things came off.

They couldn't play our type of rugby and it was at this time that they bought over skilful English players. The Aussies learned that type of game to go with their intensity and toughness and now they have done that we've never beaten them in the Ashes, World Cups or anything else.

I signed originally on a two year contract and then they wanted me to improve it so I eventually signed a five year contract. In my third season they wanted to tie me to the club to the end of my career. Mr Cowan used to say that as long as we're involved in this club, you will be going nowhere so the price was right.

It was so lucrative; they bumped it up to $28,000 a year from the $19,000 contract I had negotiated after the club had signed Bob Reilly. It gave me more scope with the bookies and the women; I lived my lifestyle accordingly to the pay I got.

While playing I had a great rapport with most of the rugby league press and media. I worked for 2KE radio doing advertising. It was crazy advertisements. I tried putting on an Australian accent and was National Tyres. I would say "Tell them Billy boy sent you and get your discount from Billy boy" with an Aussie accent. I felt like a prat, but it paid well.

The only bloke I ever fell out with, well he fell out with me, was one of the television presenters, Rex Mossop who had played as a forward for Manly and Australia. We had a very important game against Easts at Penrith on the Sunday in my third season.

He had a programme on television on Sunday mornings. It had a passing competition on it from the Elephant Bank and he wanted me to go on. I said "No".

He asked "Why?"

I said "If you think I am driving into Sydney on the morning of our game against Easts and driving all the way back to Penrith Park. I'm sorry I'll come on any other time."

It was a three hour drive either way because there were no motorways then. But because I didn't go on his show I thought that he tried to ruin me because he said that I had let him down. He completely fell out with me from then on; I thought that all his comments about me were negative.

I wasn't worried, he was an Australian anyway and my performances spoke for themselves. I had a superb third season, he and everybody else in the media knew it.

19. Here today, gone tomorrow

My third season finished successfully on the field. Off the field I was heavily into, in my own words, keeping up the team spirit with the lads when not playing and training and working at the gym. Five out of seven days and nights, wine, women and song. Things had been brewing and building up as the playing season came to an end between me and Sheila and it dramatically came to a head.

Sheila caught me with another woman on the golf course, although we were just playing golf. I made some excuse, but she knew I was lying. I suppose there is a big difference between suspecting, knowing and having it thrown in your face.

Sheila had had enough and decided that she wanted to return to Wigan. She wanted me to come too. She was leaving me and I had to face the fact that we were separating and that she meant it. There are times you know these things; we had been together that long and before we came to Australia she was thinking of divorcing me.

I didn't want to leave Australia. I was quite happy with my lifestyle. With the new five year contract I'd negotiated I was on $29,000 a year. I wanted to make sure she took her mum back with her as well, so that was another plus for me.

Not the plus that Sheila was leaving, that her mam was leaving and everything that went with it, so she decided that she was going back and her mam and family were going as well. I went to the club and told them that Sheila and I were getting divorced, that I didn't want my family struggling back home. I asked them if they would advance two years of my contract money so that Sheila could set up home in Wigan with my four kids. I still loved them all and when they got home I would be at peace knowing they were all okay financially and everything would be alright. The club listened to what I was saying. They accepted my proposal and were brilliant.

I gave her the contract money and she went to Wigan with the children. It took a while, but she got a house just outside Wigan in Platt Bridge. Her mam, dad and brother, the honest reason why I went back to my old ways went back as well, they got a house in the next street so they were still close together.

I still loved Sheila and my kids Carl, Graham, Kathleen and Billy. Billy was born in Australia and has dual nationality. We kept in touch by telephone and by post. Sheila has still got the letters and shows them me every now and again.

Pre-season started and within the first few weeks I started to miss the kids. There was a polio scare in England and everybody had to queue up for sugar for polio.

I was worried about my kids and I asked Penrith could I have a few weeks off to go home and make sure my kids were alright. I spoke to Roger Cowan; he put it to the committee and they refused to give me permission because I had signed the new contract.

I had said that I would come back when I knew they were okay. I knew I was in an awkward situation when I asked, especially because they had given me the advance of the contract money. When I was told about their decision I was very pissed off. I thought I'll go and have a word with this shower. Two years earlier Stevo had been allowed to go home for personal reasons, but not me.

I couldn't see the difference between his request, which was granted, and mine which was not. At that moment my mind was made up; no-one at the club was going to stop going home to see if my children were okay. I was worried about the polio outbreak. My children hadn't been struck down with it, but I needed to be home with them. If Penrith hadn't said 'no', I wouldn't have done what I did to them. As I said earlier no-one beat Bill Ashurst, Bill Ashurst beat himself.

The problem I then had was that when Sheila and the kids went back home she had the family passport. We didn't have individual passports. At that point I was stuffed. I telephoned Sheila and told her what had happened. I asked her if she would send me the passport back because I was going to come home.

Sheila sent me the passport to me in Penrith and I just went through the motions in pre-season. When the passport arrived, I never told anyone apart from a couple of very close friends, Glenn West and Ross Gigg, they knew what I was going to do. I booked the flight at Sydney Airport, got the money out of my bank account, got a money order and emptied the account that I had in Penrith. I took what I could in clothes, drove the club car to the airport, got on the plane and flew back to England.

Glenn and Ross knew what time my flight was and at the exact time the fight was due to leave Sydney Airport they let Bob Reilly know who they knew I had a lot of time for. He rang one of his close rugby league press contacts and said "Bill Ashurst is just flying over the Blue Mountains. He's off back to England." The shit hit the fan. Bob got $500 off the press for the story, but never gave me $250 when I went back in 2006. It was probably the easiest $500 he had ever made. At the time I couldn't care less, I was on my way home.

Just for the record, contrary what has been said elsewhere, when I left for Sydney Airport for my flight no furniture was moved from my house. I just booked the flight, got in the car went to the airport and flew home. Never touched a stick of furniture, I left at the house and there were three Penrith lads there. Paul Marino and two others who they had just signed were in the house after Sheila left and shared with me. I left them at the house, I just took the things I could carry, left the rest and all the furniture. Nothing else was taken from the house, no dramas. All the club had to do was collect the car from Sydney Airport.

It was a relief; I knew I was coming back and could make sure that my kids were okay. That was my main worry. People may think why did he go back, why did he do this? Well, when you love your kids so much; this epidemic was all over the news; people were queuing up for emergency vaccinations, sugar tablets. I was worried about my kids and it was a relief when I saw all four of them and everything was okay.

I had had the advance money from Penrith, and taken any other cash from accounts in Penrith leaving nothing in them, the Aussies can't take a joke. I didn't have any visits from any solicitors because of what had happened and what I had done. Penrith's Roger Cowan did get in touch with me...

All I can say about my three year Australian adventure is I made some wonderful friends. I thought that I would make enemies and I think my ability as a player outweighed what I did as a person, including flying back home and everything that went with that.

Penrith flew me back in 2006 as one of the greatest players ever to play for the club; some said the greatest player to ever play for them. The club paid for my three weeks stay, the flights, all the directors who were still alive from when I played there met me. That Friday night in 2006 at Penrith we all got drunk together, so rather than forgiveness of a person for what I did, the forgiveness of the player I was outweighed everything else.

I have no regrets whatsoever. It was a fantastic experience both on the pitch off, the friends that I made, no enemies.

Photo: Bill with Billy in Australia, who seems to have a good hand-off.

Setting up an attack for Penrith (Courtesy *Rugby League Week*)

20. Coming back from Penrith

When I had come back to Wigan, Penrith got in touch with me. I spoke to Roger Cowan about playing rugby league, would I be able to play in England now I was home? I was told if I went back that everything would be okay, I could carry on playing for Penrith. Sheila had set up home with the kids in Wigan. I was back in Wigan, but was missing the game.

No clubs here were interested in me. I was still a Penrith player and decided to go back. I booked a flight to Sydney, but didn't let the club know. I became aware when I got over there what Penrith were up to. From Sydney I made my way to Penrith and stayed with Daphne, 'Daff', who I knew at that time. I had been there two days when Peter Langmack, who was a really good friend of mine, came round.

She told him I was back and he came over straight away. He said 'They are not happy with what you did. I know that they are going to get the tax man onto you...' Peter was a very close friend and someone I could trust and rely on. To be quite honest I don't know if I paid tax while I was in Australia. The club hadn't told me. I suppose I should have asked when I got there. I wondered what to do.

I didn't have the money to fly back to England. I was panicking: no funds, no money for a flight home and the possibility that the Australian tax man was after me. An innocent man being chased by criminals; what a turnaround for Australia. I didn't leave Daff's house for a week. I didn't walk around Penrith or anything because I would have been recognised straight away. I didn't let the Penrith Panthers know that I was in town, given what Peter had told me. Whatever trust I had had with the club had gone.

I had had time to think at Daff's and was still in a panic, wondering what to do. I decided to ring Peter Carroll in Wigan. I told him what my first intentions were when I had returned to Australia, what was happening, what they were trying to do and that I'd no funds to get back. When I had finished talking to him and put the phone down it was a feeling of huge relief.

Peter went to see Sheila to let her know what had happened to me and that he was going to get me back home. He went to a travel agent and booked a flight to get me back to Wigan. Peter rang me, gave me the time, date and flight number and that the ticket was at Sydney Airport. I've not yet paid Peter back the £400 it cost for the flight, which even though it's a lot of money now, was worth even more nearly 40 years ago. I'm in lifelong debt to him to Peter and with Sheila he has always been there for me. I can only thank him for everything he has helped me with and supported me through thick and thin.

It was now becoming like a spy film. How could I get to Sydney Airport from Sydney without being recognised and the Penrith club, or more importantly the taxman, finding out? Daff had done enough letting me stay at her place, Peter Langmack had let me know what was going on and I didn't want to get him in trouble. The evening before I was to leave Australia for what I thought would be the last time, I rang another good friend, Billy Morris. He didn't play rugby league and wasn't connected to the club.

Billy was a Welsh lad who lived in the Cambridge Park part of Penrith. I explained what had happened, that I was getting a flight home the next day and needed a lift to the airport. Billy picked me up at Daff's; I made my farewells and stayed at his place that night. We had a few beers before he took me to the airport the next day. Thanks to Billy I boarded the plane for home. It had been one of the longest weeks of my life.

When I first returned, if everything would have worked out I would have told anyone in the rugby league media that I was back. I didn't, and didn't want them to sniff out a story. I kept it in-house with a close-knit, trusted group of friends that I had in Penrith. The first time I flew home the media didn't know until my plane was flying over the blue mountains of Penrith. Bob O'Reilly got his money for doing that.

Peter Langmack is one of the best friends I have ever had. It was a privilege to speak to him when I went back 30 years later. At the time of writing, he is still alive. There are a lot of people who were wonderful. I had so much respect from the players. Possibly because I got them winning pay more than anything, but I had respect for those players and when I went back for the 'Legends' team every one of the squad, apart from Stevo, rang me or came and had a beer with me. Even people like Glenn West and Ross Gigg, who sadly passed away in May 2014, who lived in Newcastle and Queensland, came and had a weekend with me at Penrith. It was fantastic.

I got back home for the second time with a result. I had beaten the Australian taxman, having gone back originally to do the right thing again. Nobody else knew that I had gone back to this day; the only people in Penrith were Daphne, Peter and Billy. Only Sheila knew over here and then Peter Carroll, when I had to ring him. If you have a close knit family as well, you can keep secrets in-house, now everyone will know. I was glad to get back to my roots in Wigan and happy to be back home

When I came back for the second time, for good, there was still no British club interested in signing me. I was hoping to get back into rugby league. The only problem was that I was still a Penrith player. I've never been a bighead, but I knew someone would not let the talent that I had go to waste.

I believe that as a result of my actions, at that time or just afterwards, Australia and Great Britain enforced a transfer embargo for players in both countries. A lot of people say, and said at the time that it was my fault. Whatever. Players used to say to me 'I'd have gone two years earlier only for you', or 'I would have gone 12 months earlier only for you.' Sometimes people can't take a joke right, so, at the end of the day I did what I did. I think that if they had had the Great Britain-Australia relationship like it is today, I don't think that there would have been many problems.

They were two separate entities then, as it is now, but there is free movement both ways now, with more British rugby league players taking the plunge and going to play in the NRL. Those players will only get better, given time, and enhance the game in our country, which the NRL doesn't rate if we're honest. The next step is for us to see those players bring their NRL experience into the international jersey, which will see England or Great Britain beat Australia in Australia and in the UK in meaningful competitions.

I decided to start training with my brother-in-law, Terry Parry, who had married Sheila's sister, Mary. I was the worst trainer in the world, but I knew that I had to get some semblance of fitness. Terry lived more-or-less across the road from us. He had a shed with his own gym, with dumbbells, bars and weights. I had a bench to do press-ups and sit-ups. I wore a big plastic bag under an overcoat to get a sweat and a rubber tyre around my waist because I'd gone up to 21 stones.

It was hard work. I gave it 100 per cent; I knew what I had to do. I had no one watching over my shoulder; I didn't have a trainer like Bob Tapper who would push us all the time. I did my own thing and got myself some semblance of fitness. I used to consider myself fit and ready when I was playing around 16.5 to 17 stones, so I began to get rid of the excess four stones.

I was in that shed every morning and afternoon. In the evening, when nobody was watching, I ran along the canal bank. I think I wore a path because I used to do the same run every day, but I got there eventually. Terry was a good trainer, we worked off each other, but I did more of the running. I needed it for my stamina as well as strength; I had been used to running from playing rugby league.

Terry was a weights and gym man. To give him credit, he tried hard with me and did a lot with me. Usually we did about an hour-and-a-half in the morning and the same in the afternoon. We went for a run at about 6.30pm for about 30 to 45 minutes, gradually increasing it each day. As all this was happening, I heard a rumour that Wigan were interested in signing me.

While getting fit, I was also looking for work at the unemployment office. I had to sign on for unemployment benefit until a job came along. They weren't like they are now, so nosy. They didn't know what I'd brought back from Australia. A lot of it was spent on furniture and everything else for Sheila and the kids. I was just waiting to get the opportunity to get to play rugby league again

One day, Martin Ryan and Billy Woods from Wigan came to my maisonette in Platt Bridge. They said that the club was working on a deal with Penrith. They asked if the club sorted it out, would I come back to Wigan. I told them that I would grab it; I was missing rugby league so much.

Wigan had made the initial approach, and I was getting a second chance to play for my home town team. Little did I realise what playing staff they had then. Credit to Wigan, they got me back into the game; I didn't get a lot when I signed on again. I wasn't a money man for myself; it was always for my family.

The first time I had signed for Wigan I got £100 in one pound notes. When I went back all I asked for was £1,500. For a person of my ability that was cheap. I just loved playing the game; I got that payment and it tided us over. Also, Wigan got me a job.

So I signed for Wigan on Thursday 1 September 1977 for the second time, this time in my living room. Sheila was there, along with Billy Woods and Martin Ryan. In that Silver Jubilee year I was celebrating after months of worry. A big 'thank you' is due to my personal fitness trainer, Terry, who was ahead of his time. Wigan had paid Penrith £6,250 for my transfer; I was back in the fold at Central Park.

Martin Ryan, a Wigan legend, was a great bloke. What I liked about Martin was that you got what you saw, no bull. He didn't spin anyone a yarn, I could be straight with him as he was with me. I love people like that. That's how I've always been, never a 'yes man'. I never sucked up to anyone. I've always believed in what I did and if people didn't like it, lump it.

The coach at Wigan was Vince 'Vinty' Karalius. I had never met him. I knew who Vince Karalius was from being a kid, who he had played for and what he had done in the game. He had the nickname of 'The Wild Bull of the Pampas' following his appearances in Australia for Great Britain in 1958.

21. A second spell at Wigan

There were a lot of local lads in the side, along with some good players who we had signed from Widnes, where Vince had played and coached. Alan Taylor was one of the best stand-offs I'd seen There were also Steve O'Neill, John Woods, Jimmy Nulty and Nicky Nelson. I thought I was a bad trainer, but I thought that Nicky was worse than me; he made me look good.

Wigan now played all their home games on Sundays. The training days and routines had changed. Vinty would change it when he wanted; we came in when he told us to train. I had had a good fitness trainer in Penrith in Bob Tapper, but Vinty, to give him credit, was one of the best fitness blokes I have ever known. We trained accordingly.

At that time, the BBC had the television show *Superstars* and Vinty was into all this competition. Wigan had just built a gym under the popular stand and with him we had the longest session that I ever had at the club. We started at 6.45pm on a Friday and we finished at 10.40pm, four hours. We did stuff in the gym and had competitions, press-ups, sit-ups, star-jumps and more. I will honestly say I have never had a more enthusiastic fitness coach.

I was happy with sit-ups and press-ups because I had spent hours doing those in Terry's gym. I used to win some of Vinty's sit-up and press-up competitions. With weights, Steve O'Neill and people like that were so strong. Steve was one of the best forwards I played with in that era at Wigan; a cracking young player. Jimmy Hornby was on one wing, Denis Ramsdale on the other. Geoff Aspinall, Billy Melling and Terry Hollingsworth, whose son I have coached, were honest players who would try and try, but were not as good as those I had previously played with at the club.

I made my second debut for Wigan, two-and-a-half weeks after signing for them, on Sunday 18 September 1977, ironically at home to Wakefield Trinity. I was fat as a pig and still had some weight on even after my training regime. There is a photo of me training; I looked six months pregnant.

I remember the ovation I got from the supporters when I stepped onto the pitch at Central Park ready to play; it was fantastic. I played for an hour and it was certainly good to be back. George Fairbairn for us and Terry Crook had swapped penalties and it was 2–2 at half-time. My kicking game was going well.

Vinty wasn't happy, and in the opening minute of the second half I was involved in giving us the lead. I drove forward and put a beautiful delayed pass out to David Willicombe, who found his winger, Green Vigo, and he scorched in for a try. George added the conversion and we were in control, more so when I dropped a goal, which was worth one point. Geoff Aspinall scored to make it 11–2. When I came off on the hour, we had a comfortable lead. Green then beat three men to go over and the final score was 19–2. I pleaded with Vinty to let me back on, which he did after that last try. It was a great feeling being on the field when the game finished, although I was knackered.

It was great to start off with a home win as I had when I made my home debut for the club all those years ago. After the game, people were saying 'We'll kick on now that you're back' and all that. They also asked 'Why did you leave in the first place?' They said that me leaving was the start of the disbanding of that Wigan side. I did listen to the fans, but I knew that I had made my debut in a side that had won its opening five games that season in the league and cup.

My next game was a week and a half later, at home to Warrington in the semi-final of the Lancashire Cup. The last time I had played against them was when Murph and I had a misunderstanding that saw him carried off and me sent off. They still had some good players in Ken Kelly, John Bevan, Steve Hesford and Bob Eccles. We won a hard-fought game. We had reached the final, everyone was happy and we had a very good night celebrating.

I missed the next game, but was back for my first away game, to play Bradford Northern. It was a narrow defeat and the first of six starts for me. The next at Central Park was on Sunday 16 October. We won and I scored my opening tries of the season, going over for a little double. By that time I had got to my playing weight and got some pace back. The fat had gone; I was a bit more streamlined.

Then came a trip to play Leeds in the John Player Trophy. This was probably one of the team's best performances of the season and certainly one of mine. It was Green Vigo's game. Fans from both clubs, with the BBC television audience who watched the second half live, saw the best and full potential of Green. He made one of the best wingers of the previous decade for Leeds and Great Britain, John Atkinson, look out of place beside him.

We were trailing by 10 points after 55 minutes and it looked as if we were going to be knocked out. Green then scored three of the best tries I have ever seen. John Atkinson, who was trying to mark him, briefly retired after that game and I also witnessed the worst racial abuse I have ever seen and heard from a crowd. Green scored his third try and some ignorant idiot among the Leeds speccies threw bananas at him after his hat-trick. It was disgraceful. We won 25–22.

People would never get away with that racist stuff today; they would get kicked out of the club and the club would be heavily fined. Green just took all the abuse. At the end the supporters cheered him and the team. He blew kisses to the fans and beat his chest. Green was a heck of a winger; he could have moved to Wakefield and should have come, listened to common sense; things would have turned out better for him.

He was so good; I think his potential was wasted. When I moved to Wakefield Trinity later that season, I told Wakefield to sign him. He met our great chairman, Trevor Woodward. We sat Green down in a restaurant in Castleford and gave him a meal. The chairman said "Green, we want to sign you. How much do you want?" His contract was coming to an end at Wigan.

Green said "I want £10,000."

The chairman said that was not a problem and he verbally agreed. Green went back to Wigan. The next thing we knew was that he had signed for Wigan. I rang him and asked "Why have you signed for Wigan?"

He said "They told me if I didn't sign for Wigan that they would deport me back to South Africa." They terrified him into signing for Wigan for far less. In my opinion that was devious.

Continuing on throwing bananas at players; I know everything's a lot different now in most countries, but I thought it was brilliant how the Barcelona footballer Dani Alves ate the one that was thrown at him this year. I also cringe when watching the national football team when they are subjected to monkey chants in some eastern European countries. They shouldn't be allowed to get away with it now in any sport, and there should be heavy fines imposed. In this country, in the 1970s racism was part and parcel of the culture. However, rugby league had always had a multi-cultural history of black players playing the game, whereas football didn't.

I had played against black players and I probably was as bad, calling them 'black this, black that' because they were the opposition stopping me. I remember Colin Dixon, who sadly died when he was 49 years old and had become a good friend of mine. I used to have a drink with him on occasions. Colin Dixon played for Salford and Halifax; the things that we called each other when we had played on opposing sides. It sounds nasty to me, but it was friendly abuse really; we left it on the pitch never took it off. I recall like Colin coming on the blindside and I'd say to him "Don't come blind today, Colin."

He would say "Why?"

I would reply "Because I'll give you the biggest white eye you have ever seen."

"White eye?"

"I can't give you a black one." Stuff like that was banter; it was not meant to be offensive.

We used to be called 'white' on the field. It was part of a rugby league culture; we would laugh at it after the game. But to throw bananas at players, that was disgraceful. Green had the last laugh at Leeds by scoring his hat-trick to win us the match and a winning bonus for himself and the team with his superb efforts.

The following game we went to play Hull KR in the John Player Trophy. It was a long journey home after a defeat. The only consolation was that I kicked a drop-goal. Everything now was getting ready for the Lancashire Cup Final, at Wilderspool against my friends from Cumbria, Workington Town.

I had always had an enemy, if you want to put it that way, from Workington and he probably had me as an enemy from Wigan. His name was Bill Pattinson. He had two brothers and Bill and me, we just didn't like each other ever since I played at Wigan and came into the side as a youngster. More so when I moved into the pack, don't get me wrong, together with their team these brothers were good players.

I was looking forward to the game and my form was really good now, I was expecting to win, even though they had been losing finalists to Widnes the previous season. They had good players such as 'Boxer' Walker, one of the best English scrum halves at that time. In Iain MacCorquodale they had one of the best kickers in the game. To top it off, they had John Risman at centre and at full-back their captain Paul Charlton; what a player he was.

Our team on Saturday 29 October was: Malcolm Swan, Green Vigo, Dave Willicombe, Steve Davies, Jimmy Hornby, Alan Taylor, Jimmy Nulty, Brian Hogan, Geoff Aspinall, Bob Irving, Bill Ashurst, Bill Melling, Bob Blackwood. Substitutes John Burke, David Regan. We wanted it to be a physical game, but knew that if we overstepped the mark that we would get penalised and that 'Corky' could kick us off the park.

It turned out that way. He kicked four goals that day, and Bill and I had a continuous running argument. I scored a good try in the corner, beating Paul Charlton. Paul broke his shoulder trying to tackle me and went off. It got really physical after that with a lot of off-the-ball stuff. I'd put a good hard tackle and the other player I thought spat in my face. I didn't say anything and got on with it until it was my turn.

The next confrontation I tackled him and maybe the red mist came down. I saw his face and knew that I had to do something. I head butted him. It looks as if it was a bad thing to do; and can be seen on You Tube or the video. Obviously it was, it was a coward's way out. I butted him, but he had started it. I was going to finish it. It could have cost us the game, but I think the referee, Billy Thompson, saw what he had done and must also have been disgusted, I'm not proud of it now, but I was then.

When we got penalised for it, I looked at him and said "It's not over". I knew I'd get another opportunity; I just wanted to break his face that day. We put a set move on; I was the dummy runner and had to run past him. I just happened to lift my elbow up and he ran onto it; we were penalised again. Fortunately Corky couldn't kick that far that time, so it didn't cost us two points.

That was the daft game that was rugby league then; a physical game, a nasty game and there was no such thing as the sin bin. A lot of the times we would just be penalised, sometimes we weren't. It was all part and parcel of a stupid, physical, nasty game, although it was great as well. Even the great commentator Eddie Waring blamed it on someone else for that one, I got away with it on the commentary, but obviously it was me.

I knew what I was going to do, but that's the way I answered him for what I thought he had done. I have never spat at a player in any shape or form during my career, I've never kicked anybody, I've used my knees, head, elbows and fists, but I've never kicked anyone or spat at them.

It was like dog-eat-dog in the forwards, particularly that day. What I loved about my game when I played was that we could tell who wanted to play and who didn't want to play. In some games the opposition would play with four forwards because they didn't want it nasty, didn't want it tough. I had learned from Danny Gardner years earlier and would have followed Danny into war or anywhere else. That game just carried on like that to the end, with hard hits, even after I had taken him out with my elbow. I had won that particular war for the day; I never saw him after the elbow. I saw the other forwards, they toughed up, but he didn't after that.

They won the final 16–13 and played well. Corky won it for them with his goalkicks and probably a couple of points were from my indiscipline. We were only trailing 9–8 at half-time and thought we were still going to win. We were in a position where we could win. On the day, to be fair, they were the better side.

Wigan were the underdogs, comparing our squad with Workington Town's players. I was gutted for the young players playing for Wigan because they were not Wigan class. I knew the class of Wigan when I was there before with Ashton, Robinson, Laughton, Tyrer and Francis.

I wasn't sure how Vinty would react; he was alright, although disappointed the same as anybody else. He said to me that it was a great performance from me and was pleased with the way I was getting fit. But at the end of the day, whatever the coach said, it was a matter of how we consoled ourselves in defeat and how we celebrated a win. We didn't need a coach to tell us when we lost.

The following week we played New Hunslet in the John Player Trophy at Central Park. It wasn't pretty, in front of just 5,447 fans; we narrowly beat the resilient Yorkshire side to reach the quarter-finals. We were drawn away to Widnes, but the first team had a problem with the club in the lead up to the game about the bonus for the win over New Hunslet. It was so bad that the first team squad met up and decided to take the serious action of going on strike. We did not play in the club's next game, at home to Warrington on Sunday 13 November.

This was something new to me and I thought I had seen everything in the game; but we all agreed on the decision. The spooky thing was as becomes clear later is that it happened to me a second time 11 years later, also on Sunday 13th and again because of bonus payments and in the John Player Trophy; ironically the opposition then was Wigan.

The club put the 'A' team out and found some trialists. They lost 24–9 to a good side. It was a brave and courageous performance. Wigan raised the bonus payment from £55 to £70, but the players wanted £75 and were still in dispute with the club. The Wigan chairman, Ken Broome, wasn't happy. The board decided to stand firm on their offer and sent the 'A' team to play Widnes in the John Player Trophy quarter-final. Widnes had only lost in the league once all season. Their team included Stuart Wright, Eric Hughes, Reg Bowden, Keith Elwell, Jim Mills, Mick Adams and Doug Laughton. They got through to the semi-final with a 25–0 win.

The following week the situation was resolved for the rest of the season, and I became captain of Wigan. Given that I always led from the front and had now got to the stage of taking charge of games, it was a tremendous honour. It was not the best way it had come about. I thought playing for my country was the ultimate honour, but being captain of this famous club was right up there, especially with the great captains there have been in the history of the club. The irony was that in my first game as captain, we were at home to the team that had caused the problem in the first place, New Hunslet, in the league. We had won the cup tie 9–7, but lost the league match by the same score, after we had been in front 5–3 at half-time. I missed our next two games, which we lost.

139

I returned, still with the captaincy, against Hull. They were struggling and were later relegated. Both I and the team played well and we won 31–10. This was the start of a 10 game run for me leading out the side. We followed this up with coming from 5–3 behind at half-time to win 8–5 at Dewsbury. This brought us to the Boxing Day clash with St Helens.

The game was at Central Park. More than 10,000 were there, which was good, but nothing compared to past crowds. But it was a game I was always up for and the team were as well, especially the local players. That day we were not good enough and were well beaten 24–13. We were 16–7 behind after 40 minutes. We had the effort, fitness and a coach who just wanted to tough it and fight. He wanted us to be physical, but we were restricted in what rugby we could play because he didn't like the fancy stuff.

I had been having problems with my employment by the club as a groundsman for some time, over my working arrangements and pay. It came to a head when the secretary gave me the nod to take Sheila to hospital. Later I opened my pay packet. The club had docked me £10 for taking the time off, so I slammed in a transfer request. The tightness of the club was shown when they put me on the list for £20,000. They had only paid just over £6,000 for me, so this was a bit of a joke.

I felt disgusted, considering what I had given to the team since my arrival and my form. I believed I was catching the eye of the England and Great Britain selectors. I still wasn't happy with what they had done, but wanted to continue playing for the team. Next up was a trip to play Warrington on Monday 2 January 1978; just what we needed after losing to St Helens. We all put in a big performance and led by 10 points well into the second half. I kicked what turned out to be three match-winning goals with my immaculate right boot. My kicking had been in fine form throughout, giving us attacking positions. Alex Murphy's team made a late comeback, but we just held on for a good win after the St Helens defeat.

The following game was at home to Bradford Northern. The second half was going to be shown live on BBC. Like in Australia, I always showed up well to a bigger audience. It was no different that afternoon. I was different class, leading as the captain from the front – tackling, defending and kicking. I went over for two traditional Bill Ashurst tries and kicked a drop-goal to show everyone at Wigan what a contribution I made.

The club must have realised what they would miss if I was left. On the Friday before the game at Widnes, I went to the club and had a lengthy meeting with Mr Broome, the chairman, and the board of directors. We sorted out our differences. I got the money back they had taken from my wages and I agreed to come off the transfer list. I was happy, but for how long?

At Naughton Park I was off quite early in the game, but this time on a stretcher after eight minutes instead of being sent off. I had put a good hit on big Jim Mills early on to let him know I was in charge, but Jim had the same sort of red mist I had. Our heads clashed and butted into each other; it all kicked off and left me out cold on the pitch. Fair play to Jim, he had done me good style. He was one of the hardest I played against. He was sent off for the 17th time of his career, a record I equalled. Vinty had coached Jim before and had said to wind him up and he could get sent off. It was not part of the plan for me to be carried off.

In a volatile game, Widnes won to go top of the league. Billy Melling clobbered Dave Hull, but stayed on. Just before half-time, Green Vigo had an early finish after taking Mick George out. I ended up with just a plaster for my troubles, although my head was still ringing. It is good that the game now takes concussion seriously, both here and especially in Australia, where they take a more serious view than the British authorities.

I'm glad that they didn't at that time, because we were off to The Willows to play Salford. This was a game I needed to play well in against Eric Prescott, because we were both in contention to be called up for England to play Wales at Swansea. This was a triangular tournament with France, who England were playing the following month. Wales and France had played the previous weekend with Wales winning, so the game against them could be a championship decider. It would also give me an opportunity to get up close and personal with Jim Mills again. He had played in Wales's win over France.

I always enjoyed my nights out in Salford and Manchester with my two friends. First though, it was down to business and I was that good in our win that I won the sponsors' – Burtons Tailors – man-of-the-match award. I was given a brown suit which lasted me for years, it was a great prize.

I'll never forget that day because when I first went to Runcorn, Eric Prescott was there. The first thing he said was "Have you still got the brown suit?" He was a great player.

Wanting to impress from the start, I scored a sublime drop-goal after only five minutes. From a play-the-ball I played it to myself, fooled two Salford defenders, aimed and slotted it over from 30 yards for a 1–0 lead. Salford had a chance to take the lead, but David Watkins missed a penalty. From then on we got stuck in and I led the team around the park, dictating what we were going to do. My radar right boot was on overtime and I created a try for Adrian Foster. In the second half we continued to control the game. I charged over for a try, as did Dave Willicombe, to win the game.

I also won the battle with Eric Prescott and was selected for the England squad for the game against Wales. This meant attending two England training sessions at Huddersfield in February, to prepare for the game England needed to win. As always, I was proud to be selected for my country. All that hard work with Terry had paid off, together with Vinty's training and fitness regime. I was going to get a full set – an England jersey to go with my Great Britain one.

Five days later, we beat Castleford at Central Park. It looked as if we were on a roll because we had now won four of our last five games. Castleford played well, but our confidence was high and I was doing everything right. I used all my skills to set up three tries before going over for the match winning try in the final minute. Life was good.

A funny game rugby league, it's always there to bite you when you don't expect it. The trip to Belle Vue to play Wakefield Trinity, who were struggling, was no different. They turned us over; even though I thought we still had a chance at half-time when we were only seven points down. That's what I told the players after Vinty had said what he needed to say, but it was not to be. I had a couple of beers with Toppo who scored one of their tries. We reminisced about Penrith. I got a lift home from one of my friends, rather than coming back on the team bus.

We lost away to Hull KR the following weekend. I was away with the England squad and for the next two weeks our games were postponed. The first was a first round Challenge Cup tie against amateurs, Dewsbury Celtic. They showed some guts when they refused to switch the tie after what I thought was a mean offer from the club to do so. Dewsbury Celtic wanted £1,500, but Wigan only offered them £250 plus £690 gate share. The following week the club should have been at home to Workington Town and I should have been playing for England in Swansea.

The double whammy was that the international game was also postponed because of the weather in February. The irony for me was that England beat France in Toulouse, which had happy memories for me, in March and battered Wales in the rearranged game in May to win the championship. I missed both games; this was a recurring theme in my international career.

I didn't play in the Challenge Cup tie against Dewsbury Celtic on the infamous slope at Batley, which was much worse than now, and it isn't good now. Fair play to the amateurs, first of all they held firm to Wigan's offer and more than 4,000 fans turned out on the day. We laboured through it after leading at the break. When we played an amateur side then, rightly or wrongly, we were expected to win easily. We didn't have our best side out; the 10 point margin spoke for itself.

The following week we travelled to the Elland Road Greyhound Stadium to play New Hunslet. In the first half we played like startled rabbits and trailed 12–7. I kicked two goals as first choice kicker because George Fairbairn was missing.

A message came onto the field after 10 minutes. Vinty said "Take Lindsay Proctor out. This guy's a good player, he'll do damage to us." He was a New Zealand international. It was just a full blow; I just drove in a tackle into his stomach, hit his ribs with my shoulder and drove him back. I think I cracked a couple of his ribs. It wasn't a dirty tackle; it was just one of the best hits I ever put in. It was clean, believe it or not, and he was carried off for a short time. We won.

Another reason I remember that game was that one of our players ran dead instead of putting the ball down. New Hunslet had American Football type posts instead of the traditional ones. We came up field, went forward, and Jimmy Hornby thought the tryline was where the post base was. He put the ball down there, five yards behind the dead ball line. We were gobsmacked when it happened, but were still laughing in the dressing room afterwards. We had never seen posts like them on a rugby field.

We were slightly better than them in the second half and edged a win. I kicked the match winning goal. New Hunslet had come so close to doing the double over mighty Wigan. They were relegated that season and the third goal I kicked turned out to be the last points I scored for the club.

Six days later, on Saturday 11 March, we were at home to Bradford Northern in the Challenge Cup second round. I had been struggling all week with a hamstring problem. The physio and backroom staff did a great job getting me ready for the game. We had lost a close game there earlier in the season and beaten them at home. Our form wasn't consistent during my second spell at Wigan. Bradford Northern were going really well and finished the season in second place.

The second half of the game was shown live on the BBC. If the viewers were hoping to see me they were in for a shock, as were the Wigan fans, chairman and board of directors. I was sent off near the end after a brawl and we were turned over in the second half and lost 22–10. It wasn't long after that I was put on the transfer list again by the club. They wanted £20,000 for me, a £14,000 profit for less than six months service.

In one of my last games for Wigan I fell out with Vinty Karalius and, in all honesty, it had been brewing. I recall being brought in and we had worked on a set piece move. We attacked and I threw an inside ball, a disguised pass. We walked in under the posts. In the break something happened which I'd never experienced from a coach. Vinty made a beeline for me and grabbed my shirt with both hands. He said "One thing's for certain, don't ever throw another pass like that in my team."

I looked at him and said "What do you mean?"

He said "I didn't even see where it was going. It was lucky that he did."

I said "It was a set piece."

He replied "I don't like those passes, don't do it."

I said "Look, is it not called football?"

He said "Just do what I tell you."

I said "I won't. I don't want to do what you tell me anymore." I gave him my shirt and said "I don't want to play for you or this club anymore."

I would not play for that guy again. Although I could play it tough and fight, whatever, but I was a footballer as well. I didn't want to play for Wigan after that, I didn't want to play for him. Soon after that, Wakefield Trinity came for me.

I found it very hard to talk to Vinty because he had a bombastic attitude; 'I'm Vince Karalius, I'm a tough guy.' Don't get me wrong, I watched him play and he was one of the best loose-forwards in that era. A lot of people think that Rocky Turner was better than him. It was hard to get my ideas across and we did a few things on our own when Vinty wasn't there.

Summing up that spell, I played 21 games and was on the winning side 11 times. With nine games left, I finished fifth on the club's leading try scorers list with seven. I was the top forward. I also kicked four goals and six drop-goals for a total of 37 points; very good figures. Also, I got into the England side for a game which was postponed and had the coveted captaincy of Wigan.

Bill with Billy. (Courtesy *Wigan Observer*)

22. Record transfer to Wakefield Trinity

I was finished at Wigan. Straight away after that cup tie, I wrote a quick letter to the board saying that I wanted a move. Within the next 24 hours Wigan banged me on the transfer list for £18,000. I was surprised with the fee to be paid. It was going to be a British transfer record at that time, a hell of a lot of money and a second record for me.

All I was interested in was getting away. I was still a young player and hadn't started getting so many injuries. My knees seemed to be standing up to it and weren't giving me problems. I thought somebody would come in for me given what I had done that season, and would negotiate a smaller fee with Wigan. Clubs would put a player on the list for a fee and end up getting less. I didn't think anyone would pay the full price. That weekend I cut all my ties with Wigan. I wasn't going to train there anymore and I didn't want anything to do with Karalius. I had had enough.

Hull came to see me and said that they were rebuilding and thought that I would be the ideal start for them; would I be interested in going to play there? I weighed it up and thought 'It's a long way away.' I was living in Wigan then and wondered how long it would take to get there and back. Whichever club I went to, I wanted to give it 100 per cent. I decided I didn't want to travel there two or three times a week. I'd be knackered by the time I got there, trained or played and then got home.

So I said "Thank you, but no thank you". It was another clever move; they signed a lot of good quality players after I declined their offer. They had great success under Arthur Bunting in the late 1970s and early 1980s with Sammy Lloyd, 'Knocker' Norton, Gary Kemble, Peter Sterling and James Leuluai. They were relegated and came straight back up winning all 26 league games, the only time it had been done. League champions, Premiership winners, Challenge Cup winners and runners-up, Yorkshire Cup winners and runners-up; another great Bill Ashurst decision.

The following day David Topliss and Trevor Woodward, the chairman at Wakefield Trinity, came to see me. Trevor was aware that I had played with Toppo at Penrith. I was good friends with David. Like Hull, they were struggling in the First Division. They wanted me there so that the players would look up to me during a game. They knew I was a leader on the field, an organiser, space creator, try maker and scorer with a great kicking game. They wanted me to keep them up.

There were some very good teams in the First Division, and Trinity had a couple of good quality youngsters coming through. They also said that they would be bringing young players into the team such as Trevor Skerrett, Keith Smith, Les Sheard and the Rayne twins. They thought that I would help them fulfil their potential.

Although I had always had a deep, close, meaningful relationship of hating Yorkshire clubs and Yorkshiremen, I listened to everything they said and outlined other things I wanted out of the move. Although there would be less travelling than Hull, I needed a house and a job. I knew that Wigan wouldn't let me keep my job at the club once I'd signed for another one. As much as anything, the final reason to go was Toppo, having played with him for a spell at Penrith I knew what he could do. He was already a great player; I had seen his ability at first hand.

I asked them to let me discuss it with Sheila and they agreed to come back and see me. We had four children and Sheila was happy to move even though she was a Wigan girl. They agreed to sort a house out for us and we later moved into Cock Lane. Whether that was appropriate, I don't know, but Sheila was very happy; it was a lovely house. There was even a pub at the top of the lane and it was not far from my job. David Garthwaite, a board member and former player at Trinity, ran a brewery. I worked for him, second mate on the wagon. I was happy and the job was a good one. Everything was hunky dory.

When I signed on the dotted line I asked for a £2,000 signing on fee. I was happy with that, it wasn't about money. A few years later I told a player how much I got from Wakefield after leaving Wigan. He said he left the club just after me to play in Cumbria and got £8,000. I thought that he wasn't good enough to lace my boots.

As when I had signed for Wigan for the second time, I hadn't met my new head coach or any of the players apart from Toppo, although I knew some of them who I had played against earlier. The coach was one of the great players who had played at Wakefield Trinity at centre, Ian 'Brooky' Brooke. He had taken charge from the beginning of the year and was the coach when Wigan had lost to them at Belle Vue. It was a privilege when I went to Wakefield Trinity; I know that I didn't play many games because of injuries catching up with me. However, I got coaches who let me do what I wanted to do and the players responded to me.

When I was doing that, I was happy. All through my career I always wanted to do what I wanted to do because I was that type of player. I found it was hard to follow instructions. There were coaches who would never beat me, Barry Harris in Australia and Vinty Karalius. I would beat myself up at times because that was the player that I was. At the end of the day I lived and died by what I did and not what someone told me to do.

I did not have a car at this time and needed a chance to sort one out so that everything was done and dusted. Trevor Woodward came to Wigan and picked me up for my debut on Good Friday, 24 March 1978. It wasn't a home debut though; we went to Post Office Road to play our neighbours Featherstone Rovers. I'd missed the game earlier in the season when Wigan lost, but this was a different time and occasion. On the journey, Trevor told me that they had signed John Burke, a prop from Castleford, as well. From what he said about him, he made me feel like a choir boy. He had just finished a six month suspension after being sent off for the 20th time earlier that season, playing against St Helens. Either, like me, he didn't like Saints, or, unlike me, he didn't like Lancastrians.

It was busy when we arrived at the ground with its infamous slope. Given the short distance between the clubs, apart from the threat of relegation, it was about bragging rights which I knew something about. As I got out of the car with my kit bag I could sense the atmosphere. I was there as the big signing for the visitors. No pressure; I was sure I would get a big welcome from the home fans when I stepped out onto the field.

146

The first time that I met the Wakefield Trinity players, apart from Toppo, was in the dressing room at Featherstone Rovers. I know I may have played against them and knew their faces, but I went onto the park not knowing any of them. It was the same with Ian Brooke. He told me to go out and do what I do, but to stay on the field. Some people recently said to me that it was the best ever performance they saw from any second-row at Post Office Road.

I had an awesome debut for Wakefield that afternoon. The players listened to me when I was shouting and barking out orders to them. I wasn't the captain, but led from the front as always, which is why they bought me. It was one of those rare games when everything I did turned to gold. That was until the last few minutes when the referee became 'Fool's Gold' and cost us two vital league points.

I had already kicked two penalties and a couple of drop-goals, so my goalkicking was on song. I had made a superb 20 yard pass which put Trevor Midgley in. I also started and finished a try with my trademark chip over the defence and caught the ball before Harold Box could gather it, and then passed to Terry Hudson who looked a certain try scorer. He got tackled by the posts. From the play-the-ball I fooled them with a dummy, left them off balance and dived through.

For all that, we still trailed 19–16 as the seconds ticked down with the Featherstone Rovers fans whistling for full-time. I shouted for and got the ball. I went for a try and again put a chip over, beating two defenders in the process. As I went for the ball and touched down, the referee disallowed it. He said that I did not have full possession of the ball. Rubbish!

I did everything, and was named man-of-the-match by the home sponsors.[7] I even set up a try for Featherstone. I gave Keith Bell an interception pass on their 25 yard line and he went the full length of the field and scored what turned out to be their winning try under the posts. I had made four tries that day.

It was an extraordinary game. We were robbed in the closing seconds as the referee blew the whistle seconds later. I thought it was an awful decision. My try should have been the match winner because it was near the posts and the kick would have given us the points. It would have been a perfect ending for my debut for Wakefield and for the fans who from being elated were deflated. Today's video referee would have given it.

When I came off that park the Wakefield players and supporters were in awe of me even though we had lost. I had got those players in the palm of my hand and I knew that they would follow me anywhere in the fight to keep us up in the First Division and that it would be a fight to the end.

---

[7] Mike Rylance comments that "Ashurst made a sensational debut at Featherstone... exerting as much influence on a match as an individual can. If his late try had not been disallowed... it could have been claimed that he had won the match almost single handed." (*Trinity – A History of the Wakefield Rugby League Football Club 1872 – 2013*, League Publications Ltd 2013)

Three days later, on Easter Monday, my home debut for the club was against Warrington. By their standards they were having an indifferent season, but not fighting to avoid relegation. After being robbed at Featherstone we knew we had to win. It was going to be us, New Hunslet or Hull for the drop. How I wished Wigan had beaten New Hunslet when we had played them at home earlier in the season. I did a training session with the team and found out what Brooky wanted from me: the same as Good Friday.

Les Sheard and Trevor Midgley who played at full-back were injured, so Brooky brought in one of the youngsters at the club, Paul McDermott, what a baptism. But he put up good display as did Ray Handscombe who controlled the scrums so we could get the ball moving. We defended when we needed to and attacked when we could. John Sutcliffe's three tries made sure we got the two points with a 15–11 win. It was important for us because we got out of the bottom four and the team had shown its character to win a close game.

Next was a trip to Knowsley Road to play St Helens, who were top of the table and going for the championship. The coach had been hoping to pick John Burke after he had completed a run out in the reserves. But he did what I had done a couple of years earlier, got sent off in a reserve game.

Then, I had played for the first team the next day against Barrow. Times had changed and John was given a two match ban. That meant he missed the St Helens trip and our home game against Hull. I couldn't read the Saints' minds, but I bet they were relieved when they knew John wouldn't be facing them. He was looking forward to going head-to-head with them.

Our loss was Saints' gain and all the great work that we had done in the two previous games went for nothing, especially in the second half. It was our biggest defeat of the season, 36–5. We were in the game up to half-time, only 12–5 down, and were confident that we could come back. But their forwards were in rampaging form. We were on the edge again and I doubt if John Burke would have made an impact.

In the relegation run in, each game counted; but our next match was definitely the one that mattered, especially after the Saints defeat. Hull at home; 12th against 13th.[8] Everything depended on this. We all knew that we had to win and went out to do a job, but they played really well and wanted it as much as we did. Both packs were absolutely brutal with some big hits and it was like that all through the game.

Our hero that day was Keith Smith, who has sadly passed away. Usually a centre, he could also play at stand-off and did so because of injury problems. He made his mark in the final 20 minutes. His three drop-goals and a solo try – probably his best performance for the club – saw us edge home 9–7. The defence tackled their hearts out as Hull battled to get over the try line but sheer grit, determination and bravery saw us hold on. Relief all round for the players, coach, chairman and directors and, most importantly, the fans who

---

[8] The bottom four teams in the 16 team Division were relegated; finishing 12th therefore was safe.

must have bitten their nails down to the knuckle, such was the tension. We could see what defeat meant to Hull from the looks on their players' faces. We had a two point advantage over then and a better points difference with three games to play. Then we lost away to Hull KR 17–16, despite my four goals.

Colin Tyrer, who I played with at Wigan, was playing full-back for Hull KR. I don't know whether I felt sorry for Colin or not, I should have scored. I got the ball three yards offside and I should have walked straight over him, but I tried to go round him and go in at the corner. He pushed me in touch so I cost us the game twice as I got sent off. John Burke joined me for an early bath.

John's start to his career at Wakefield was nearly as bad as mine at Penrith. John played two first team games and one reserve game and was sent off twice. At least when the next season began he would have a few weeks rest. He was up to 22 sendings off, I was in double figures it would be an interesting day at Red Hall for that one.

We were both suspended for three games for the following season, but on his return he was the foundations of the Wakefield pack that saw us travel all the way to Wembley. He was a strong forward runner, superb tackler in defence with supreme ball handling skills.

In 1980, following injuries to players in the Great Britain Ashes squad down under he was called up to go. No hesitation, John went and played nine games, but didn't play in a test match. Typical of him he threw his boots in the famous Auckland Harbour and retired from the game. He may only have played 24 times for Wakefield, but he made an impact in all of those games and an impact on me.

St Helens, who had embarrassed us at their ground two weeks earlier, now came to Belle Vue. We all trained really hard and our confidence was up there. Saints were coming to us confident after getting a draw away to high-flyers Bradford Northern four days earlier, which cost Northern the championship. None trained harder than John Burke. He was chomping at the bit and over the moon when he knew he was in the side.

There were over 5,000 at Belle Vue that day. Although Saints brought some fans with them, it was all about us and our fans were simply superb. They sang and cheered us on for the whole 80 minutes. In the first half we blasted St Helens apart and led 21–5 at the break. At half-time it was decided that I would come off because I was injured. But in those first 40 minutes, Saints certainly knew who Bill Ashurst of Wakefield Trinity, not Wigan, was now. I was running hot and showed a full array of my skills in defence and attack. I set up all the tries. Before the game revenge wasn't mentioned, but in the second half we led 36–10 at one stage and looked likely to kick on to 50 points. We certainly didn't look like a side that had been staring at relegation when I had arrived. Saints came back into the game, but there was no way that the boys were going to blow it, especially with John Burke tearing into Saints. We won 36–23 in the end. The whistle went and the speccies charged onto the field. They knew that we were safe because Hull had lost. We had won two of our last three matches; the difference between success and failure.

We had got used to each other by then and my teammates had begun to have a lot of confidence in me. Toppo helped me a lot by telling the players "This guy can do it, listen to him because he will win us games". At Wakefield I had a much underrated pack to work with. One of the best ever prop forwards I played with was Trevor Skerrett, who went on a couple of Lions tours.

There was Graham Idle, the Rayne twins, Andy Kelly, me; John Burke was on the bench. A great pack of triers, a couple of class forwards; Mike Lampkowski was one of the hardest toughest forwards I've played with. I was the ball player, the brains and these guys would follow me through a brick wall.

Toppo was a gentleman and one of the fittest guys ever. We had a cracking time in Australia. When Toppo had just arrived we played South Sydney at Penrith Park. They had a forward called 'The Body', Mick McCarthy. An absolutely massive player, built like a brick outhouse. Toppo tried to tackle him and was left with stud marks from his boots on his head as McCarthy trampled over him. I remember coming in at half-time and looking at Toppo. I said "Toppo, you're knackered."

He went "Bill, that bastard, how do you tackle McCarthy?"

I replied: "There's only one way mate, just move to one side and let some other bastard do it."

He was great, I loved playing with him, he was an extraordinary stand-off and very underrated. Watch the Hull versus Widnes Challenge Cup Final replay at Headingley; he won the Lance Todd Trophy that night and was awesome. He was very modest and unassuming, but what a great football brain. I used to go across to Wakefield regularly after I had left the club and meet up with Toppo, Trevor and Graham and have a few beers. The day before he died, it was a Sunday, we were all together at Wakefield.

On the Monday Toppo rang me at 1.30pm because there was a dinner at Huddersfield; we were meeting up the next weekend and I had to pay my £30. He said "Bill, I'll pay the money; you give it to me when you come over."

At 3.25pm Trevor Skerrett rang me and said "Bill, Toppo's dead."

I said "You're joking man; I've just been talking to him."

He said "Bill, honestly mate, he must have rang you, gone on the five-a-side football pitch, come off and died as he came off."

I didn't, couldn't, believe Trevor and rang Andy Kelly and he confirmed it, that he had died within an hour of speaking to me. I was deeply shocked and couldn't believe it. He was a fitness fanatic, awesome, every day he was playing five-a-side or was in the gym. I was probably the laziest person ever to play rugby league, I wouldn't train, I drank, smoked 20 cigs a day. The first thing I said to Sheila was "If that's what not smoking does for you, I'm going to light up and having another cig"; so I went in the back garden for a smoke. I still smoke today. I'll carry on taking my chances, if a dear friend like Toppo could pass away like that, I might get another 15 years yet.

23. Wakefield at Wembley

I was well and truly settled at Wakefield Trinity. My family were settled as well, and I was enjoying my job – heaven, working for a brewery and getting paid as well. It was hard graft, but kept me fit in the close season which made it easier when we began training at the club under Brooksy.

In that close season the club had been as good as its word to me when I signed. They said they would bring new players into the first team squad, and did so. Welshmen Brian Juliff, Steve Diamond and Adrian Barwood came from rugby union and Cumberland hooker Alan McCurrie was signed from Whitehaven.

This season, 1978–79, Australia were coming to Great Britain and after how I had played at Wigan and Wakefield Trinity last season and broken into the England squad, only for the game to be postponed, I was confident that I would be in the selectors' minds. Injuries and a match postponement had prevented me from playing for England after being selected. However, the season was one of a catalogue of injuries which saw me only play nine games, disappointments, comebacks and a bitter sweet finish in the last game of the campaign.

I missed the first three games after being sent off with John Burke in our final game of the 1977–78 season, so my first start was on Sunday 10 September with a trip to face St Helens. They had battered us in the third game I played for Trinity. They had won their first two league games and we knew it wouldn't be easy. But we were confident; our pack got on top, gained control and we led 11–5 at half-time. We thought we could do the job in the second half. Unfortunately it wasn't to be and although we fought the good fight in the second half, we lost by a converted try, 20–15. I had a good start and was looking forward to the rest of the season; I knew the Aussies were coming that month.

The next match was at home to my former club, my beloved Wigan, who were still coached by a certain Vinty Karalius. I was looking forward to facing them. Like St Helens, they had won their opening two league games. There were nearly 6,000 in Belle Vue and there was a great atmosphere; the city was buzzing. It was different for me, seeing it from the other side of the coin, only ever having played in England for Wigan.

Our coach and squad were up for it in training and our supporters certainly were. We tore into Wigan from the kick-off. It was an almighty battle in the first half with some big hits. I was making an impression with my drives as I led the team round, leading Wigan on a merry dance. We took the lead after only 10 minutes; I drove forward, dummied the whole defence with my footwork and passed to Mike Lampkowski who went over to give us a 3–0 lead. The crowd went delirious.

We had a problem soon afterwards; John Burke had to go off with a back injury. This was a blow because he had been charging at the Wigan defence all the time, giving them problems. We carried on; were in control and dominating the game with five minutes of the half left when the team and I were literally hit for six. One minute I was fine, the next I was laid out in extreme pain and agony, sensing and knowing there was a problem with my face. I got a late forearm that I didn't see coming. I just hit the ground senseless, not knowing where I was.

The next thing I remember I was in the local hospital. I was told that following the forearm from one of the Wigan forwards I was stretchered off and straight into the ambulance. I was told that I had a fractured cheekbone, a broken nose and that I would be out for eight weeks. As they putting my face right, the news came that we had lost to Wigan. My chance to play for Great Britain in the first test was over and that Wigan forward had been the fall guy for Wigan. He had been Vinty's sacrificial lamb to take out the player who was causing damage to his team. It was the same as when I volunteered to do the same at New Hunslet when I did Lindsay Proctor. The difference was mine was a legitimate hit and broke his ribs; this hit wasn't by a young kid wanting to make a name for himself with his late hit which broke my face and good looks for a time.

I was gutted with what the hand – or in this case the forearm – of fate had done to me. I knew I somehow had to get back quicker to have any chance of playing against Australia. The expression 'no gain without pain' comes to mind. I came back early after the hospital specialist had given me the all clear. If he asked me, I was going to say I was okay, no pain. After four weeks out I turned up at training to my coach's and team-mates' amazement. I said I was okay to play in a practice game, but had trouble with my vision, a blind spot which was always a good excuse when going to the RFL Disciplinary Committee.

I wanted to get back to playing because the team were on a bit of a run while I was out, but Brooksy and the medical staff wouldn't have it. I kept training and badgering them and I don't know if they got fed up, but I was picked to play at Huddersfield. Although I was always confident before and during the game, I was feeling slightly worried about what would happen if I got hit again. I was not right or ready yet.

After a few minutes I settled down and was back in the old routine. I dominated the game as if I had not been away. Although not match fit, I came through it. I took the first hard tackle and hit on me and didn't flinch. It didn't matter whether I was hurt anyway; I wasn't going to let Huddersfield know. We won comfortably. Keith Smith, who had come on really well from the previous season, scored three times for the second time in two weeks, but this time picked up winning money.

Now it was game on to try and get into the Great Britain squad, which had already been chosen for the second test in seven days time at Bradford. The selectors had already picked a new front row after the first test defeat, Phil Lowe and George Nicholls were in the second row and Steve Norton at loose-forward.

Sadly, from my personal point of view, Great Britain won the second test 18–14. The pack played really well, including my second row rivals Phil Lowe and George Nicholls. It was the old fate thing again. The following Sunday I needed a belting game against Salford; I gave everything and ended up with another injury. From a team view, playing strong winds and heavy rain, we came from 10–5 down to draw 10–10. For me it was a dream over, but a point gained for the club.

I returned to the side again and played a few games. We beat Halifax in the John Player Trophy and reached the last eight with a trip to Bradford Northern. I had unfinished business after getting sent off against them previously, but focused on the game. They did their best to wind me up, but in this game it wasn't the players who did that, but the referee. It was 13–13 and Bradford came driving down our end. They got the ball out to their winger, Henderson Gill, who scored an iffy try. We all protested to the referee, but were wasting our time.

At this time I played when I was probably only 60 per cent fit. I shouldn't have done, I suppose it was pride; I'm never going to be beaten. It came to a head though in December with my knees. I couldn't take much more pain, so I had my first trip to Middlesbrough General Hospital. From that first visit, over the next three years and recovering from five operations and other tiresome injuries, I spent more time injured than I did on the field. I can only apologise to the fans. Perhaps I shouldn't have rushed back every time, but that was me, lazy in training but I always wanted to play.

I remember a cartoon on the operating theatre door. It was by one of the lads, Mike, who was a theatre assistant. He'd drawn this guy going in on the trolley with his head covered up. Just his knees were showing: 'Not that Ashurst again?' It seemed as if John the surgeon always did my knee operations on New Year's Eve. For three consecutive New Years Eves I was in Middlesbrough Hospital. I suppose he didn't want me bladdered and I saved some money.

During one of my stays in hospital, Sheila was pregnant with our Leanne. I remember saying to the nurse "I've just had a phone call. My wife has just had twins." She said "Awe absolutely fantastic Bill". She bought me a cigar, smoking in hospitals was allowed then, and got us some whisky. The nurses went to the Chinese for our supper that night. Sheila came up the day afterwards with a big fat belly. The sister came after us when Sheila had gone. She said "By the way, Bill, that wasn't your missus was it who was pregnant?"

I said "No, that's just a good friend. Don't tell anybody."

Every time I went into hospital it reminded me of my lengthy stay at Wigan Infirmary when I was a kid. I was in for ages. Then I went home to rest and was treated by the club. Then I would begin the long road to recovery. By the time I was fit again to play it was late April, four months had passed. Brooksy had been sacked by the club in January. He only lasted 12 months. I thought he had done a really good job, but obviously the board didn't.

Bill Kirkbride had been appointed as head coach. I'd had a drink with him after games before. That 1970 Lance Todd incident was done and dusted and we were friends off the park. Bill is one of the nicest Cumbrians, men and coaches there is. The team had an up-and-down run while I had been out, but a fantastic run had got the club to the Challenge Cup Final for the first time in 11 years. It was sponsored for the first time by cigarette brand State Express. It didn't bother me, I'd smoke any brand. To reach Wembley, Trinity had won at Featherstone, won at Oldham and beaten Barrow at home.

In the semi-final we faced St Helens at Headingley; not far to travel for us and our fans. More than 11,000 packed the ground and with three minutes left it looked like we were out, because we were behind for a second time. Saints had led 4-0, but an Andy Fletcher try, Keith Smith's conversion and a drop-goal made it 6-4. With three minutes remaining Les Jones scored in the corner to make it 7–6 for Saints, but then Toppo intercepted near his own line and was tackled, but a couple of tackles later the genius broke away from his own half, wrong footed the Saints defence and got the ball out to Keith Smith. He found Andy Fletcher who became the hero of the hour again as we went 9–7 ahead. The defence held firm as Saints came at them; the hooter went and we were at Wembley. We would face cup kings Widnes who were be heavy favourites in their fourth final in five years.

The last league game of the season was at Belle Vue against already relegated Rochdale Hornets. They had nothing to lose and we needed a boost for Wembley. We won comfortably and I struggled because of the length of time I had been out, I was just glad to get through without another injury. Although I wanted to play in the final, who wouldn't, I didn't think I deserved to or would get in the squad because I had only played one game. Our win was the perfect tonic for the players who had got us to Wembley.

It was all down to Bill Kirkbride; he had to choose the team, and when he announced the 17 I was very, very surprised that I was even included in the squad. I would have been pleased just to be in the party, that's all I expected because I hadn't played in the Cup. The lads had done a great job. We went to London on the Tuesday, but I didn't train until the Friday morning.

It was only a ball session and Bill Kirkbride said "I'm playing you".

I said "But Bill, I'll need painkillers."

He replied "No problem, we've got it all set up."

I pleaded, but he said "I would rather have a 50 per cent Bill Ashurst, who could win a game on the turn of a key, a drop-goal or whatever, with one of your passes, rather than you doing all the graft." After he told me, that sudden tingle, a surge of excitement and pride kicked in. I was going to play at Wembley for the second time in my career, albeit on dodgy knees.

On Saturday 5 May we arrived at the twin towers and as we drove in our team coach towards the stadium it was something else. I was hoping I could take it all in for years to come. We did the usual, went onto the pitch and hit the cauldron of noise as our fans cheered us, then went back into the dressing room. Bill had already told us how he wanted us to play and we knew we would have to step up to the plate against a very good Widnes side who had finished third in the league. They had lost only seven games compared to our 16. Our team was: Les Sheard, Andy Fletcher, Keith Smith, Steve Diamond, Brian Juliff, David Topliss, Mike Lampkowski, John Burke, Alan McCurrie, Trevor Skerrett, Bill Ashurst, Keith Rayne, Graham Idle.

Anyway, I had four pain killing injections in my knee before the game. It was a dour, forward-driven battle between two hard and physical sides who cancelled each other out. Or put another way, a boring spectacle for the game's purists. It was 0–0 at half-time. The pain killers had worn off and I told 'Kirkie' that they had worn off, put 'Twinnie' Rayne on.

He said "We'll give it another 15 minutes."

Unfortunately, it was that moment when perhaps sentiment and the heart ruled Bill's head. A coach has to step away and not let sentiment affect them. I always say that that cost us the game. In that opening 15 minute spell Eric Hughes got a ball and just tried to run around me. I made sure he didn't, gave a penalty away, and Mick Burke made it 2–0.

Toppo had a golden opportunity moments later, but a heart stopping tackle by Mick Adams saved the day for Widnes. My former team-mate Stuart Wright then chipped over the defence and crashed over. The conversion and a drop-goal gave them an 8–0 lead. Andy Fletcher brought us back in the game when he scored a try. As we pressed with the momentum, Widnes got possession and with 10 minutes left Dave Eckersley dropped a goal. They had a six point lead and Hughes finished us off with a late try.

I gave it my best shot on the leg that I had left, it didn't work, we only lost 12–3. It was a good performance by our lads. Toppo was the stand out player on both sides and was a rare loser becoming a winner by collecting the Lance Todd Trophy. If I did let anyone down that day, which I felt I did, I can only apologise; none of them made me feel guilty.

I know that it's all about, being the winner on the day and money doesn't come into it. But if we had won we were on £3,000 a man. When I lost with Wigan in 1970 I got £7. This time for being gallant losers we picked up £1,500, there was a lot of sponsorship and we did well out of it.

The losing money helped, but there is no consolation in defeat. Wembley is a massive occasion, but I was a born winner. Any game whether we lost it at Wembley, or a friendly, or a seven-a-side competition, I just absolutely hated losing. I think that's what I have tried to bring across to my players when I'm coaching. I hate people who can lose and then laugh and joke after a game. I was down for two or three days when I lost. I think sometimes we make too much of a runner-up. I have always believed in the saying that I heard the late great Bill Shankly say once, and it's so true: 'Winning's not everything, it's the only thing.'

The 1979 Wakefield Trinity team.

24. Knee trouble

After the disappointment of the Challenge Cup Final at Wembley, we began the new season, 1979–80, really well. However, for me it was another frustrating season. I continued to have problems with my knees and other chronic injuries and only managed to play eight games up to the middle of November. Then it was back to hospital to look at the problems I had with my knees again. I knew the club, coaches and supporters were frustrated that I didn't play more that season, but when I did I gave it everything.

I missed the two opening games of the season; wins in the Yorkshire County Cup Hull KR and Bradford Northern. It looked like being a very good season and in our opening league game we were at home to Wigan. In the build up to the game at training I was conscious that the last time I had played them at Belle Vue, Vinty Karalius was still in charge. I didn't know who would be their henchmen in the game. I knew I would have to be very alert the whole time.

We took them to the cleaners and after leading 12–0 at half-time kicked on and won 22–6. I was at my creative best. I made two tries for Kevin Rayne, one with a sublime reverse pass which I was delighted to see wrong footed the whole Wigan defence. I made a try for Alan McCurrie after some great work by Paul McDermott and, to rub their noses in it, kicked two wonderful drop-goals.

Wigan simply had no answer to me or the team. It is always nice to beat your old club; but a little bit of my heart was still at Wigan. However, it was a great feeling for the whole team when we beat Wigan. Although I kept my eyes on anything around me, it wasn't the same for Steve Diamond because his jaw was broken during the win. I don't know who did it, but Steve must have been highlighted as the player to stop that day

But then on 2 October came the news that Vinty Karalius was being replaced as coach. A week later they appointed Kel Coslett, the former St Helens legend as head coach and he was in charge when they were relegated at the end of that season.

We then played Leeds in the semi-final of the Yorkshire Cup and were confident of getting to the final. It was down to the pack to lead the way and we went at them hammer and tongs. The problem was that Leeds had the same attitude. Something had to give and it kicked off between me and Roy Dickinson. We both got sent off. This gave Leeds an advantage; we had lost our creative player leading the team around the field, they had just lost a big forward and edged home 12–7 as we battled to get a draw. I'm sure even in defeat our fans enjoyed it as much as we did.

We beat Hull at Belle Vue in the John Player Trophy. I put in a good performance before a two match suspension for the misunderstanding with Roy. When I came back we had beaten Featherstone Rovers and I returned for a home quarter-final against my friends Workington Town.

It was tasty and feisty for the whole game. I directed operations and their pack tried to take me out. That was the challenge for me; my kicking game repeatedly put them on the back foot and in their own half. Our backs and forwards played off me which saw me create tries. We put the work in on defence and won comfortably to reach our second semi-final of the season.

I missed the semi-final and sadly we lost to Bradford Northern 16–3 at Headingley. My knee problems had flared up again and it was back to 'Emergency Ward 10'. Again I was told that I could be finished for the season. I had a spell of playing five games in two weeks which created problems. Time was catching up with me. The heart wanted it; the legs and knees didn't.

That's how it turned out and while I was in hospital the club got rid of Bill Kirkbride in January 1980. I felt sorry for him; he couldn't do anything about injuries, especially when it happened to his main playmakers. The club appointed Ray Batten as head coach who had been coaching in the amateur game in York. They also brought in former Castleford legend Alan Hardisty to run the 'A' team.

The chairman who brought me to the club, Trevor Woodward, also stood down. I had a lot of time for him. With his drive and enthusiasm I did everything in my power to keep us up in my first season and we did with a game to spare. Trevor had his own restaurant and regularly invited the players for meals. It was good business for him; people came in them after seeing us eat there. He used to always say to me "Bill, I don't care if you never play another game for Wakefield; that was the best 18 grand I ever spent." When someone like Trevor said that, I knew that rugby league was not about what I think, or what the fans think, it's what people in rugby league think.

While all the turmoil was going on at the club, I was well out of it; although I wanted to play. Once I'd got the nod for rehab it was back to the daily trek to Featherstone Sports Centre to slowly coax some strength into my legs and knees. I was under Stan Timmins' direction; doing it slowly, slowly and waiting to find out from the surgeon how it was going. It had been injury, operation, recovery all the time; with no time to build up my strength and muscle. There were the boring, monotonous, cycle exercises – just pedalling on a static bike with nowhere to go apart from looking in front; soul destroying. I felt like a hamster in a cage on a treadmill, but I could not run fast in case I broke down again.

Eventually, after 10 months away from the smell of grass, I was given the green light by the surgeon and training staff to slowly come back into training with the first team players for pre-season for the 1980–81 campaign. We had lost some great players: Trevor Skerrett, Graham Idle, Kevin Rayne, and Paul McDermott all left. Graham Brown and cash were swapped for Terry Day to come in, with his former teammates Alan Agar and Harold Box. I suppose I could be seen as a new signing, the length of time I had been out.

We began the season with a trip to Hull KR in the Yorkshire Cup and hoped that we could do what we had done the previous season when we beat them at home. Ray Batten told us how he wanted us to play and I made the team for the opener, which was a real statement from me and the coach. It was like I hadn't been away. I was leading from the front, taking the team around the park and I kicked them all over the ground. Everything clicked into gear showing why the club had paid that record fee. The swagger was back, or so I thought. We were leading 10–0 and then bang; someone I won't want name had a word with my jaw and I had to go off. From that moment Hull KR took over and, although we played really well, we lost 21–17.

The jaw recovered, or I was used to the pain as we went up to Barrow and came back with nothing; not an ideal start in the league. I then played in our opening home league game against Leigh. I was really looking forward to it; my third game and the supporters would get the chance to see me back for the first time in over 10 months in a much changed side. I had already begun a great understanding with our scrum-half, Alan Agar, and it showed in this game. I was aware that Wigan, who were now in the Second Division, had come over to watch the game; not that it mattered. I certainly put a show on for them, especially in the first half. I inspired the team with the way I played and led Leigh a merry dance as we led 25–4. Although they came back in the second half, I was still in total control with all my skills working and we won by 13 points. I was happy, as were my team-mates and the fans.

Next came a trip to Knowsley Road. Over the years my success there had been limited and for Wakefield we had lost every time. They had done the double over us last season. We went into the game with the same record as them, won one and lost one. After the win over Leigh we were confident. I was putting a run of games together and my confidence was sky high. I cajoled and coaxed the team around the field and once again was in the zone with my kicking. I did some superb touch-finders and our prop, Colin Forsyth, was leading from the front with big hit after big hit.

We were ahead 6–4 at half-time. I was in control and dropped a goal. With Alan Agar's try we had a seven point lead and it was looking good. Then the game changed and Saints had a three point lead. I couldn't believe it, but I got us the momentum back after we had to defend our line. We went downfield with some lung busting drives and more tactical kicking. From one of those Mike Lampkowski drove over from the play-the-ball with 10 minutes left and Keith Smith kicked the goal. Don't ask me how our defence held out as Saints tried to retake the lead, but we did for a 16–14 win, three tries to one. The Saints hoodoo was gone, we deserved that win and I was walking on air. A few months later we won at home to do the double over them, although I wasn't playing.

We then met Halifax at Belle Vue. I and the team produced another great performance and won 22–11. Three league wins; heady days and we were near the top of the table. Next up was our biggest challenge of the season, at home to the champions Bradford Northern. They had a great side including the Redfern brothers, Jimmy Thompson, Brian Noble and Jeff Grayshon.

We went into the game with the same record as them, three wins and one loss, and with two other clubs, Widnes and Warrington, were a point behind leaders Hull KR. We were up against the second best defence in the league. There were nearly 7,000 jammed into Belle Vue. The atmosphere was absolutely awesome. The game had everything including sending offs, a touch of sheer genius that will be remembered by those present and those who say they were there, and a sensational finish. It was one of the best games I ever played in and brings back great memories.

In a red raw battle between the two packs in the opening period, Northern were on top and took an early seven point lead. I was trying to get my side into the game, and from nothing inside our half, I saw something was on in a flash. I put my trademark delicate chip over the Northern defence, the bounce worked for me, coolly I re-gathered the ball and came inside, running towards their full-back, Keith Mumby. With Toppo backing me up and shouting for the ball, I dummied big style and left Mumby flat footed. I smiled and went in for a magnificent 50 yard try. Class, genius, wizardry, magic given the occasion – it had all that. To score from 50 yards out on my legs was a miracle. If I could have bottled that moment, I would have made a fortune. It was that good. Playing in a run of games I was getting fitter and stronger, or so I thought. We kicked the goal and a penalty and went in at half-time level and well into the game.

Whatever we took in at half-time, we certainly left it there because with 12 minutes gone we were playing catch up again as Northern went 15–7 ahead. The game got hotter and more frenzied. Alan McCurrie was sent off for a difference of opinion with Jimmy Thompson and Jimmy was sent for an awful hit on Harold Box. I tried to bring Toppo more into the game, but as soon as he had the ball he was wrapped up. We got five points back and it was game on again. As we began to gain possession and territory we went downfield and with five seconds left we scored a try. I joined in the line and we got the ball out to the overlapping Steve Diamond. His pace saw him score in the corner to give us a 15–15 draw. We had shown that never-say-die spirit, will and determination we had when I first came to the club.

I don't think our fans could believe what they had seen. It was an abiding memory they would never forget and I haven't. Two weeks later was a trip to The Shay to play the return game against Halifax. We were all buoyed by our amazing draw. Later in the season, although I was not involved, we only lost 7–6 to Bradford Northern, who retained the championship.

I then found I had another tragic problem; another major injury to my knees. Words failed me; the knees of fate had touched me again. I'd already had a 10 month layoff and this was the beginning of another long injury nightmare for me and more perseverance to recover my fitness. I thought 'This'll teach me to hate Yorkshiremen.'

After my last 10 month layoff I was looking forward to a season with no injuries. I knew they were always part and parcel of the game, but surely I was due some luck. I used to try my best to play, bravely or recklessly; but I could only take so much anaesthetic in my knees and so many painkillers. I hated needles to start off with and now my other knee had started to go as well. I was having four or five injections in each knee to try and play.

I think later on I was pleased to pack in playing and I did have a wonderful time at Wakefield Trinity when I did get on the park. If you are as only as good as your last game, what a privilege it was to play in the draw against Bradford Northern. I weaved my magic wand for 80 minutes. I played six matches and was now having my sixth operation.

What I loved about Wakefield was that it was a family club. I'd been to Australia and played twice for Wigan. At Wakefield, irrespective of the injuries and number of games I played, it was the nicest club I was ever involved with.

I had a lot of wear and tear, I'd had my knee cap taken out and scraped a couple of times, I had cruciate ligament damage and more or less had a knee rebuild. With the pressure on my other knee and that not being good enough, it also started to go and I had all the cartilages removed. I'd had some tendons transplanted as well. I think I had more screws in my knees than B & Q, it was time to think about packing in playing. It would be a long time to recover this time.

The Wakefield Trinity team which won the Wigan 7s, coached by Bill. Back: Stan Timmins (trainer), Keith Smith, Alan McCurrie, Brian Juliff, Bill Ashurst (head coach), Terry Crook; front: Jamie Lyon, Harold Box, Nigel Day, Dale Fennel, Ben (physio).

25. Welcome to club coaching

While I had been recovering from that operation we had come to the end of the season. I decided that I was packing in playing. My knees were virtually shot and I couldn't go through what I had endured over the last three seasons. It wasn't fair to the club, the coach, teammates and especially not the fans who had always supported me during the lean times. I went to speak to the chairman. While I had been recovering, John Scaife had replaced David Garthwaite in that role. I told him of my decision and the reasons behind it.

Ray Batten had taken the club to fourth place in 1980–81, their highest league position for 15 years, a great achievement. But he had decided to step down from the role because Alan Hardisty, who had been appointed as 'A' team coach at the same time as Ray took the job, had been dismissed.

I said earlier that you need luck to make your way in the game and so it was with me. I was asked to take over as head coach of Wakefield Trinity, a club with a great history. Although I had never coached a side before, I thought I could build on what Ray had achieved, using my playing experience in England and Australia. I had my own beliefs in how I thought a side should play: discipline in attack and defence, team spirit and professionalism. We had some great players, which was a base to start from, or so I thought. How wrong I was. I had a 12 month verbal agreement which seemed to be how the club did its business. Terry Crook, who I played with at Wakefield, was brought in to replace Alan Hardisty and take charge of the 'A' team. One minute I had stopped playing, the next I was the first team coach.

The club had big financial problems and had to sell its stars. Toppo, after finishing his testimonial year, went to Hull; Alan Agar left and had a superb first season as player-coach at Carlisle; Steve Diamond went to Fulham; Adrian Barwood had started a new job in Wales and joined Cardiff. The club brought in some real good ones, John Lyons from Batley and in October Ray Baxendale, a New Zealand test forward. But all of a sudden these great players, the spine of the side, had gone to pastures new. I was left with players who perhaps were not up to their standards, echoes of my last spell at Wigan.

We had brought a player in who would have to be coached into the professional game from the amateur game. We still had some good solid pros, and youngsters such as Andy Kelly and Colin Maskill were chomping at the bit to play in the first team. I had seen them train and knew they could step up to the plate and give it their best shot.

This was my first coaching job and I said that we were all in it together. That was something I learned. Whatever you do, do it together to build a fantastic team spirit. We had lads who never gave me less than 110%. That effort though doesn't make up for two players who had more ability than any of them. A couple of players with more ability, effort and team spirit would have seen us not finish where we did at the end of that season.

My first game in charge was on 16 August 1981, against Dewsbury in the first round of the Yorkshire Cup. Our performance gave hope to the fans, we won 18–6. That was as good as it got in the Yorkshire Cup. In the next round Hull KR turned us over by 10 points, not satisfactory.

Seven days later we began our league campaign with a defeat at Hull, but improved the following week with our first league win, 18–12 over York. In that game for the first time in my career I saw something I couldn't believe. Keith Smith was the most gifted stand-off; he had ability, thinking and vision, but I thought he lacked self-belief. He always looked to come off. I'd pat him on the back, didn't bruise his ego, and never told him off. At half-time in that game I needed, for the first time, to tell him off. He took his shirt off, gave it to me, got in his car and drove home. He never came back. I'll never forget it. Absolutely awesome player, awesome – but he retired after that.

After that win, we had a disastrous September and October and lost our next seven games, including 27–22 to Second Division Keighley in the John Player Trophy. During that period there were coming and goings; more than I can remember. Also as coach I upset a few former teammates by playing them in the 'A' team, based on how they'd played in that losing run. There were some big departures that I wasn't happy with. Our captain, Terry Day, went to join Toppo and Trevor Skerrett at Hull, Alan McCurrie went to Oldham, after he had been substituted after a heavy loss at Hull KR and put in a transfer request. He was joined there by Billy Harris and Wakefield Colts player Tony Rose. Those decisions were down to the board, I just had to work with the team.

I put five new signings in for our home game against St Helens on 1 November. We won 16–9 after being battered there five weeks earlier. We followed that up, again at home, with a shock 11–8 win over double champions Bradford Northern. It reminded me of my last game for Wakefield. I thought we were on our way after that victory which came at a cost. Andy Kelly celebrated his 21st birthday by breaking his arm in the game. It was a big blow for a youngster who was the future of the club and needed to be kept at all costs. I knew I had to do everything possible to get him playing again; he was that good a player at that age.

I thought with those two wins that we would kick on and climb the table. However, Wigan, Leigh and Widnes saw it differently and beat us, so we were in the bottom four. December came; there was a cold snap and we did not play for five weeks. Although I had told John Scaife that I had packed in playing, the club had kept my registration. I decided to train again to play and assist the team on the field. I could lead from the front. Along with training I did exercises to strengthen my knees. As always, it started off well, but after a fortnight I broke down and a specialist suggested I finally call it a day. I didn't make a decision either way.

Going into our game on 3 January, we were second bottom above Whitehaven, who hadn't won any of their opening 12 games. They were our opponents in Cumbria. If we won, it would put us within a point of three sides ahead of us on nine points. If we lost well ... we drew 9–9 and the Cumbrians had their first point of the season.

They only got six more from two wins, two more draws and finished bottom. Before that game I thought we needed to win 10 more games, I didn't know where they would come from and I was trying to be positive. We had crucial games coming up against fellow strugglers Castleford, Featherstone Rovers and Fulham.

The weather did us again for the next three weeks before we went to Fulham and lost 13–12; so they pulled four points clear of us. Next up was the return against Whitehaven. We knew we needed to win. I don't think the fans were bothered; only 2,626 turned up for our first home game for over two months. It wasn't the best, but we dug in and Andy Fletcher's hat-trick was the highlight of a 15–12 win.

A trip to The Boulevard followed. I tried to instil into the players that we needed to put a winning run together. We knew it wouldn't be easy as Toppo, Trevor Skerrett and Terry Day would turn out for Hull and we knew how good they were. I took a gamble and picked 18-year-old Colin Maskill at hooker. He deserved the chance. Despite us losing narrowly, Colin justified his selection with an outstanding performance. He made some great runs and won the scrum contest in both halves.

With the weather having been bad over the past three months, I put it to John Scaife that to help team spirit a trip to warmer climes might be beneficial before the Challenge Cup first round tie at Bramley. He agreed and we went to Majorca for five days straight after the Hull defeat. The bonus was that we could train in the warm every day, the players got to know each other better; but we needed to beat Bramley. We were getting a load of aggro for what we had done. If we won great; if we lost – what a waste of money. In the Challenge Cup it was justified as we won at Bramley 16–4, beat Oldham at Belle Vue 18–12 before losing to Leeds 20–2 at Belle Vue. But in between the cup ties we lost two away league games, at Leeds and Leigh.

Now we had to focus on not getting relegated to the Second Division. Due to the awful winter we had 11 games to play in six weeks; seven at home. We hadn't won away all season. Any away win would be a bonus; the key to survival was the games at Belle Vue.

The first home game was against Fulham, who were down at the bottom with us. We had lost there by a point earlier in the season; a win was crucial. It wasn't the prettiest of games, but it was about winning and we did 18–13.

I had to keep being positive; the fans had already made up their minds that we were going down. At York we came from behind to win 13–11; but then had a setback in the first of three consecutive home games, Warrington edged it by a point 18–17.

In the second one I made a coach's call against Barrow. First I picked Andy Kelly who had put himself through the ringer as I had challenged him to get back into the first team before the end of the season. He was in on merit; I didn't do sentiment. I needed players who wanted it more than I did. Andy was one of those and showed my faith in him as he went nearly half the length of the field late in the game for a try. I also decided to ignore the specialist who just before Christmas had told me to retire and made a comeback against Barrow. Call me crazy, brave, foolish whatever; I had made more successful comebacks than Frank Sinatra. This was no different. I did what I had always done; led from the front and by example. I played for an hour by which time the agony was too much. I was literally playing on one leg. By then we had scored five tries, but still had to defend hard on our line for a 23–20 victory.

That win had seen us move up to fourth from bottom. Next up at Belle Vue were Wigan, who were two places ahead of us. It was quite simple, we had to win. No sentiment, if it was us or Wigan to go down, it would have to be Wigan. We led 13–7 at half-time; but from us being in control, Wigan went a point ahead. Harold Box kicked two vital, match-winning penalties; one from 50 yards that I would have been proud of in my pomp. We won 17–14. It felt like my first season at the club; in that relegation fight we had the momentum and only lost three of our last six games.

We had six games left in three weeks to save our season. A local derby at Post Office Road against Featherstone Rovers was lost 14–3. Then came another local derby, against Castleford. Our destiny was still our hands; we needed another victory to put ourselves in a great position. We were struggling for players; but I put out a team, although some players were clearly not fit. It was also my birthday and there was only one present I wanted.

The lads put on a brave performance and somehow produced a win; we beat Castleford 14–5. Once again we were out of the bottom four. It was a great birthday present; I'll never forget that day and our win. It was a double celebration which gave us a chance to stay in the First Division.

One more win and we would be safe. Two days later, at home to Hull KR, we knew what we needed to do. The fans were behind us and believed we could do it. All the squad were knackered and more busted now than against Castleford. Hull KR were up there challenging for the Championship, so the result meant as much to them as it did to us. That day we finally ran out of steam and lost 25–11; another blow.

We then had a trip to the champions, Bradford Northern, who wanted the points for a third consecutive title. There is no sentiment in rugby league and feeling sorry for anyone, it was all about the team and how much they wanted it. Bradford Northern wanted it more than us. We were running on empty and their big pack and talented backs showed what they could do. They took us to the cleaners with an easy win.

It was down to our trip to Castleford. Whoever won stayed up; the losers were down to the Second Division. Our destiny was in our own hands; whatever happened there, no-one else was to blame. We had lost a lot of class and star players, playmakers and that was the difference about where a team finished in the table. I was one as I'd proved against Barrow, but my knees had gone. I couldn't risk playing; I had my family and Sheila had always been supportive of my career. The good thing was we had a week to prepare for the game, but day-by-day the tension grew. The supporters got behind us. The players who were fit enough to train just did what they needed to; if they weren't match fit now they never would be. It was the biggest game of their careers.

Sunday 25 April – the day had arrived. Castleford's Wheldon Road is a tight knit ground and was packed. Their fans roared their team on. As good as we played, we lacked a middle man to control the game and Castleford won 15–7. There was not much else to say. We were relegated. There was a sort of numbness; I was proud of my players and felt sorry for them at the same time. Sadly, the table never lies and Wakefield Trinity were relegated for the first time in 78 years. I had the distinction of being the coach in charge. Sport is all about inches; we were a foot short and got our just rewards, relegation. After the defeat I got a vote of confidence that I would be back for the next season.

Three days later, it was our final game in the First Division for at least 12 months, at home to Featherstone Rovers. I was confident I could take the team back up the following season. Perhaps some of the players who knew they wouldn't be there went through the motions and we went down 23–8 to one of our local rivals. It would be a hard summer for our fans.

The simple final facts were that we only needed a win from one of our last four games; we lost all four. More importantly, when I got the job the club sold all the star players for financial reasons and did not bring in the same quality we had let go. Doesn't that sound familiar at Wakefield? I was never able to play the same side in back-to-back games and that season we used 49 players which says it all.

The final irony was that I began my career at Wakefield Trinity playing my first game at Featherstone Rovers and losing and finished it as a coach at Featherstone Rovers losing and the club was relegated.

Bill at Belle Vue during his time at Wakefield.

26. Murphy and me

A few days after the end of the season we had a do at the club; it was fancy dress. I can't remember what I was dressed as, but it must have been as a prick because within 10 minutes of it starting, the vice chairman came up to me.

He said "I'm sorry Bill, we had a vote yesterday at the board meeting and it was agreed to let you go." What could I do? Well, it gave me the excuse to get drunk. I had a great night with the lads, told them all. I think I always had a good rapport with the players I was involved with, and we all got bladdered together.

So that was it. Sacked. I hadn't had a contract; they had just said 'Do you want to coach the side?' I didn't sign a contract; I was just put in charge of the team. There wasn't a pay off if I got the sack, nothing like the mega compensation deals in football now; if a manager is sacked in the Premiership he is made for life. It wasn't anything like that, it was never about money, it was always about being involved in the game.

I wanted to succeed in whatever I did, it was really my first opportunity in coaching; I had never coached anyone before. I can guarantee that if we had kept the players that we started the season off with when I was given the job, we would not have got relegated. With the financial problems that Wakefield had – and continued to have all through the years – at the beginning of that year in charge they sold all their top quality players. I was left with some good players, don't get me wrong, I signed some good players like Billy Harris, Clive Pickerill, Nigel Day and Harold Box, but they weren't the same as Dave Topliss, Trevor Skerrett or the Raines.

After that bombshell, and drowning my sorrows that night, in the early morning I had to break the news to Sheila. She was disappointed because we lived in Cock Lane in Wakefield. We had a nice home and all of a sudden we couldn't afford the mortgage payments for the property. Fortunately, Mr Woodward, the previous chairman when I signed for the club, wasn't the chairman anymore.

He had contacts though and Trevor got in touch with people in Wakefield Council and got me a house opposite the ground which had just been built. New homes owned by the council, we lived in a house and it felt royal, Buckingham Drive. We lived there for the next few months and it was during that period that Wigan came in for me.

To be quite honest, I was flabbergasted after being sacked by Wakefield. I knew that we had done a good job even though we had been relegated. I knew the work we had put in and I knew some of the young players that I had brought in would come good. I even tried playing myself to keep us in the First Division for a couple of games. I was playing with five pain killing injections in each knee. I wasn't fit; I was as fat as a butcher's dog.

I went on the park to give leadership and I must have been an idiot because by the time those injections had worn off I was in pain for the rest of the week. I couldn't train or anything, I tried to show leadership and on the back of that we did win some games.

I was trying to put the effort in until the painkillers wore off. I could probably do half a game or just over. I remember players like Clive Pickerill saying "Come on, if he can get there we can get there."

I always tried to show that leadership, even up to when I finished in rugby league a couple of years ago. It's all about leadership, believing in yourself, passing that onto people for them to believe in themselves. I've never felt down about anything, apart from what happened at Wigan, which we'll come to and that wasn't my fault.

As well as getting the sack from the club, I lost the job at the brewery a couple of days later. They said they had to let me go from that job. I'd been struggling with my knees and started having operations.

Once again I signed on the dole. A few weeks later I got a visit from one of the Wigan directors, Jack Robinson. I've known Jack all my life. He has his business in Ince, where I now live. He had a massive stroke a few years ago, but has got better. He said that they had just appointed Alex Murphy as head coach at Wigan and that he would like me to go back to Wigan as his assistant.

I said "Can I speak to Murph about it?" I was a born-and-bred Wiganer. Sheila and I came over to Wigan from Wakefield; Sheila went to see her mum and I met Murph. He said that even though I had got relegated with Wakefield Trinity, he was impressed with what I had done there. He had taken the Wigan job and was looking for a good assistant; would I like to go back and assist him at Wigan? I didn't need convincing whatsoever.

Sheila had had enough of living in Yorkshire, I was jobless; it was the chance to move back nearer to our families. We'd spent four years in Australia, a brief return to Wigan, four years in Wakefield. Now was the time to return and settle back in my roots. I'd been an adopted Yorkshireman for four years, quite something considering that I didn't like them.

It was great coming back. We were around the corner from our families rather than a four hour round trip. We could walk and see our families. If I had any problems I could walk to see my mum, any problems Sheila had she could go to her mum's.

It was great to see all my friends again, back to the pubs that I used to go to before; life was good, as well as knowing the women I used to know in Wigan. I was back where I should be and that was at Wigan.

My relationship with Sheila had mellowed, though even when we were in Yorkshire Sheila's mam was that big, it felt as if she was at the side of me. So it didn't make any difference if I was in Wigan or Yorkshire, her presence was always there. Later on, we did mellow to each other, but at the time there was still a rivalry between Sheila and her mum.

I respected what Alex Murphy had done. I had always admired him as a player, arguably for me he was the best scrum-half I ever saw, better than everybody else, Andy Gregory or Peter Sterling. He had got a great record as a coach at his previous clubs.

We were both strong-willed individuals with firm opinions. I always said what I thought as I do to this day. As I saw it, Alex became my assistant as I thought I was doing everything else at the club. I didn't know what would be expected from an assistant coach because I hadn't had one at Wakefield. As I look back on my time as an assistant coach, I really enjoyed it.

I was really looking forward to working with Alex. It wasn't about money again, because I knew he was on a big contract. Believe it or not I got £53 plus I had to apply for Family Income Supplement. So once again it wasn't about money, but about keeping in the game.

I was coming back to the club I'd loved as a boy following his heroes to being Murph's assistant in 1982. Wigan had been in the doldrums after being relegated in 1980. They had been promoted back into the First Division in 1981, and had survived their first season back while I got relegated with Wakefield.

It was an opportunity to get back to Wigan and live there; they promised me that they would sort a house out, which they did. The club got me a council house in Norley Hall, just outside Wigan and we lived there.

I had a great time that year. For the first seven weeks of the season I never saw Murph, he was in Australia. We won seven games out of our first 10, drew one and lost two, including a defeat in the Lancashire Cup. We were building a team who didn't half work for each other, with a great team spirit. Great players are great, but if they don't work together that's all they are, they don't win games.

We had some good players at the club, some old players, like Glyn Shaw, David Stephenson, Danny Campbell and Nicky Kiss and we brought in players such as Brian Juliff and Mick Scott, who make for a good hard working team. We had a fantastic team spirit; we would stay out, as we did in my era. I taught them how to stay out together having a drink after the game; none of them went home.

We had a great season and finished third in the league. Also, Wigan won their first trophy for many years. We won the John Player Trophy at Elland Road, Leeds against Leeds 15–4. Also, we just lost to the Australia tourists 13–9.

For Wigan it was a great year, but a sad year for me at the end of it because I lost, I really lost hope in rugby league when I was sacked by the club. I really did and the way I got sacked was baffling. I knew why I got sacked and to be honest the reason I knew I would be on my way was because I was doing so much.

We had a few idiots playing in the side, such as Lee Bamber who sadly later in life was shot and murdered. He could have been a heck of a prop forward, but he got on the wrong side of the tracks, a bit of a gangster. Twelve, 18 months later he got shot in a pub in Widnes and blown away. I think he got the man-of-the-match that night we played Australia.

Murph would ring me up on the Tuesday and ask what I was going to do that night, he would turn up and I was doing the session. We had a great fitness coach in place at the club, Alan McInnes, who was superb at his job and got the players fit. I could talk to Alan.

One particularly disappointing result was when we lost at home to Castleford in the Challenge Cup. The match was due to be played on the Sunday. It was a bit frosty the night before, but we came in early for breakfast and went onto the pitch, we knew that it would thaw out by dinner time. But a local referee was called in to come and inspect the pitch and he called the game off. Later we trained on the pitch, and Castleford turned up at 1pm, went on the pitch and were absolutely livid because the pitch was fit for play.

The thing was that we were prepared and ready, but the match was put back until the Wednesday. Those Castleford players were so incensed that they just toasted us that night; I don't think anyone would have beaten them on the night after what they had gone through on the Sunday. We could have played that game then and won, but we lost 17–7.

For the John Player Trophy Final, I knew the team I wanted to pick, and I used to work the set pieces. We scored a try in the John Player Final where I had Brian Juliff coming off opposite wing and Brian went over under the posts.

I knew I was on my way out, the week before the final at Elland Road we played away to Workington Town and were winning well at half-time, 26–4, and went on to win 31–12. I recall we came in and I said to the lads "Great win, fantastic result, put it to bed. Let's have a few beers, get ready, extra training session this week, lets prepare for the John Player Trophy Final next week." But I remember Murph coming in and starting to criticize the players, which I wasn't happy about and told him so.

I didn't give a toss at that point; I had to say what I had to say. For me when I had said it or if anybody would have said that to me, it would have been done, dusted and put to bed, move on – no grudges. Don't bear any grudges, it's said and done, I mean I've been in the wrong and said so, to me alright it's said, done, I'll take it on board.

What really topped it off when we won the John Player Trophy at Elland Road and were coming back on the coach. All the players start singing songs. I remember them 'We've got the best fullback in rugby league' and they started going through the playing positions and substitutes anyway when it came to coaching they sang 'We've got the best coach in rugby league, his name is Bill Ashurst …'

I was there until the end of the season when I found out that I was sacked in the *Wigan Evening Post*. I was going to training on the Thursday night and had bought the local paper. There it was on the back page 'Wigan fire assistant coach'.

That's when I found out and I couldn't get to the bottom of why and who at that stage, but later on I found out what had happened. I believe that only Jack Robinson stood up for me when push came to shove. I think I had become the boss in the players' minds, they were coming to me for advice, and the press were coming to me as well.

When I did ask Murph, he said he said it wasn't him, he blamed Maurice Lindsay. He never said to me it's you or me Bill, I'm the head coach you're the assistant, you might be doing the coaching, but it's not working. I'm going have to ask you to stand down and recommend to the board for you to stand down. In the end I suppose that there was no room for both of us. Murph didn't last long at Wigan after I left, and was sacked by Maurice Lindsay at the start of the next season.

In that season at Wigan they had the 'Gang of Four' directors; Maurice Lindsay, Tom Rathbone, Jack Hilton and Jack Robinson who I've mentioned. Maurice did fabulously for Wigan, I mean you have got to give credit where it's due. Maurice and those guys just dragged it back up to the penthouse again, and did a fantastic job. I remember my first team talk, Murph was in Australia and I was halfway through my team talk.

I'll never forget Maurice's red face, he opened the dressing room door and walked in and I just said "What the f... do you think you are doing?" I swore then. Maurice said "What do you mean?" I said "Don't come in my f...ing dressing room when I'm talking to my players, just leave and close the door behind you please." Maurice left the dressing room; that was my first real chat with him.

As far as I saw it, I was in charge in the dressing room, this is my team, this is rugby league, it was not the board room. This is me and them because that's how I work, because they and I have got to get that result. I've got to do what I've got to do and say what I have to say; they have got to take that and take it onto the park. It's me and them, I'm separate from them, but I'm part of them; I'm the boss, but I'm part of them, we're together.

I'm not a shirt and tie man who can just give orders and stand five miles away. I have got to be part of that, to be part of them because they are taking me on the park with them in respect of that. I always had teams that would go through a brick wall for each other, for me that's mutual respect, if I was separate from them where's the respect?

All the directors, including Maurice, used to come in after the game and congratulate the players, but never before a game. I used to get on with Jack Robinson, Tom Rathbone and Jack Hilton. I knew Jack Hilton when I first played for Wigan. Jack was a director at Wigan when I first signed for them; I used to be a mate of Jack's son John, so I knew Mr Hilton very well.

Training days were still the same from my playing days at Central Park, the only difference being they had a built in sauna, the players still trained and could come in, during the daytime if they weren't working, for a sauna. I used to love the saunas. I used to meet up on a Monday morning with Westie, John Pendlebury, Danny Campbell and Shaun Wane who was there then.

I coached Shaun who had just started at the club; Shaun always had potential when he was at Wigan, a Wiganer through-and-through. When he played for Wigan Shaun always bled for the club, probably cherry and white cells and it's great to see him eventually get his chance and coach his home town club where he started his playing career all those years ago. He's brought home-grown Wigan kids into the team and look at the success he has had doing it his way. It makes you think doesn't it?

He would have been about 16 or 17 then, and been signed on for a couple of years before I got there playing in the 'A' team when I coached there. We had players like Glyn Shaw, Nicky Kiss, John Pendlebury, a side doing well though Shaun started some games and also played coming off the bench. I first saw him in the pre-season training and he was in the first team squad when then they separated the first team and 'A' team squads.

The fitness side was really down to Alan McInnes. I didn't get involved in the fitness side of it I would be there watching the players train, encouraging them and talking to them as they were training, "Put the effort in, don't cheat yourself" everything that goes to motivating and coaching. Alan was a superb fitness coach. He had a circuit which he used, it was brilliant the way he worked it, and the players enjoyed it. We had no lazy trainers; they all put the effort and commitment in.

One of the best trainers I saw at the club was Graeme West, once we signed Westie I was in awe of him. The way he spoke you knew that he was a winner; at that particular time Murph had made Colin Whitefield captain of Wigan.

In my opinion, Colin was affected by the captaincy, it hampered his game and I told him what I was going to do, take it off Colin and give it to Graeme. At Central Park the referee's room was where I used to get changed. I called them both in and I recall saying "Colin, it's obviously affecting your game. I want the pressure took off you go and enjoy your rugby, Graeme you're the captain of your country, a born leader, will you accept the captaincy?" and he said "Yeah." They both shook hands and wished each other all the best and they went training. I came back into the dressing room after training, Murph came in sat them all down "I'm going to change this captaincy". But I had already done it; I had made Graeme West captain.

Captaining the team, I remember he played at Featherstone and we could have won the game with Colin's goalkicking and one particular goalkick. Colin used to look at Murphy on the bench; Graeme was captain and said 'go for goal'.

He looked at the bench, Murph said tap it, so Colin tapped it and we lost possession, coming off that pitch Westie was livid, he was looking for Murph. Murph didn't come back in the dressing room after that game. Westie was looking for him.

A win would have got us the one point behind leaders Hull in second place, three points ahead of Hull KR, with the final league game to come. As it turned out on the final day of the season Hull and Hull KR won their games, we lost 21–17 at Widnes and finished third on points difference. We went on to lose at home in the first round of the Premiership to Leeds, 12–9, who we had beaten at Central Park a month earlier.

It took a while to calm Graeme down. He was like me, he wanted to get it off his chest and then put it to bed, that was the way he was. He led Wigan for many years as captain, a born leader and he knew who'd done it. When he turned to coaching he won everything on offer including that magnificent World Club Challenge in Australia against the Brisbane Broncos. He couldn't put any blame on Colin, Colin was doing as his coach Murph had told him, but Westie's never forgotten it.

During my third spell at the club, a dear friend of mine, Keith Mills, was still there. He sadly passed away two years ago, after over 40 years involvement at the club. He was Mr Wigan; he used to be the physio, sponge man, take the kicking cone out and had various jobs at the club.

I knew Keith before I went to Australia. I played for a year in the 'A' team with Keith at Wigan and the odd first team game with him and I've known him all my life. I was talking to their Maurice some time ago and we always had a mutual admiration for each other.

For who he was and what he did, Keith had it for me as a player and a friend. Keith was the first bloke who nicknamed me 'Walt'; I had it all my playing career thanks to him. It was a sad day for rugby league, for me, especially in Wigan and for Wigan Rugby League Club on the passing of such a good friend.

So that first season, with me as I saw it doing so much, the club finished third, the John Player Trophy was won and there were some great highlights for that season. I always enjoyed playing against the Australians here and over there. This was my first time coaching against them, a cold October night at Central Park. We lost against a side that went through the tour unbeaten and became known as the 'Invincibles'. To go down by just four points was a phenomenal effort. It was the closest anyone got to that side.

The players drained themselves to a standstill; the work rate that they put in was remarkable, so near yet so far, the Australians were sweating as we went all out for a winning try and goal with over 12,000 fans cheering us on. Despite beating us three tries to one, Henderson Gill's try and three Colin Whitefield goals gave them a fright.

The other highlight was winning the John Player Trophy Final, the first trophy that the club had won for a long time. To beat Leeds at Elland Road in their own town; It was remarkable and superb achievement by the players; I really loved that one in front of thousands of Wigan fans who had travelled over to support us.

To be involved with players like Nicky Kiss, who had just started developing, and watching Glyn Shaw show his experience and Danny Campbell, David Stephenson, as well as young players coming through like Denis Ramsdale. They weren't big names, there was only the odd big signing, but the work rate they put together was fantastic. Players like Mick Scott just did it for each other, hard on and hard off the park which created a great team spirit which as I've said can win games.

I didn't get any bonus for our John Player Trophy success. All I got was the £53 from the club, the FIS, plus child benefit for my children. It wasn't about money for being the assistant coach at the club, although that was one of the excuses made to me at the time for sacking me after I'd read the news in the paper.

It was a bombshell. I turned up for training and read it in the paper at the end of an outstanding first season when we were getting ready for the close season. I didn't take training that night, I just went in said my goodbyes to the lads, the players were as gob smacked as me, as devastated as I was, and still are today.

I meet Nicky Kiss and he always says that I was the first coach that really taught him how to play hooker and that there have been some great coaches at Wigan. He played under John Monie, Graham Lowe; with the team I had he thinks I was probably the best.

People like Nicky have said that the team that Wigan did eventually buy, and you know no disrespect to the coaches, Donald Duck could have coached them. They had so much quality, I mean if you looked through those sides, Andy Gregory used to say to me we didn't need a coach we had a great team.

They bought really, really well and I had had the privilege that year, one season of coaching Henderson Gill. There is a funny story about Henderson Gill and Glyn Shaw. In the winter it was always bad at Wigan and we couldn't train at Central Park. We had no other training pitch apart from the one at the top at the back of the Spion Kop, so I sent them on a run one night.

I sent them on this run from Central Park up Whelley, through Haigh Hall Plantations, down the other side, turn left at the Boars Head, back past Wigan Hospital and back around Central Park. I would say it was about four miles. Usually I would follow them, in the car of course, to make sure that they didn't cheat. This night, however, I didn't.

Anyway they were all coming in, no Glyn Shaw, no Henderson Gill. Keith Mills was asking "Where are they?" An hour later there was still no sign of them. Next thing the phone rings in the office, Keith picked it up "It's for you Bill, its Henderson Gill and Shawy." I got the phone and said "What's the matter?"

He said "Bill, where do we turn left?" I said "Why, where are you?" He said "We're ringing from a pub called Henry Africa's", which was a pub just off the motorway. Instead of turning left they had turned right and gone all the way there, so I had to send Keith in the car and go and pick them up.

So that was Gilly and Glyn Shaw, at the next training session Gilly came with a new car, did a wheel spin and straight into the wall, banged his car in the wall. He was certainly a character, but that was him and the side was made up of characters like him. What an entertainer, he turned out to be on the field for years to come, for Wigan and Great Britain, with his famous wiggle at Wembley and in Australia and that gigantic smile of his.

That's what I loved about coaching, being part of that of that camaraderie. Coaching's not all about working hard, it's about fun as well, you become a squad you have fun together, you have hard times, you have good times, winning times, losing times, and it's all part of that togetherness.

27. A Wakefield return

After I had been sacked by Wigan as assistant coach to Murph, I knew I had to use painkiller injections so I could try to continue playing. I went back to Wakefield Trinity who, although they sacked me as coach, had kept my playing registration. Before I had taken up the offer at Wigan, I had offered to continue playing for the club. I wanted to try and play again, because I just loved the game.

In the 12 months I had been away, Ray Batten had returned as coach and got them promoted back to the First Division at the first attempt and then resigned again. This time it was after the club, in a cost-cutting operation, decided to get rid of trainer and conditioner Stan Timmins. That was a poor excuse after what they did in December 1983.

I felt sorry for Stan; he was great while I was playing at Wakefield. He did everything he could, and used every trick in the book to get me back on the field after every operation. He always offered words of encouragement when he knew I was feeling down and fed up. He did his best for me when I coached the side; getting players fit to play and twice in my own attempts to play again, which I did against Barrow.

The head coach now was a legend, Derek 'Rocky' Turner. He was a former player and captain at the club. He had coached at Castleford and Leeds. The only problem, in my opinion, was that he had been out of the game for 10 years and the game had moved on. The club and coach were happy to have me back, even though I was totally unfit and had piled weight on. The difference between being assistant coach and training is I didn't need to train because I wasn't playing. At Wigan I was doing all the things a rugby league player shouldn't do and doing them to excess. No change there.

I went about getting right slowly; I wanted to give it a good shot. I knew that if and when I played, whether in friendlies or competitive league games that I needed painkillers before a game. I had no problems with the physio and doctor who administered them, and trusted my body in their hands.

My first game of the 1983–84 season was a friendly against Batley. I went into the game confident that my fitness was okay and that I was ready. The pre-season training had been different to say the least, but it had got me here without breaking down. I had a magical comeback and – apart from my age – it was as if I had never been away. I led from the front, took the team around the park and barked out instructions even though I wasn't the captain.

The RFL had decided that if a try was scored, it would now be worth four points instead of three. This was to give more reward for tries over conversions and penalty goals. In the match with Batley, with the new scoring system, we won 54–20. I made three of the 10 tries we scored as well as being involved in several others. The best one was when I drove through the tackles, went one way and flicked the ball out the other way for Harold Box. I also worked well with Nigel Stephenson, who was at stand-off so he could play with more freedom with the backs. Also, it was great to play with Mike Lampkowski again. The big positive outcome for me was that I completed the full 80 minutes after the painkillers and I was okay in training the following week. I would like to think that Rocky was happy with my game.

The following weekend we played a charity match at Hilton Park against Leigh. It was a good hard game and step up in the strength of the opposition from the previous week. I wasn't as involved as the previous match and Leigh got in my face, but we all gave our all and went down to a close defeat, 15–14.

I was disappointed with my overall performance. Next up was our first game league game of the season, at home to Fulham. I had done the training in the lead up to this game and didn't feel I should play, it was important that we got off to a good start. I went to see Rocky and asked to be left out of the side. Rocky didn't agree with my reasoning, but respected my request. We managed to grind out an 18–14 win. Two penalties from young Colin Maskill got us home.

We had another home game which was memorable for different reasons on Wednesday 24 August 1983. It was against Wigan, who I had played for and coached up to the end of the 1982–83 season. Rocky chose me for Wakefield and I was up for it, I didn't feel I had anything to prove. Everything had gone well in pre-season and I thought lets go for 80 minutes and win. Wigan had a good side out including Graeme West, Brian Case, Nicky Kiss, Glyn Shaw, Henderson Gill and Mick Scott.

Murph was still in charge, but having coached them the previous season I knew their strengths and weaknesses and how they would play. Having said that, any coach will say that knowing how they play and how to stop them is a different kettle of fish. Wigan put in a great opening 40 and I thought were waging a personal war against me with some hard and often foul hits. I took it as a compliment. They were attacking a knackered 35 year old with dodgy knees. I didn't bite and just kept smiling at them. I knew mine and our team's time would come. I was bruised and battered and they led 12–0 with two converted tries at half-time.

Rocky wasn't happy, but as I remember we stormed back in the second half and had Wigan panicking. I got my kicking, probing and handling game going between our backs and forwards. I made tries for our centre Paul Coventry and his winger David Jones. Paul scored the try of the night, which I created. I saw a gap, went through it and was away. I drew Barry Williams in and flicked a sublime reverse pass to Coventry to score. Colin Maskill added the goal and it was game on. Jonesy showed his speed to score in the corner and I dropped a goal so there was one point in it.

The painkillers had worn off and my knees had gone. The adrenaline was still flowing, but I was in agony and came off. I wanted to stay on, but there was no way and we lost a little direction. We threw everything at them, but Wigan soaked up the pressure and scored a converted try late in the game for a seven point lead. They held on to win, but we had certainly given them a fright.

At training a couple of days later I had one of the funniest experiences in my life with Rocky Turner, although it turned out to be momentous. I couldn't train properly because of my knees, which he knew about. He had a reputation as a tough loose forward. At Wakefield, by the pitch there are the iron railings.

He shouted "Right guys, the length of the pitch, length of the pitch, over the railings, over the railings, up the steps, over the walls, back in over the wall." I started walking back to the dressing room and he said "Where are you going?"

I said "I'm having a bath."

He replied "You finish this ... session."

I said "Look, I'm a rugby player. If you want someone from the SAS go and buy somebody. I'm not climbing walls and fences, I can't even run on a rugby pitch."

He was so old fashioned Rocky, he was unbelievable. In my opinion, the club had got the coach it deserved. I thought that he was 10 years behind the time. It showed because they yo-yoed back into the Second Division and won only six more league games that season. The only highlight was the signing of 'King' Wally Lewis who came over for 10 matches and was on £1,000 a game. I thought that he was only half fit through injuries at home. They won five games during that spell and he scored six tries, what a good return. When he'd taken all their money and gone, they lost their last nine games and went down with a whimper.

You reap what you sew in this game and I was happy with my decision and reputation intact. I just walked away, finished, and retired there and then. I had had my last hurrah and rode back home to Wigan to depression and reality, or so I thought.

Coaching at Rose Bridge.

28. Backwards for the future

As throughout my whole career I always had plenty of confidence in my own ability, but reading about my sacking at Wigan in the newspaper left me disillusioned about the game and people within it. I was on such a low, to get kicked in the teeth the way I did and knowing what I had done, what I had achieved, all of a sudden I was sacked for being a success. What's the point?

So I had to sign on the dole because I didn't have a job. No other rugby league clubs rang me up or knocked on the door, I think that if others had come in at that stage I wouldn't have wanted to get back into the game. Depressed, I had not even gone to watch a game of any sort, I was so fed up, I didn't want anything to do with rugby league again, I had fallen out of love with the game.

This lasted for between nine to 12 months, during this time I still enjoyed a drink or two and put myself into a bit of a cocoon as well with my bout of depression. I was on that Prozac and finished on them after about three, four months, I thought 'bollocks to this', I was sick of sleeping. They used to make me go to sleep and it finished up that I couldn't keep taking them, so I kicked myself away from them.

Where we lived at Norley at the time and there was a field at the side of us, after I had came off that Prozac I could see the odd game through the upstairs bedroom window where I used to have a smoke. I would watch the kids playing rugby league and I slowly started to get my enthusiasm back by watching them play the game. I had never been involved coaching or playing with kids; it was later in my life that I got involved with that side of the game.

Although slowly regaining some enthusiasm, I didn't want anything to do with rugby league again. I had only been off the Prozac for about a month when one of my friends for life, Billy Melling of Rose Bridge, the club I used to play for before I signed Wigan, came to our house to see me.

He said "Will you come and coach Rose Bridge?"

I replied "I'll think about it Billy."

He said "We've got one or two good players, we need a good coach. We know what you can do, you played for us, get back in the game."

I hadn't wanted anything to do with rugby league again, but when Billy came, he was so enthusiastic at getting me back to Rose Bridge that it made me go and watch a training session. I had a chat with Sheila and I think that she was pissed off me being under her feet all the time and not working, so I took on the challenge of coaching the Rose Bridge Open Age amateur team.

I was surprised how quickly I got that energy back into my life. I was laughing again, enjoying it, taking the piss out of lads that I was coaching, watching them work rather than me working and it was good. It revitalised my energy, getting back into rugby league.

Being given the sack at Wigan became a memory. It's not a good one; it will always be a bad one.

When I got involved with Rose Bridge there were still a couple of lads playing that played with me at school, Cliff Darby at scrum-half and people like that had gone back to amateur rugby league. I had a squad that could be made great and we eventually did, with that side we had a lot of fun, some good wins, the players improved got better.

I brought Denis Boyd in who was a friend of mine, one of the hardest forwards I played with, he came as my assistant. Then I had Terry Crook who came from Leigh as an assistant as well and we made that team into a very good side.

Believe it or not that team should have got into the *Guinness Book of Records* on two occasions. We played a team from Sutton, St Helens in a cup game and we won 138–0 or something like that. They had just brought the four point try in and David Worrall, a young kid who played for me, kicked 16 goals and scored eight tries which is 64 points in a game. It was never recognised, never put in, we sent it to them and they didn't publish it.

That year end of that season I had 13 players sign as professionals in rugby league with four clubs, Blackpool Borough, Batley, Dewsbury and Keighley. The players included: Freddie Turner, Mark Dwyer, Frank Mooney, Cliff Darby and Tony Sanby, who is now the chairman of Ince Rose Bridge.

Including the good wins we had some fun after the games; I remember when we played in a semi-final at Mayfield. How unwise were those Mayfield players, they sold white raffle tickets after the game. Then they came to me saying "Give your players two of these raffle tickets for a pint, there were 70 raffle tickets. My lads were legless, I was legless using the white tickets for free ale."

The Mayfield players came over to me afterwards and asked who was in charge; I said "It's me". They said "We got it wrong Bill. You have been using these tickets for free ale, look at the bill." The bill was for about £300 and I said "Don't worry mate I'll sort it", all the lads were together and again I said "I'll sort it no problem."

Anyway their player turned his back and I finished up putting it in my mouth, chewed it up and swallowed it and said "That's it it's taken care of now." I'd swallowed the bill. I became an idiot like the ones I coached when I went back to the amateur game. There it was, gone, swallowed.

One day in the Premier Division we played Wigan St Patricks. Rose Bridge and St Pats just hated each other and I put Denis Boyd at prop. I've said how hard he tackled. Anyway we were just leading when they brought on their so called dangerman, Dave Regan, who was an 'A' teamer at Wigan when I played there. I shouted from the touchline "Denis they have just brought your breakfast on". First tackle, Denis absolutely ate him up and they carried David off.

Anyway, that night it was the first time I was banned from a club. We were on Tony Sanby's stag do, a pub crawl and we called in at St Pats just to take the piss. David, his brother Peter, and dad Freddie were in and Freddie started at me saying "You got our David franked." I said "I never f...ing touched him, I was standing on the touchline."

He said "Well, you got Boydy to do it."

I said "I didn't."

They wanted to fight and I said "Let's go in the car park." The late, great Cliff Fleming, a gentleman at the club came to me and said "Bill, would you leave and don't come back for a while." So I was barred from St Pats as well, it makes you think. I've mellowed and learnt that it's not all about Rose Bridge and St Pats; it's about the players playing and the coaches who are coaching them. It's not about rivalry, it's about the young element, not the club, and when people start putting youngsters first, they become a different person.

Cliff though was 100 per cent Wigan St Pats. I once heard a story that he loved pies, money was a bit short then, somebody said "Cliff they have put the pies up at St Pats."

He said "Why, how much?" and was told "No, not the cost. They've put them up so you can't reach them."

I've never changed in as many places as I did in my time at Rose Bridge. We started at the Conquering Hero and built showers, we moved to St Williams Club and built showers, we moved to The Imperial and built showers. It became a joke around Ince, with Rose Bridge you don't go for a pint and a pie, you go for a pint and a bath because every pub had showers in the back. We were just everywhere, like stray dogs and it was after that third year I left.

I left for the simple reason that the club was tearing itself apart, they had lost a lot of players, the committee wanted this, the players wanted that. I just finished up saying "Look, to bring it all together I'll give it up. I'll just call it a day. Bring in a new coach and I'll walk away," which is what I did. The club thankfully brought itself together, got one group out and eventually they got their own club.

I was then approached by Jeff Sutcliffe who was chairman for many, many years of the Wigan Amateur Rugby League; he has a walking stick now and is getting on. He asked me if would I take the Wigan Open Age Town team on, they had never got past the first round of the open age competition. I agreed to as long as they let me do what I wanted to with the team and selection.

Normally they picked Rose Bridge and St Pats players. I had the opportunity with not coaching anybody now to go and watch different games. I became impressed with players from St Cuthbert's, St Jude's, Spring View and Crown Springs, so I brought in a number of players from Division 1 and 2 clubs who I thought had ability. I used to take them to an all-weather pitch at Skelmersdale for training because then it was winter rugby league.

When we had big games I used to bring them in for breakfast. The league had to pay for all this and I treated them like professionals. I had one of the best captains and loose-forwards I had seen in amateur rugby at St Pats, Martin McLoughlin. He's coaching kids there now. Martin was the captain and in the first year we got to the semi-final at Hull and were losing by two points. I remember Tony Sanby made a break at centre. Paul Topping was his winger and he turned the ball inside to him. He only had to catch it, put it down and we were in the final. Unfortunately he dropped it and we lost.

The following year we got to the final against Halifax at Thrum Hall, Halifax's home ground. In the build-up we stayed at Mick Scott's pub in Halifax for breakfast. I knew him from playing at Wigan when I was assistant coach there. A great experience; I told the lads that they were ambassadors for Wigan, nothing stupid, let's have a good time in the pub. We had not been in there five minutes and two pairs of shoes were floating in a fish tank. So from 10 years old to open age, it doesn't make any difference they are still daft as brushes at times.

There had been a big freeze, no games in Wigan for six weeks leading to the final; they Yorkshire teams had played, so fitness played a big part in the game. A young Karl Fairbank, who finished up going to Bradford Northern and playing for Great Britain, played for Halifax amateurs then. We lost that final 12–10. We had gone from the Wigan Town team not getting past the first round to making the semi-finals and then the final.

At the reception after the game Harry Jesson, who was involved in the amateur game in Lancashire, approached me and said "Have you got a [coaching] badge Bill?"

They had just come in and I said "I've not Harry, I don't believe in them."

He said "Why?"

I replied "Because it doesn't make you a good coach. At the end of the day if you can't do the job it doesn't matter how many badges or pieces of paper you have, it doesn't work."

Harry said "Well, the thing is, if you had had a badge we would have given you the Great Britain team."

I thought it was ridiculous, but from memory they appointed a good young coach instead to coach Great Britain.

29. Runcorn

In the close season after the 1986–87 season, following the Wigan Town team's loss in the final a few months earlier, I got a call back to coaching in the professional ranks. It was a complete shock and came out of the blue. I had never even dreamed of a team like Runcorn Highfield trying to ask for my services. The telephone call was from Tony Almond, who was the club secretary; he told me that Matt Cusick, who was a friend of mine from Ince, was doing interviews for a coaching job at Runcorn.

I knew Matt; he used to have his own gym and the lads would go training at Matt's, he was also the conditioner and fitness man at Runcorn Highfield. Tony had had a word with Matt, who had told him I had a good pedigree in rugby league. Tony asked me would it be possible for me to go for an interview with everybody else interested in the job. I wanted to stay in the game and I'd looked at Runcorn. Everybody had looked at the joke Runcorn were then. The games that they couldn't win, not the games that they won sort of thing

I went for an interview on the Friday night at Canal Street, the old Runcorn FC ground where they played. Tony and the chairman, Terry Hughes, a businessman from Liverpool, a really nice man who was so enthusiastic, interviewed me. I went in with an open mind about what they were trying to do; what I wanted to do was sell them my ideas. I told them I'd seen videos of the previous season's performances and was impressed with one or two players. I told them whether it came down to money or not, I was pleased with what they had and would just bring decent amateur players in. With my background in amateur rugby league I find players and build them around what they already had. It wasn't going to cost them a lot anyway.

Whether it was my ability or the money I asked for I don't know, again it was never about money. I got a phone call the day after from Tony. He invited me to take control of Runcorn Highfield. I jumped at the chance and accepted, telling him I was looking forward to working with the chairman.

It was a verbal agreement. The chairman said 'see you later'; it was see you later. I've always been a man of my word and a handshake is good enough for me. I didn't need to put pen to paper with solicitors and lawyers when I was signing a coaching contract, with players you do, to me a hand shake was the sign of a deal. The money was enough to survive on, buy the milk, bread and butter, enough to provide for Sheila and the kids, never anything over the top.

I just loved being back in professional rugby league. It was a funny club, Runcorn, but I had a great time there. I'd played at Wigan; we went onto the pitch and waved to the crowd. When we went onto the pitch at Runcorn the crowd waved at us because we knew every one of them; they knew us by name because there were so few of them; they were great people. It was a great little club, we had a fantastic team spirit and I really enjoyed my spell at Runcorn, although it came to a sad end.

At the first opportunity I got the players together. In coaching at that time I was the coach, motivator, conditioner, fitness man with Matt, I did everything. I had some good players there already, such as John Cogger and Tommy Rawlinson. I brought good players in like Chris Middlehurst, Steve Moylan, Terry Rose from West Bank, Geoff Dean from St Jude's and Paul Durnin; a team built around experience.

We trained away from the ground in the close season, a lot of it at Haresfinch in St Helens in the light summer nights. I wanted to get the lads in early so we could get their fitness up to a peak before we played again. The ground was central for everyone; we had players from St Helens, Wigan, Widnes and Liverpool. We worked hard, played hard and that has always been my philosophy as a coach. In training, I wasn't the best of trainers myself so I knew all the short cuts, all the twigs and tweets which they would try to get away with. They all did running circuits and my car was always right behind them, as a player if I would have been asked to do what I told the players to do, I don't think I could have done it.

We used to leave for a pretty good run and in Mossbank, we used to run up to the top of Mossbank Hill. I would drive up in first gear in my car. We found an open space at the top and did 45 minutes circuit training, bodywork, press-ups and sit-ups using your own body weight. We would then carry on over to the other side of Mossbank Hill, right towards Carr Mill Dam. We would cross at the traffic lights on the East Lancashire Road, right at the roundabout and back down to Haresfinch, shower and change for home. There were one or two stragglers when we started this type of training, but there were a lot of fit players as well by the time they had finished.

The players had all bought into it. All the teams I have ever been involved with bought into it and we had a great team spirit. From a coaching point of view, I have always believed that 70 per cent of a team is team spirit; rather than a team of 100 per cent ability. Everyone must work for each other. We used to have fun and laughs in training; we did everything together. Sometimes we had bike competitions – work hard play hard. The fitness side was important; with their past history I didn't want them to be cannon fodder for the rest of the clubs.

There were no modern gym facilities like today; no treadmills and players didn't use a lot of weights then, it was a matter of breathing, and body weight to use instead of weights to get fit. It's the way I had trained, been brought up to train, although before my second return to Wigan I did a bit of training in my brother-in-law's gym in his shed. All the hard work that we did before the start of the season stood us in good stead.

The new season approached. It was my first in charge and with the record Runcorn had, our only aim at the beginning of the season, to be honest, was to be winning at half-time and full-time. Anything else was a bonus. The lads kicked into defence; I loved the defensive side of coaching because I believe that if a team scores two points more than the opposition they will win games. We put in a tremendous defence effort and work rate. Our record for that year shows we didn't concede a lot of points. Six games in that 1987–88 season we lost by only two points, including two cup matches, so it just shows how well we played, we had a good season. We could have had a tremendous season if a bounce of the ball, the referee's whistle had gone our way in some games.[9]

1987–88

We started off with a couple of wins; 8–0 away to Rochdale Hornets and 23–16 at home to Fulham. I think we shocked everybody in that first game at Spotland and to win and have no points scored against us. Traditionally, the club struggled, so it was a memorable win to begin with. Against Fulham we played well and deserved the victory.

Then came a Lancashire Cup tie with Widnes; a true local derby, with 2,679 on. They had come over the bridge which must have been open that day; there were times when I wished it was closed.

It was the first game that Martin Offiah scored in for Widnes and I have always said, there is Billy Boston, but I will always maintain that Martin Offiah is the best finisher I have ever seen as a winger. Billy was the winger for me, but Martin was the best finisher. It may sound strange, but it's not. Billy had the all-round game, defence, tackling everything; but Martin was an out-and-out finisher and a superb athlete.

I had never seen him. We had all heard about his reputation and how fast he was supposed to be. I had a young kid on the wing called Ian Smith. I said to Smithy "Look mate, he's come with a reputation. You stick with him wherever he goes; if he comes off you come off and sit next to him."

Anyway Martin scored two of the best tries I have ever seen and made an instant impression on me. At half-time we came in the dressing room and just looked at each other. I said to Smithy "What happened?"

He said "I'll be honest; I never saw which way he went." We laughed together.

They toasted us 40–6, but also physically battered us, I was in awe of Martin Offiah and Widnes; they were a top quality side. It was good experience for my team to face a team that won the First Division and thrashed better sides than us.

Doug Laughton was their coach. He was probably one of the best coaches involved in the game and I knew his qualities as a player from when I played with him at Wigan. He had those qualities as a coach. His teams took his orders onto the field and Doug would want to paste us physically because of the history between us as players. At the end of the day, good luck to them but we had a tremendous season.

We brushed ourselves off and came back to win our next three games against Mansfield Marksman, York and Workington Town. At York we were losing by three points late on, Chris Middlehurst took a tap, scored under the posts and we won by three points. In our win over Workington Town, Terry Rose broke a club record for points scored by a player in

---

[9] Runcorn conceded 469 points in 28 league games, 74 less than the previous season.

a match first set in 1931 when he scored 24 points from two tries and eight goals. Terry was our top points scorer that season with 126.

After the New Year, we had the return game at Fulham, we had won 10 games and lost four and we were in line for going top of the Second Division. Runcorn Highfield top of the league, a nose bleed. The supporters would think that the table was upside down.

We needed to draw or win, Fulham played somewhere near Heathrow on a sports recreation ground. I wish that day that they had been on a plane with their heads in the clouds. They scored a try in the last seconds out wide, and it put them level, so we were top of the league.

The BBC were there. They were going to interview the players. Runcorn were top of the league. It was shocking weather, raining and windy. I said to my assistant coach Arthur Daley, who was the best assistant anybody could have: "Let's go and do the interviews mate, we're at the top with a draw." Then Steve Guyett kicked the winning goal from the touchline. I couldn't believe it. We were all so dejected, not just because we had lost, but because Arthur and I didn't get chance to do the interviews. It's never over until it's over; I was gutted for the lads because they deserved to be top of the league.

Then we went on a bad run, we lost four on the trot home to Oldham, at Keighley, at Whitehaven and a Challenge Cup home defeat to Springfield Borough. They had a player called Kerry Gibson an Australian, who had one arm, believe it or not. We lost by two points and he had a good game at stand-off.

I can't say whether it was novelty or not, but the chairman said that we were going to sign this guy with the one arm. So the chairman, as is his right, signed him and he joined the club and became a novelty within the squad.

"He's got one arm Bill. Where are you going to play him?"

I said "The side where he can catch it and not on the one he can't." Anyway it wasn't Kerry's fault, he lasted a couple of games to appease the chairman as he'd signed him.

From that loss at Fulham we had a bad run to the end of the season with only four wins and 13 defeats. We finished 12th with 28 points, 14 wins and 14 losses. There were so many games which ended in narrow defeats a couple of points here, a couple of points there. It was frustrating from a coaching point of view where we finished at the end of the season.[10]

With another 10 league points we would have been fourth, the bounce of the ball, the blow of the whistle, costs you games, points and championships. That's what happened in that first season at Runcorn. We achieved at the club winning games and had a great rapport with the speccies. Crowds rose, to 500 or 600 and 2,400 when we played at home to Oldham, they were good games. The side was full of ability, team spirit, a will to work for each other, camaraderie; it was old heads and young legs that got us to where we got that season with those 14 wins.

---

[10] In 1986–87, Runcorn finished 11th in the table, but with only 21 points from 28 matches.

We went through 35 players that season and got some good ones in. Glyn Shaw been there, done it, read the book, I had so much time for Glyn Shaw, he was one of the most outstanding trainers I have ever seen. He was an outstanding example to young players and people, or to anyone playing with him. Work rate is the most important thing, Glyn got everything out of the game that he put in and I loved the guy as a leader.

John Cogger and Terry Rose got nine tries each and were our joint top try scorers. John was a young blond Australian loose-forward from Western Suburbs and a really good player for me. I had a beer with John when I went back to Australia in 2006.

I had Eric Prescott with us, the father of Steve, who so sadly lost his battle against cancer last year. Steve was a true man of steel who will be remembered for his deeds both on and off the field, a real sporting hero.

Eric had been there, done it and read the book. He was another great leader and another who never knew when a game was lost. He was a bit volatile, like me.

When I saw him at Runcorn when I took charge he asked me about the suit I had won when playing against him at Salford which got a good laugh. Eric was a blond bombshell and a great player in his whole career and would probably still play today if he could; he was that type of player and character.

Arthur Daley was my assistant coach and trainer who had coached the team the previous year. He also played seven games and come off the bench for me. There were odd times when we had to play him when we struggled with injuries. He was an old head who brought the threequarters through. I had no qualms whatsoever putting Arthur in the side; he was a good loose forward and so fit. He trained every day, a great assistant and he never let me down.

The disappointing thing at the end of the season was to reflect on those close defeats. It was sad for the players who had given their all. For some reason the chairman wasn't very impressed. I was told that he was disappointed.

He pulled me in and said "The situation in the future is we are going to have to let you go, we can't keep on paying all this winning pay." The players were on good winning pay, but that was between the players and the committee. It was very disappointing because now the team and I were getting a kick up the arse for winning instead of a kick up the arse for losing. The club had just had its best win-loss record for 12 years.[11] I was very, very pleased and proud of what we had done in my first season. I knew what I wanted to do in the close season.

I'll never forget the end of season fancy dress do at the Canal Street ground. I went dressed as Miss Runcorn, I had the swimming costume on, the wig, makeup and I nearly caused car crashes where we lived in Wigan waiting for the minibus to pick us up. It was so funny and we had a great night. It was one of the happiest clubs I've ever been at; they and Wakefield Trinity were the best professional clubs I was involved with.

---

[11] Looking at the club's record as Huyton as well as Runcorn, it was their best performance since the 1974–75 season when they finished seventh, with 26 points from 26 games.

I sat down and spoke to Arthur of what and who we needed to plug the gaps and build on what we had done. It seemed to be that the players we wanted other clubs wanted as well, and went in for them before us. I don't think we had the chance to bring those players in though, because when I approached the chairman and the board they said that there was no money.

Although I didn't get the players I wanted and had the squad from the previous season I was confident in my own mind we could have a positive second season. I had sat down with Arthur and we had given the players a sheet of paper saying how we wanted to have them coming back after the close season. 98 per cent of them came back fitter than we expected and better than the training sheets we had given them.

We used the same pre-season training regime as we had in my first year and it didn't take long for them to reach for the fitness levels we asked of them. We concentrated then on ball handling training, unopposed sessions, everything revolved around the ball. The players were all positive and we were all ready for another big season.

1988–89

Geoff Fletcher came back to the club when I was in my second season as a director of the club, he was straight in, he wanted to do this, he wanted to do that, I was restricted in what I could do. He wanted to take a lot of decisions that I thought were not his place to make about the playing side. I thought that he disgruntled a lot of the players, who became unhappy. I know a couple of years before he had become known as Mr Runcorn, and had kept Runcorn going. At the end of the day, whatever he did for Runcorn, look at the stats and the league table and they speak for themselves; that was the situation we found ourselves in with the restrictions of what we had and what we could do.

We got off to a bad start, losing at Dewsbury and at Leigh, who were becoming a yo-yo side getting relegated from the First Division and then gaining promotion the following year. We didn't have the skill or class to compete with them. Leigh were a good side with a good coach in Billy Benyon and had too much fire power for us. I was very impressed, that season they returned to the First Division as champions.

We won our opening home game of the season against Batley. We could score points, but the defence was shaky. Things sadly got gradually worse with Geoff Fletcher, the board of directors and my role; we suffered several losses, six defeats running. Prekkie went over with more than 2,000 watching as Warrington hammered us in the Lancashire Cup, they were three or four classes above us. The side gave their all, we never dropped our heads and went on to the end. We didn't get the score against us we deserved, given the quality of Warrington; we did put a great effort and commitment in to lose by less than 50 points.

Our next win was at home to Fulham on 30 October. That turned out to be the last win we recorded that season. The following week we lost away to Chorley Borough, so things were getting better slightly, a closer away loss. This brought us to the biggest game in the club's history and defining moment for me as a person.

190

30. Debacle at Wigan

I think there is still the excitement and magic of the Challenge Cup, our only cup competition now compared with nearly 30 years ago when there was the Lancashire Cup on this side of the hills and the John Player Trophy. The only difference now is the less likelihood of giant-killing cup shocks, semi-professional sides defeating full-time professional sides. One of the biggest for many a year was 1998, although Sheffield were a Super League side, and being a Wiganer that's as far as it goes.

Back then though there was excitement for everybody connected with Runcorn Highfield and none more so than me, we had been drawn at home at Canal Street to play Wigan in the first round of the John Player Trophy. Because of our limited capacity, the club decided to concede home advantage and play the game at Central Park to attract more support and a larger gate to make extra revenue for the club.

We had played Warrington at home in the Lancashire Cup earlier that season and been turned over which was an experience for the lads and then we drew Wigan at home. The World Champions the previous year, Challenge Cup holders and they had won the Lancashire Cup a few weeks earlier. The excitement was tremendous, the players were looking forward to it as I was, being a former Wigan player and coach. I was going home to where it had all started for me. The match proved to be eventful both in the build-up and the game itself for me.

I understood why the club had forfeited home advantage to Wigan and I was looking forward to going back to Central Park with my side, playing against the quality of players and side that Wigan were at that time. They would be playing at one of the world's most famous stadiums in rugby league where I had been lucky enough to play.

That Wigan side was awesome: Hanley, Gregory, Edwards, Lydon, Goodway – the list was endless. My lads were looking forward to playing them, testing themselves against some of the world's best, and playing at Central Park. In the lead up to the game we trained well, spent some time together and organised a couple of extra sessions.

After the Tuesday training session the lads wanted to know how much money they were on, all we could get off the board of directors from Mr Fletcher was 'You will get £150 for a win'. The lads wanted a guarantee win, lose or draw and I didn't blame them, I'd been a player myself. They and I knew that the club were going to get a good gate from Wigan having given away home advantage. All the club were saying was that they would get £150 a win and otherwise their normal pay; so to the lads that meant their normal losing pay. They were going to get toasted by Wigan.

Losing pay to the players wouldn't be much, £20 or something like that. The players knew, they were not thick, what the gate would be, they knew what Runcorn would get from the game. They wanted a guaranteed win, lose or draw because they knew they would be going up against top quality world class international players who were full-time professionals. Better in class, more physically ready than they were, and there was always the risk of injury. The Runcorn Highfield chairman and board of directors would not give them a guarantee, so the players decided to go on strike. I took that to the board and they said was that the players could go on strike, so they did.

I had been negotiating on the players' behalf with Geoff Fletcher and the rest of the board, mainly with Geoff, who I felt was the stumbling block. Although the players had said they were going on strike for the game, they all turned up for training on the Thursday and we trained well that night. I wanted them to continue to negotiate with the board. On Thursday I met the board again.

Friday passed nothing, on the Saturday I spoke to the captain, Chris Middlehurst, who said that the players had had a meeting and that they would play against Wigan. I rang the chairman "Listen Mr chairman, I have got good news the players are playing tomorrow, I've spoken to the captain." His reaction was "They are not playing."

I said "Why are they not playing? We have got to give them a chance, you have got to give your first team players a chance to play."

He replied "Geoff's already sorted it."

I said "What do you mean Geoff's sorted it?"

He said "We are playing Sutton Amateurs against Wigan tomorrow."

I said "What do you mean you are playing Sutton Amateurs, Mr chairman?"

He said "Geoff's brought a team in from Sutton to stand in for the first team."

I said "But Mr chairman, I don't know any of the players or have worked with any of them."

He said "Bill, we've got 13 players and they are playing tomorrow, that's all." He continued "Well, Geoff Fletcher has got these players and offered them £150."

He had got these players and offered every one of those £150 win, lose or draw which if he had told my first team players that there would have been no problem. Geoff had got his way and gone and done it his way and I wasn't aware it was Geoff's lure to the amateur players. £150 is a lot now, it would have been a fortune back then when he had made them that offer, you couldn't blame them, even though they were amateurs.

I had no inkling, none whatsoever of this. Geoff Fletcher had taken it on board and did it himself. That Saturday telephone call was the first time, when I spoke to the chairman, that I had heard about it. I then rang Arthur Daley and found out that they had only got 15 and needed two more subs. I said "Well, look mate I'll be honest with you, if they are on £150 we're going on the bench." Apart from the money, it would save the club getting fined for not having enough players.

The first time I saw the players was on the day of the game, I had no idea who they were, all I knew was what the chairman had told me that they were from Sutton Amateurs from St Helens. I met them at Central Park; I didn't go to Runcorn, why should I go to the club after what they had done when I only lived around the corner from Central Park.

Two hours before the game in the away changing rooms, I didn't know or recognise any of them, not one. Geoff knew who they were, what positions they played in; it was his team, his baby. I got the team on a piece of paper, Geoff gave it somebody and I finished up with it, the positions that they played in. I think there was only one of my first team players who was under a proper contract who turned out that day and that was John Cogger who played loose-forward. I just looked at them and looked at his team sheet.

With what they had done behind my back, normally I would have blown up good style. But within that month I had mellowed, become a Christian, a 'Born Again Christian'. It wasn't upsetting me as much as it would have done weeks earlier. I had told my players, who said that they knew something had happened. In a short space of time and during training, I had stopped effing and blinding, stopped swearing and everything else so they all knew the situation.

With what had happened, the attitude of Geoff Fletcher, the Runcorn board and chairman following his shock announcement, it was hard to grit my teeth and not say this, that or the other. I'm sure I'm not perfect, there's probably nobody who is. I probably did eff and jeff up to and even when I got into Central Park before this game. It was a laughable situation you couldn't make it up really, if you had it on the *League of Gentlemen* today it would be seen as hilarious, ridiculous. That's the situation it was, but at that point I hadn't actually gone public.

I had just learned how to pray, so there was a few of those going around in my head. I said to the players "Play where you play", but I gave them a short motivational talk. It was extraordinary and there were 7,233 speccies at Central Park that afternoon. I remember I always used to walk out last as a player onto the field before a game, so I decided to walk out last as a substitute as well. I got a fantastic ovation when I walked onto the pitch, and an ovation from walking through the tunnel to taking my place on the bench on the Dougie side, it was superb. I just felt so proud for myself, if not the club given the circumstances of where we were that day, but how the mighty are fallen.

I took the bench with Arthur as the coach and a substitute on the bench watching this Wigan side, the way that they were demoralising those young lads from Sutton. I felt sorry for them many times. I turned behind me and looked at Geoff Fletcher sitting in the directors' box and thought "Are you ... pleased with yourself and what you have done here today?" Arthur made comments as he saw Geoff Fletcher in the stand.

Those kids on the park had got to cope with it, because they were an open age team, but they were only kids as well if you know what I mean. Wigan put a good team out that day – Gregory, Hanley, the Iro brothers, Hampo, Goodway, Shelford and Dean Bell to name just a few of the side. We were getting battered and I thought to myself, the old rugby league brain kicked in, not the clever one, the old rugby league brain kicked in: 'You can still do it, get on and make a difference.'

I said to Arthur "I'm going on".

Arthur said "Don't go on Bill".

"Arthur I'm going on mate." Anyway, I ignored him. I think I went on after about 15 minutes and Greg (Andy Gregory) sometime later said to me "I couldn't believe it Bill, you couldn't walk and two of your passes split us open like nobody's business and then the next thing you was walking off."

I had passed the ball out and got hit in the cheek bone with an elbow. I felt the swelling straight away and thought to myself 'it's broken, my cheek bone's broken.' I didn't see it coming, it was too quick for me, don't forget I was over 40. I couldn't move or turn around quickly enough. I thought the old rugby league head, not the Christian head, the old rugby league brain kicked in again "If it's broken I'm not going to get my own back, I'm going to do it now."

The first person I looked up to and saw on realising it was broken was Andy Goodway, I immediately thought that he had done it. That old rugby league brain kicked in again. I went after him and gave it to him. I head butted him like nobody's business; it was a cracker – full on, spot on and down he went. I hit him on the forehead.

I hadn't been on 10 minutes although it was reported I'd been on 11 or 12 minutes. I had got an ovation coming onto Central Park, the referee Dave Carter pointed to the dressing room and said "Off" the last time I ever heard those words in my career.

The sad thing is that I got the wrong person. It was Adrian Shelford who got me and not Andy Goodway. Sadly Adrian is not with us anymore – he has passed. His wife and children are still living in the Wigan area now with Steve Hampson; Curt played at Wigan St Patricks and Kyle trained with us and was on a scholarship with Wigan.

It was the worst moment of my life, from cheers to jeers and tears; from hero to dickhead. A short space of time, that's all it was really, the speccies let me know that as well, calling me an idiot, a gobshite, dickhead all in that space of 50 yards walking off the pitch. That walk seemed a lot longer, especially with tears in my eyes, I was so ashamed at what I did in that first half. That is the one sending off I will always regret.

I have never heard as many boos in all my life. I was sent off a number of times in my career, which are on record, but I'd never cried. That was the first day, the first time walking off a rugby league pitch crying for the stupid thing that I had done. I thought I had let down the whole Christian Kingdom as a 'Born Again Christian.' walking slowly towards the tunnel into the dressing room with swells of boos as I sat near the bath and cried.

We were getting well beat and were down to 12 men thanks to me. Arthur did the half-time team talk, I kept out of the way until they went out again. I couldn't even go back onto the ground after I had changed because of the sending off, I just stood in the tunnel and watched the rest of the game.

Watching on, the sad thing was that the first team had played Warrington in the Lancashire Cup and not got toasted, but were beaten by 40 points. We would have put up a proud performance at Central Park, the lads had looked forward to it. The board and the chairman, I thought it was their stupidity to more or less listen to one person, Geoff Fletcher. With his decision his team had let the club and the young kids from Sutton suffer the humiliation of a 90 points hammering and defeat on the pitch, it was ridiculous.

At the end of the game, the crowd gave the players representing Runcorn Highfield a standing ovation, those brave players acknowledged the crowd. It was their moment even in defeat, I just went into our dressing room thanked the players for what they had done, and praised them for their efforts which I always did.

194

Sent off at Central Park when playing for Runcorn. (Courtesy *Wigan Observer*)

I went upstairs, but didn't speak to my directors. I had one beer when I apologised to Andy Goodway. I was ashamed at what I had done and how I felt; I should have never have let it happen. I walked home bitterly upset and told Sheila and the family what had happened.

What was so phenomenal was that I had become a Christian a couple of weeks before, not many people knew, the following morning the local radio reporter came to my house. "What happened yesterday Mr Ashurst?" (They came to take the piss.) "We believe that you are a Christian. Why do you call yourself a Christian after you did what you did?"

Granada Reports came, so it was on the television and in the local papers. Well, from that worst day of my rugby career, it was probably the worst day of my life. The way I was regarded at Wigan, what I had just done at Wigan, and what I had become.

From that day forward I stood up and said "I am a Christian and I'm so proud to be a Christian" and I apologised for what I did. They put it in the paper, on television, they on the radio and from that day my life completely changed regarding to the Christian side of it. From that day I could stand up, not with pride, because pride is a sin, but with a swelled chest and a big heart and say that 'I am a Christian, and that I will truly follow what I believe in' and that's what I have done for the rest of my life.

No one from the club got in touch with me on the Monday or say anything on the Tuesday when I went back to training with my first team. None of the amateur players who had played against Wigan were there. Geoff Fletcher had just brought them in for the humiliation of one game on the Sunday, see you later. Non gladiators thrown into a pack of lions, that's what it had been, it was disgraceful, For someone to make a decision like that I believe that no thought was given about the kids on that park. They didn't deserve to go through what they went through for the sake of £150.

On the Tuesday at training all the lads did in the full session was take the piss out of me for getting sent off. On the Thursday I was pulled in by the club before we began training. Tony Almond, the secretary, told me that the board had made a decision about last weekend after I had been sent off against Wigan. They had said I would not receive my £150 match fee, that it was an internal discipline thing. They had me by the .... At the end of the day it was just, well management are always to clever to a coach, when it comes to finances a coach will never win. I didn't win that time.

I took it on the chin; I didn't want to stay there anymore. I decided I was finished on the Sunday. I bit my tongue with Tony. It was the disappointment of the whole episode. It was an amateur decision made by a professional club which was the sad thing about it. I know we were called semi-professional players and I'm sure semi or professional people should run those clubs, but at Runcorn I thought that didn't happen.

Before the home game against Rochdale Hornets I told the lads "I'm finishing, do me a favour, play well, it's up to you guys." The words were good luck with what you will have left, Mr Fletcher, because soon he took back the reins after John Cogger had a short spell as player-coach. I said "I wish you all the best, let's go out singing."

There were 325 on that Sunday, one of the better crowds that season, after that heavy defeat at Wigan. They were really good with me when I walked onto the pitch and went to the coaches' bench. I had a great rapport with them, just a great part of a close knit club. Not many of them, but they were top class I never heard one player suffer from abuse yelled at them whatever happened, and we and they had had it tough that season.

Sadly we lost 28–10, but the lads gave it their all for themselves and me despite the loss. After the game I went to a pub in Widnes and had a few beers with Arthur, Terry Rose, Tommy Rawlinson and John Cogger; the other lads went their own way. I told Arthur that I wouldn't be back and hoped he got the job because he had been at the club so long.

I didn't say anything at all to the chairman or the board of directors after the game and that night. The following day I rang Tony Almond and said "Mr Almond I am just ringing to let you know I won't be coming back to Runcorn anymore." They couldn't sue me, I had no contract, it was a verbal agreement and a handshake. It was goodnight from Runcorn and on benefits again. I never went back there again. My resignation was announced a few weeks later, at the start of January.

It went downhill very quickly. They never reached those heady heights again. We used 35 players in the first year, the following season 59 plus 15 amateurs. The sad irony of my last game in charge was that I had begun my coaching career at the club with a win at Spotland. How the atmosphere and people at the club had changed from 18 months earlier. It was a sad way to go, but I didn't believe I had gone on a low in putting my boots on. I had become a Christian, had a new lease of life and other good things to look forward to rather than just rugby league. I can't remember going to the disciplinary at the RFL; I was suspended for four matches. I wasn't bothered – I would never put a pair of boots on again. I didn't mix in the professional game's circles again. I didn't mix in the Wigan circles and didn't go and watch a professional game of rugby league for a very long time.

31. Discovering Christianity

It originally started when I was playing for Wakefield Trinity and living in Wakefield. My life hadn't just revolved around playing rugby league; it was everything that went with the game then. The drinking, women, gambling and I was very rarely at home; I was either doing one or the other.

Also, I was all over the place including when I was in Australia. That's why Sheila came back from Australia, although that's also why we went to Australia in the first place, to make a new start because of what I was doing. Obviously, if someone is in a peer pressure group where 'everybody's shagging everybody', they felt obliged to get involved; that's what it was like.

Sheila found me out on a couple of occasions in Australia and that's why she came home. We had gone back to Wigan and eventually went to Wakefield. Again, with being the player that I was and involved in that kind of lifestyle, Sheila started looking for companionship, rather than religion. Unfortunately for her and me, she got a knock on the door and a visit from a religious group. That was that, she joined them.

I thank God that I never saw the accident waiting to happen, so I didn't see anything she got involved with. She started going to these meetings. I went with her on the odd occasion, just for a laugh actually. I thought it was a joke, Sheila was doing her thing and I was doing my thing. From that it grew into something she did seriously and enthusiastically. She was baptised into this group. She was involved with them, but it didn't bring us any closer together.

Eventually though, when we came back to Wigan, Sheila was still a member and became pregnant with our sixth child, Laura, I was elated. One day she went shopping to the local shops and nearly got knocked down by a van. The fear of it had caused damage to her and she started bleeding and haemorrhaging. She was about 18 weeks pregnant and so I took her to the local hospital at Billinge, which has since closed down.

They took Sheila for a scan which they told us was for three reasons: that we would not keep that baby, she would lose it following the scan; that she was haemorrhaging too much and although she was 18 weeks pregnant, the foetus was only eight weeks and they couldn't hear a heartbeat. As far as prayers were concerned I prayed like a dipstick, I think we have all said a prayer in our own way when we've needed or wanted to for whatever reason.

Mine was "God make her better I'll not have another cig; God make her better I'll not go with another woman, I'll not have another drink, I'll not swear", all the promises I made. I remember Sheila's prayer. We held hands on her bed in hospital and I remember Sheila said "Lord, if you save this baby, I'll bring it up to know you and your son Jesus."

Well, believe it or not, within 24 hours she had stopped bleeding. They took her for another scan, and the foetus had doubled to 16 weeks from eight weeks with a very strong heartbeat within 24 hours. It was from then that Sheila started searching for something different, but not me. We had our Laura and 18 months later she got pregnant with our last child, Andrew, that's when it all started.

Because Sheila had been unwell carrying Laura, we didn't think she was fit enough to walk around the streets of Wigan, so she couldn't go out with her group. She got a visit from one of their elders. This bloke came to our house and started going on at Sheila about being the only one in his group that was not campaigning for them. I thought he was trying to score points using what people did for him.

I opened the front door and he left pretty quickly; I more or less threw him out of the house, but they were very persistent. He then brought someone older, older than him, who I thought was worse than the first guy so I threw him out as well. I just looked at Sheila and said: "Look, if you are in touch with God, why are you answerable to a man, why are you answering to him?"

A few days later, Sheila started being poorly because her hormone deficiency was kicking in, so they had to send a midwife round to do hormone injections. This midwife was called Mary Sackey. She was an absolutely wonderful woman and Sheila started to tell her problems. Well as soon as she mentioned her group, Mary Sackey brought a bible in, told Sheila that she was a Christian and started giving us all this about Sheila's group.

Well, I was straight out of the door; I didn't want to chuffing know about God. I went straight to the betting shop as normal and put a 'robin' on. Eventually, Mary brought another couple of young ladies round who witnessed the bible with Sheila. Again, I wasn't interested apart from on occasions when I had no money for a bet; then I'd sit and listen and began to get interested.

On one of those times my mind drifted back to three years earlier when, because of my rugby league lifestyle, I'd left Sheila and was living with another woman called Eileen. I'd gone home to visit the kids one weekend and Sheila had a religious magazine on the table. For some strange reason I just read the front cover. It said 'Is God in your marriage?' I went back that night and couldn't sleep. I was tossing and turning, I knew that I shouldn't be there, I knew where I should be; I should be with my wife and kids, four of whom were living at home.

My son Billy was living with us. I got him up at four o'clock in the morning and said to Eileen: "Listen, I am going to try and get back together with the wife. That's where I should be, not here. You didn't mean anything to me in the first place." It was a cruel thing to say, but I realised where I wanted to be, I went back with Billy. Since then I've bumped into her a couple of times and I saw her daughter regularly because her son played for one of the junior teams at St Pats.

Sheila opened the door. For two or three days we talked; I begged her to have me back and thank God she did. It wasn't easy for the first six weeks; I slept on the bedroom floor, but she took me back eventually and we grew so close it's unbelievable.

Sheila went to see her and said: "Look he's mine, he's back where he should be and if you want to fight for him, I'll fight you."

I only knew when she had told me, but Sheila just told her how it was, Sheila's not a fighter but my word she says it how it is, she calls a spade a spade. She's always been like that, sometimes she can be so cutting she doesn't realise what she's doing. I mean she is unbelievable; she is the funniest person I've ever seen and the words that come out of her mouth, she's incredible.

I knew I had got my feet inside the door again, but would have to work to make it work. I was chuffed; it was like winning a Wembley medal. I mean I'd lost twice at Wembley and Sheila telling me what she had done was like winning there. She jumped onto my side and I knew that her feelings were exactly the same for me still as they were when we were 16 years old.

So Sheila started going to a church called the Pentecostal Church in Scholes in Wigan and she asked me to go on occasions. I went and I thought, well – I thought they were crazy, because all I could hear, like people speaking in tongues; I call it 'Bedrock', because all I could hear was Fed Flintstone 'Yab ad ab a doo be doo bedoo'. Mary came to this church on a Honda, I thought what's she doing coming on a bike when it's raining hard, it was always all this language stuff.

When Pastor Belfield used to get up, he would say exactly the same at 11.30am "We will take the collection and have the word of God." I used to say to Sheila "I'm going to wait outside for you." That was for two reasons: I didn't want to know about God; second – you're not having my beer money for a pint this afternoon and I'm not giving it to him or any God. So that was it. I used to go in with Sheila and wait outside, but something happened in November 1988. I'll never forget it.

I went outside and it was raining cats and dogs, tipping down. I looked in my pockets; I'd forgotten my cigs and my matches so I couldn't have a cig outside. I thought 'I'm not getting wet through for nothing; I'll sit at the back of the church.' So there I was sitting at the back of the church. I was not trying to listen; I just wanted to stay dry. When Pastor Belfield started talking about this guy called Jesus, for some reason that I can't – and will never be able to – explain, I took it in.

I was enthralled and when he started elaborating on how the man who had done absolutely nothing wrong in his life was taken into custody, if you like into the equivalent of Guantanamo Bay. He was beaten and beaten so much so much as each layer of skin was torn off his back; he was laughed at and humiliated. I burst into tears and couldn't stop crying, I was heartbroken. Then when I heard him say he had to drag this enormous cross through the streets, up a hill and eventually to be nailed through his hands and feet onto it. He was stuck up there, crucified; again laughed at, jeered and mocked, suffering the most horrible death for me, because he loved me.

I was absolutely heartbroken. It's the most wonderful love story I've heard and I found myself sitting next to Sheila, I'd moved from the back of the church to Sheila and I didn't realise that. I had sat next to Sheila I must have been breaking her hand with emotion, a flood of tears at my feet and I couldn't stop crying.

The appeal then, it's the same today: "Does anybody believe that, does anybody want to make Jesus the lord of your life; you can't change yourself, but he can change you." Sheila and I went to the front and we wanted that, I wanted it more than anything, more than any medal, any Great Britain cap, more than anything. I was so loved and yet so heartbroken, do you understand what I'm saying?

It was the first time I had ever seen it, the first time like I say that I had heard of the most awesome thing that anybody could do for me, this guy that came from heaven and did it me and the promise. I looked at the concept and what went through my mind as I was crying; I've got seven kids because we had had our Andrew by that time.

What was going through my heart and my mind was could I give one of my kids up to be laughed and mocked and humiliated by the world? No. Could I give one of my kids to be absolutely tortured and wrecked the way he was? No. Could I let one of my kids be hung on a hill with nails through his hands and feet? No. God had one son, one and only son and he gave him, he gave himself freely because he loved me. That's awesome, absolutely awesome truth, and it was that morning when I gave my life to Jesus. Little did I know what was going to happen a few weeks later.

It was a story; it was the Jesus crucifixion story, but that morning it for me it became reality. Became real, absolutely real, I looked at the world and history, I wanted to follow this guy who had done this for me. If you want to relate it in simple terms which I did, I remember the story of Abraham Lincoln before he set the Afro-American people free.

He'd gone to a slave auction and he had bought this slave, this young lady for $300 to $400 he might have paid for her and he took her chains off. He said 'Go on your way' and she was gobsmacked: 'What do you mean go on your way?'

'Well, you're free, I've set you free.'

She said 'But I'm a slave to bondage... Look can I do what I want?'

He said 'Go and do what you want, you're free.'

'Can I say what I want?'

'You can say what you want, you're free.'

She said to Abraham Lincoln 'Can I go where I want?'

He said 'Go where you want, you're free.'

She turned to him and said 'You've freed me, can I come with you?'

That's exactly the same. In retrospect Jesus freed me from all my bondage, from all my sins, from everything that I had done wrong. I was gobsmacked. I was a dickhead. I was an idiot who deserved absolutely nothing. I didn't even deserve that Sheila should take me back.

I'd completely been set free; he'd taken my chains off just like that African-American lady's chains were taken off. Jesus took my chains off and I was a free man. I just came as; I brought everything with me and just came as I was. I knew then, and I do know now, that God has absolutely changed me into a different person.

It absolutely fantastic, the warmth and the love I felt that morning and it was twofold. I'd realised who Jesus was and what he'd done for me. I'd also realised that he'd given me the love that I'd missed in Sheila for the previous few years. It was a twofold love, that love that he passed onto me that morning from that cross; I passed onto Sheila because I knew in my heart exactly what she felt.

I was 15 again, when I met her, and from that day in 1988 for the last 26 years we have been like school kids and we don't have a penny. Most of the time we struggle to pay for petrol for the car, but it doesn't matter, we have so much love for each other. It's absolutely fantastic and to be able to pass that onto your children, great, absolutely wonderful.

That's why I love going up-and-down the country. I'm not a preacher, I don't want to be a preacher, I'm not a teacher, and I don't want to be a teacher. God picks people for that not me, thank him, I just want to tell people how my life has changed, that's all I love to do.

When Sheila and I went in front of Pastor Ray Belfield, I was still crying. He said "Do you want to make a true commitment, do you want to?" He didn't really ask me why I was the way I was.

I said "I want Jesus in my life."

He prayed for us, said a simple prayer and asked me to say a simple prayer: "Lord come into my life. I know that I'm a sinner, I know what I have done wrong, and it is wrong I can't change it. I can't forgive myself, come into my life and will you change me and will you be the Lord of my life and help me walk the way you walk?" A simple prayer and that's exactly what it was all about, giving my life to him and that's all it entails, nothing else. There's no right, no ceremony, just a symbol, "Lord come into my life and it will be different."

I'll never forget Ray's words when I'd done it, because they knew who I was, people in the church knew who I was and his words were "We'll see you in a few weeks time, because you know who this is." He gave them a story that he used to follow rugby league and he said "Let's prepare, for to be honest if God can change him, he can change anybody."

I thought to myself 'Wow, 10 minutes ago they didn't want to know me, but now God's using me as an example, so I'm being used straight away.' That's the way I looked at it and I hadn't been saved 10 minutes. A lot of other people came over to me after the fellowship who knew me, knew who I was and knew what I'd stood for as a rugby player. I just gained a heck of brothers and sisters, not friends.

I believe we are true brothers and sisters in Jesus and what I love about being a Christian wherever, whichever country I want to go to I am part of a family. I went to Tenerife with Sheila and our Kath; we went into a Christian church and it was just like being at home, irrespective of where we were.

It's fantastic. It's not a bed of roses, it's not easy and it never will be. I don't expect it to ever being easy. I know that when I played at Wembley, it was a winners or a loser's medal. I got picked for Great Britain or I didn't. In Christianity, all I know - without trying to be a preacher - is that there are two choices: winners and losers. Its heaven or hell and I'm following a winner, that's what I do know.

When I came out of the Pentecostal Church that morning, the first thing we did was go for something to eat together. I don't think we ever stopped holding hands. From that day we went to church together, we went to bible studies together and that is the only thing we have in common now. Sheila doesn't like sport, but our Christian belief is a wonderful thing to have in common.

We went to 'House Groups' where six or seven other people have their own opinion of the bible, a different interpretation of what they believe to someone else. It's all about what do you believe, the bible is so difficult to understand, yet so easy to understand. So much we'll never know; so much we need to know; but it doesn't matter. There may be that small difference of interpretation, the main thing is the belief and truth: that Jesus came and suffered and rose again for each and every one of us and no one can ever get that wrong.

I can only see it one way and that is I believe and it's a true belief. You can have all these religions: Jehovah's Witnesses, Mormons, Quakers, whatever. At the end of the day I've never been religious, I'm still not religious. If you want to put the two words together religion, salvation did Jesus come to religion or did he come to save? Religion means nothing; salvation is what it's all about, a promise of heaven.

Religion doesn't promise you heaven and when Jesus went back to heaven, he said to his disciples "I send you the comfort of something more important than me" and that's the Holy Spirit who conceived him in the first place. If it's not from the Holy Spirit, then it's not from God it's just an empty religion and I don't follow an empty religion, I follow God.

I love a Mormon, I don't like what they teach. I love a Muslim, I don't like what they teach. My concept is, love the people, hate the religion; because it's not about religion it's about salvation and that's where my belief comes from.

I love to try my best to live the life that I should and I'm a far better person. I've been to Alex Murphy and apologised for what I've done in the past, I've been to Mal Reilly and apologised, the same with Alan Bates whose jaw I broke in three places, and to many other people. At the end of the day, redemption is an absolutely wonderful forgiveness, brilliant. I apologised for what I did, so the apology was the main thing and from that day I've just been everywhere.

When I went back in 2006 for the reunion for the Penrith Panthers legends, I spoke at two churches on the following morning and I spoke at three churches all the time that I was in Australia. They would never have expected that at Penrith Panthers and we had a wonderful time. When I was playing for them in Australia I was one of the biggest idiots that you would ever meet.

I also had a wonderful fellowship with Tony Pulatua, who is also a 'born again Christian' while he was playing at Penrith. When I went to Australia for the reunion at Penrith, it was a privilege to be asked to go and to go which I'll talk about later.

People are sceptical, although they admire what you do. Even to this day, I'll see players. I go to Wakefield Trinity and I meet up with Graham Myler and Trevor Skerrett. They'll say 'Are you still one of them?' I'll say 'Yeah, I'm still one of them.' It's just a personnel thing.

Things moved on as I was out of the game. I attended the bible readings and went to church. One Easter weekend I went to Cliff College in Wakefield with our church on a fellowship trip for a day at this fellowship weekend. It was the first time that I'd been and I met this guy called Howard Mellor who ran the place. He said "Bill, I want you to give five minutes of your testimony." I went "What" because I didn't know what a testimony was. I said "What do you mean?" He said "Come on stage."

I said "Howard, there's 4,000 people here. I'm not getting on that stage." He said "Bill, give them five minutes of your testimony."

So he got me on stage and I was petrified absolutely petrified. I'd played rugby league in front of thousands of people and full Wembley Stadiums and I'd play all day. But I had never been a speaker, I'd done everything else; but never a speaker. Howard got me on stage, asked me a few questions and I responded for about four minutes, but it felt like an age. So that was my introduction, the first time I had spoken. I was so terrified not knowing what was going to happen or what to expect.

They were all Christians at that college and were thanking God really for somebody else's life. That's what you do; you are pleased that people have made a conscious commitment to being a Christian. Six weeks later I was asked to speak and really give my testimony proper at a church in Leigh. That was for more than six minutes and Howard came there as well.

I saw him and he said "I've wanted to see you. You won't believe that day when you didn't want to do it six weeks ago; you didn't want to give your testimony. There were 6,000 people there that day. Seven days later I got a letter from an old woman which she had sent to the college.

Her letter said that that morning her son-in-law had brought her and his wife to Cliff College. He just brought them for a ride; he wasn't interested in God or anything like that. He's a Wakefield Trinity fanatic and it pricked his ears up so much that he listened to you for that four minutes. He made a commitment and now he's a Christian.

I meet that guy regularly now. He's been a Christian now for nearly as long as me because of that first four minutes when I was persuaded to stand up at Wakefield and said I had given my life to it; if I can do it, you can do it. It was fantastic, but from there I eventually gave my testimony at a couple of dinners in church and I praised God. I made myself available for the Lord, my letterbox and telephone.

How ironic is it that I nearly committed suicide because of a letterbox, so that's how the devil works isn't it. From there I have been privileged to go all around the country, as I say not to preach or teach, but just to tell people the way I was and the way I am now.

I don't time myself when I give my testimony. I don't like preachers or teachers who time themselves. I just look at the Lord and my prayer is God; let's go for it together. You can go and prepare a speech, whatever, but 80 per cent of the time you'll find what you have prepared you don't talk about, God takes you down a different avenue.

I remember speaking one time at Warrington when there were only 24 people in the church. The first time ever in my life what came out in my testimony, which had never come out before, was the abuse by my dad that I took when I was a kid. Just 24 four people listening and one young girl said 'That's been happening to me' and we prayed with that young girl. It's never, never happened again and she was heartbroken as I was. We keep in touch and she is now completely free of any abuse.

You never get completely free of it, it's all emotional, it's always up there in your head as I've said earlier. By saying it that time helped release that burden from someone else. That's why I hope in any way how tiny or big that people who read this book will read stuff that will help a lot of people.

I've spoken at Sheffield University twice, at Durham University three times and at Lancaster University. I couldn't go to grammar school even when I passed my 11 plus, so now I can always say I've been to university.

I remember one young lad at university after I had spoken, he had listened to me and came over and said "I don't believe that".
I said "Oh, do you not?"
He said "No".
I said "What do you do for a living?"
He said "I'm a mechanic".
I said "Yeah, is that what you want to do?"
He said "Yeah ", so I said "How do you fix your car?"
He said "I have a book".
I said "How do you know that chuffing books is right? You might put a spark plug in the wrong place if someone's not put it right in your book."
He said "Because I believe it".
I said "That's just like my life. I have a bible; it's called the book of life where yours is a book of cars. I know for many years and years and years that whatever has gone in that bible is absolutely true, so I know that my life won't go wrong. So it's the same as you, you know that your car won't go wrong, what's the difference?'
He said "Will you pray with me?" and he gave his life to God in an instant like that.

It is an absolute pleasure to be able to stand up and say "Phew, Billy Dipstick is absolutely different to how he was" and it really, really is. To help people is what it's all about. Like I said, if I've got £50 in my pocket and somebody wants £49 they can have it. I know that God will provide me with what I need, it's all about other people, not what it used to be about when it was all me, me, me, me.

It's all about choice and at the end of the day that's what I love about being a Christian. God never takes away my choice, I can still choose. I'm not brainwashed by anyone that say you can't, you can't, you can't. Sheila was so brainwashed by the group she joined at first.

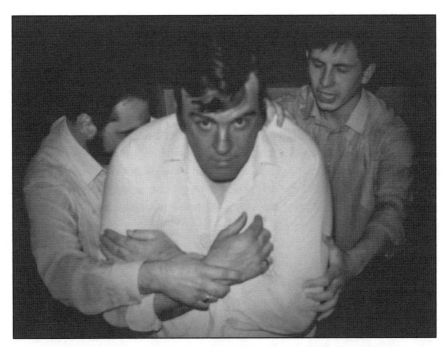

Baptism, a new creation. Steve Walsh assisting in Bill being baptised.

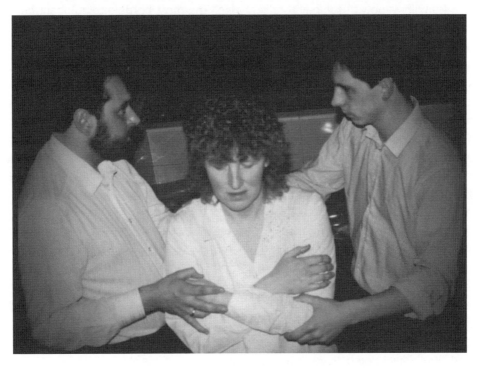

Baptism, a new creation, Steve Walsh assisting in Sheila being baptised.

We have bible study where I can believe what God tells me, not what a man tells me. Other groups have a book, they have bible studies, and every answer is given in their book for you to believe what they want you to believe. That's brainwashing. Jesus doesn't brainwash me.

Sheila has done so much walking, worn so many shoes out with the group she had originally joined, I was sick of buying her shoes. When she decided to leave them, do you know what they said about her? They kicked her out because she had committed adultery.

They make so many excuses for people who leave their religion by choice, they make an excuse up that they have got rid of them. She had a wonderful female friend for seven years; and now that young girl cannot walk on the same side of the road as Sheila. She has to cross onto the other side of the road. Is that love? Is that from God? It's unloved, not love. It's so unloving it's unbelievable, but you belong to them. They'll give you the moon, but as soon as you walk away they say things about you. It's unbelievable. Sheila is the most wonderful person you will ever meet; when people can turn on her, I'm sorry it's wrong.

It upset Sheila knowing somebody close over a period of time, as I've said it's all about forgiveness, it's all about humility. I mean I thought I was the bees' knees when I went out onto a rugby field; nobody was going to be ever better. When I went over that whitewash, whatever it took I was going to be number 1. I was going to be the best, that wasn't humility. Humility is now absolutely totally my life. The most horrible thing about humility is to say sorry when you're right and what it is to say sorry when you're right. To have a humble heart makes all the difference in the world and a humble heart is a soft heart.

My wife's one of the cleanest Christians you will ever meet. She's been baptised three times; as a Catholic, then by the other group she joined, and now as a 'Born Again Christian'. Thank God she found the truth in the end.

There are people who believe and people who don't. I love them all, to me its choice. I mean I see a lot of hypocritical things. I've pulled fellow Christians up about it. I remember one of the great lovely young Christians, Va'aiga Tuigamala who played for Wigan. We had done quite a few things together with Apollo Perelini, Frano Botica and Jason Robinson. I recall 'Inga', as he was also known, having wristbands on.

I asked "What are they for, Inga?"

He replied "I have lucky wristband."

I said "They've got a little cross on; what's that for mate?"

He said "What do you mean?"

I said "Are they a backup in case God doesn't work?"

He said "What do you mean?"

I said "Well, are you a Christian?"

He said "Yeah."

I said "Well, don't you believe in God; do you pray for a win?"

He said "I always pray for a win."

I said "Why?"

He said "What do you mean, 'Why'? Then God will help me."

I said "But did God and Jesus only die for your team? Did he not die for their team? Will Jesus favour you because you're a Christian and the lucky wristband is back-up. Does God believe in luck all of a sudden as well? Isn't it far more important in life for a defeat rather than a victory?"

I continued "Do you not learn more when you have lost than you do when you win? I pray every game with my kids Inga, I do. I pray every Sunday morning to God let's have a great game. Let each team play to their full and best of their ability, let nobody get hurt. It's about God and people, Inga. It's not about favouring one and not the other, so why be crazy? You're watching on television and you see them all praying for victory. Why? God died for the opposition as well your team."

To taste defeat is not nice, but it's good at times. You can go for the best job in the world, the second best job in the world, turn it down, not get it because you have done something wrong; you've been defeated. There's a better job that comes up two days later because you have learnt what you did not get right in the first interview. You will do better in the second interview and you get the best job in the world rather than the second best.

Six weeks after we got saved that Sunday morning, we both were baptised together. It was a full immersion; the church had its own baptismal tank and we were baptised together. I don't remember my mum telling me if I'd been baptised before. My family weren't church goers so I don't remember. I know God has forgiven me after we had had the piece of chewing gum and always got something off the plate. I've given it back 10-fold since then, call it what you want he works in mysterious ways.

Being a Christian involved in the church and going to meetings gave me a new lease in life. The most wonderful thing about what people do to you and what you do is forgiveness. It's the most wonderful thing, yet the hardest thing is to be able to forgive and move on. I see so many families in turmoil. I see so many people who hate each other 'I can't stand him...' Why? At the end of the day it's just forgive, say sorry and move on.

The sad thing is as a coach it's your responsibility to take away that absolute. Don't get me wrong, when we are playing opposition it's a twofold thing. I always told my kids you hate the opposition because they are trying to stop you winning; you respect them for who they are so it's a hate and respect thing.

At the end of the day that respect always comes through. It's all part of a forgiveness thing to respect and forgive a person. I can't hate people, why should you hate people? A personal example of this I have is with one of my sisters. She helped bring me up when I was little because I was the youngest. We fell out 13 years ago; it involved my son.

He was working on a three man job in Wigan. It was heavy work. He wrecked his back so we put a claim in against the company. We went to court and he was awarded £47,000, his solicitor advised him to turn it down because it was for life and he felt it should be double that, so it wasn't signed off.

He was on pain killers and injections in his back and had saved enough to take his two year old daughter to Disneyland. While there she fell into the pool at the hotel they were staying at, as I see it the adrenalin, pain killers whatever he was taking kicked in. He went into the pool to get her out and saved her, which any parent would.

She saw this rescue on a DVD and at the time her son-in-law worked at the same place as my son. I believe that she told him to take it into the company and he'd get some money for it. The company put a claim in saying that there was nothing wrong with his back because he had been filmed jumping in the pool to save his daughter. I understand that she got £5,000; my son was offered £2,500, I forgave my sister; it was hard.

My son got £2,500 where I think he should have got £100,000 and his back is still absolutely shocking. It was all because apparently she had asked him to lend her some money when he got paid. He told her that he was going to try and start his own business. Because he denied her some money, she did it. I think it was greed just sheer greed.

A few months later my niece – her daughter – threw her out of her home. I went round to my sister's to make sure she was alright. That was hard. She let me in, but she didn't want to know me even though I went to see if she was alright.

I said "Look, as far as I'm concerned I forgive you for what you did. I don't hate you, but I do know this: I don't want to associate with you."

The difference is we can forgive; we don't need to live in each other's pockets. It's the forgiveness that's important. I've not seen her since and we don't speak at all. I don't mix in her circles and she doesn't mix in mine. But if she wants me I'll be there. If the phone rang I would be there straight away, she only lives a couple of miles away.

I've attempted to go back, but she doesn't want to know me. That's her choice. I don't love her any less; she's my sister. I won't love her any less, like a Mary Magdalene scenario, 'I don't want to go in her company and get stoned when I've been there.' That's what it's all about. I'd rather be stoned face-to-face.

On a lighter note I remember one of the funniest things that happened. I was speaking at a church in Halifax. It wasn't in the church itself; it was a subsidiary building off the church. As I started speaking I saw a bald head at the back and I thought I know him. I was speaking and speaking and I couldn't fathom who it was.

Anyway, I finished speaking and walked off the stage down the aisle. He came walking towards me. He was five yards away from me when I realised who it was; the best number 10 that I ever played with, Terry Fogerty. He sadly passed away in November 2013. His son, Adam, played at Saints and is now an actor.

Terry knew what I was like when I played with him; he was unbelievable. Every away match he would take 50p and 10 Park Drive cigs and would always come back with two quid in his pocket, which he won at cards. Terry was a character. I looked at him, we looked at each other. I gave him a hug and said "Terry, what are you doing here? Are you searching for Christianity?"

He said "No. I heard that you were doing this and I had to see it to believe it, so that's why I came."

He didn't make a commitment, he was curious about me, everything is redeemable, as Pastor Belfield – who is now very old and retired – said after my declaration of faith: "If God can change you Billy, he can change anybody."

I don't think I'm a perfect person; am I ...! If anybody comes and says to me I'm a perfect Christian, I just say 'Kiss my arse'. There's only one and that's Jesus himself. I can try and I will make every mistake in the book. The difference now is that I have someone I can take that mistake to and I know.

I love the poem *Footprints*. It's where you are walking along the sand and there's two pairs of footprints initially and then it becomes one pair of footprints. Then two pair of footprints and you think: Why on that length was there a pair of footprints? That's when Jesus said 'That's when you had your bad times, that's when I carried you' and that's what it's all about. God must carry us through the hard times, he comes through it with us, carries us with it.

I mean, and not many people outside my immediate family know this, later even though I had seen God and was a Christian, there came to a point where I nearly committed suicide. I walked from that and I dedicated my house, I dedicated my telephone and I dedicated my letter box completely to the Lord. I gave myself over to him.

It's only the four years that I was so close to committing suicide, taking my life. I had got myself so much into debt, it was mostly interest, I could not pay the interest. A couple of loans for my daughters' weddings, I had got a credit card, I didn't know what it's like, I was fooled. I didn't realise what it, what they can do; the misery they can cause. £17,000 in debt. I'm afraid of nobody, I've never been afraid of anyone, but I was frightened of my letterbox, - something coming through - my telephone I just could not cope with it, there was a lot going on in my head.

I left a suicide note and drove right to the top of Winter Hill and at the back there is a hell of a drop, a sheer drop and you can park a car. I was standing there and I was going. I was absolutely going. I couldn't cope, I'd had enough and a voice spoke to my heart and my head and it was the Lord's voice. When people say God speaks to you in thought, he does and the voice was to me.

'Look, do not lean on your own understanding; trust in me with all your heart, your mind and strength and I will direct your path. I am your refuge and strength.'

I don't know. I knew I had turned my phone off, but as soon as that came into my head my phone rang and how it rang I don't know. I'd turned it off and it was my daughter Kathleen. She said: "Come home dad. I'll sort everything out."

I came home. Before I was coming home they had got the police. They were looking for me and everything. When I had heard those words from God and my daughter rang me, like I say I don't know how the phone rang, but thank God it did.

Within eight months my daughter had applied for a DRO – a Debt Relief Order – and we'd been working through the CCS – Consumer Credit Service – paying our bills which we could never pay. Within a year we got the whole lot completely wiped out.

When I was in Australia I was King Bill. In Wigan I was King Bill. I had everything you could think of financially. I had money, I had the material stuff, I had the women, everything that you could think of, but was I happy? If you can understand what I am saying, since I've become a Christian I haven't got the women, haven't got the money. I have not even got a bank account.

I live on a pension because of my rugby. My wife has a bank account because she has her mobility allowance paid into it. I don't have all the material stuff. I'm not interested in women; I have the occasional drink at parties. I've never been happier, I'm so happy.

God gave me back my rugby league and for 25 – nearly 26 – years I put so much into amateur and junior rugby league, I absolutely loved it. It was not putting it back in a rugby way, it was putting it back in all the round way, being a role model for young people.

To live my life then as I never did, I was helping change those young people. Don't get me wrong, obviously I had the skills to make them good rugby players. I had cracking young men in my team and I had three rules as a coach that I had always had:

1. The most important is that you don't talk back to your coaches
2. You never argue with a teammate
3. You don't 'f' and 'blind'

I had so much respect from those kids; it was fantastic. On the pitch they took it on board, at 16 they swore, but I never heard those kids swear in a training session.

To become part of that, like I say I gave it all up. When God says in his words 'Give it to him and he'll give it to you 10-fold', I'd retired and given everything up. From retiring I had 26 years in amateur rugby league, it was like starting again.

I don't go to that church anymore. I go to a quiet little church in Ashton-in-Makerfield called Cave-Browne Evangelical Church. There is a fantastic a young pastor, Michael Cornell. He's only 33 years old; he's brilliant. The fellowship is good, the atmosphere is good. They have bible studies and everything I could wish for. He is aware of my past. One of sayings on a small placard there is 'You can't do that, but you know with God you can do everything.'

32. A Penrith legend

One day in 2006 I was mucking about on my computer when there was a pinging noise which alerted me that I had just received an email. It was from a bloke called Max Cowan, Roger Cowan's son who was now one of the main men at Penrith.

The email said "Bill, would you like to come to Australia to Penrith?" I replied "Give me a minute to think about it." It took me three seconds. Yes, I would love come back to Penrith. I asked why and what for. Max said "We are having a legends evening because we have been going 40 years and have decided to celebrate it and select the best 17 that played for Penrith and you are one of the 50 nominees."

I said "Great, how am I going to get there?" He replied "We'll fly you and your wife out if she wants to come as well." I emailed back "Definitely, we'll come." I shouted to Sheila and told her about it and our invitations. She decided not to come because it was a long flight, she wanted to stay with her children and grandchildren and it was rugby league related. Sheila said that she was happy if I wanted to go. I did want to because there was unfinished business. So we decided I would go on my own. I sent an email thanking them again and that it would just be me flying over.

Max replied saying that "We'll book your flights from Heathrow and sort it out when you get to Sydney." I replied sadly saying "No thanks, I've got shocking knees. I can't drive four hours to Heathrow. Thanks, but forget it.' The next email from Max said that they would fly me from Manchester to London and I would get a connecting flight to Sydney. I replied "Great. I'm looking forward to coming."

The date was set and all my family saw me off at Manchester. I caught the connecting flight and arrived in Sydney on the Thursday morning of Grand Final week; Brisbane Broncos against Melbourne Storm. I got to Sydney Airport and was met by a chauffeur driven limousine and taken to the Hilton Hotel at Sydney.

On arrival I was met Roy Masters at the hotel. Roy was working for the *Sydney Herald* and said that he had been one of the selectors who had picked the team to be named as the Penrith Panthers Legends team. He explained that the panel had people from different eras and who had seen different players play. They had then voted for 17 legends from a list of 50 nominees. I promise you as God is my witness he did not give me any clue about whether I had been chosen, only that I was one of the nominees.

I had a shower, got cleaned up and changed into a suit because there was a fantastic Grand Final breakfast downstairs in the hotel. I sat with Roy Masters, John Gray, next to Gordon Tallis and other celebrities. It was the first time I had met Gordon Tallis.

Roy introduced me to him. I shook hands with him and sat down. He said 'Someone mentioned you were coming.' As we spoke about the eras we had played in, typical cocky Aussie, Gordon said 'Do you think you were that good?' I just paused for second, smiled and said 'Well, put it this way, I've watched you playing on television. When I came off the pitch, I'd have let you clean my boots.' We both burst out laughing, but I was being honest. Sometimes they do think they are better than everybody else.

I have a lot of Australian friends, but I find that they are different to us, especially before you get to know them. Once you become friends with them, they are absolutely great people, but you would rather walk on them than them try and walk on you.

I suppose it's that one upmanship and their arrogance at times but my attitude was that no Aussie was going to beat me on or off the field. We had the breakfast and it was a good crack meeting Gordon Tallis. He was a tough man on the field as Terry O'Connor found out when they had a difference of opinion in 2007.

After swapping pleasantries after breakfast we went to Penrith and they put me up in a fantastic hotel with anything I wanted. I met so many people at the hotel, including all the directors who were at the club when I was there. Don't forget the circumstances under which I had left. They were all there waiting to greet me.

It was like walking back in time, but not like the day I left. It was so good. One of them, Terry Hideman, the first thing he said to me was "Bill, it's nice to see you, you bastard."

I said Terry "Why?" He said "That night you left we called an emergency meeting. My wife rang and said she was having a heart attack. I said never mind your heart attack, Bill Ashurst has just flown over you." We burst into laughter and had few beers.

During the evening with them I was introduced by Roger Cowan to a Greek gentleman, Greg Maledus. He was very wealthy and owned the amusement and gaming machines in clubs in Sydney and elsewhere. He asked me what I did for a living. I told him I didn't, I was on a pension. I had terrible knees from playing rugby league and was on disability benefits.

He just said to me "Don't worry son, I'll look after you." He was a generous man, every day he gave me a couple of hundred dollars to spend and took me everywhere. In Penrith he took me for a meal with Roger Cowan and the bill come to over $2,000.[12] It was absolutely unbelievable; he didn't bat an eyelid picking up the bill. The way that Greg and rest of the club treated me, it was as if I had never done anything wrong to Penrith; it was like the 'Prodigal Son' had returned.

Fortunately, the tax man wasn't in Penrith this time waiting for me as he was when I made my second secret return to Penrith and Australia. Just to stay on the right side with the way things were going I decided not to mention my second return.

What I loved about it this time was that every player that I had played with at Penrith, if they lived in the area, came and had a night out with me, or couple of nights. The ones that didn't spoke to me on the telephone. It showed the respect that I had from those players and the respect I had for them.

The Legends Evening was great night meeting the old guys and friends that I played with in the three seasons I was at the club before my moonlight flit. We were inside a

---

[12] In 2006 there were approximately $2.5 to £1.

marquee; there were something like 2,500 people there. One reason I wanted to come back was because of the way that I left; I'd never had the chance to apologise.

I'd never had the money to go back. I'd always wanted to apologise, ever since I had become a Christian, to say sorry, but finances dictated I couldn't. Whatever I had made from the game was gone and I don't regret that.

I think the good thing now about the game both in England and Australia is that there are systems in place to help players from when they take their first steps as a professional rugby league player. It is a totally different culture and mindset now, including – rightly or wrongly – players' agents. Nowadays players are not pieces of meat. It not a contract for life, unless they player wants it to be.

As each of the nominees was introduced by Roger Cowan, who was master of ceremonies, and presented to the audience, each one went onto the stage to speak. When my name was announced there was a great applause as I walked onto the stage. I was as nervous up there then as I had been when I gave my first ever testimony.

I said "I want to apologise for the way I left Penrith. It was circumstances that were beyond my control. But I have wanted to come back for 20 years to say sorry and I thank God that I am here tonight to do that." Someone idiot in the audience shouted 'We paid for it.' And I said "Yeah, but God got me here."

Following my apology, I said a few words about the team I'd played in and the great players that I played with. I said that to become one of the 50 nominated players itself was a great honour.

The announcement of the selection from Roger was similar to the Oscars, except in that ceremony there are cameras on the faces of the nominees. There were three or four nominees for each position and I knew from those for second row that I had stiff competition. People were telling me that I would be in, as they were saying this, my mind went back to when I was told I would be in the Great Britain squads and being heart broken when not selected.

I said 'What makes you think that?' Their logic was that they not going to fly me so far and not put me in. I just said that I was proud to be a nominee, one of the 50.

It was fitting that Roger Cowan had the privilege of announcing the Legends Team from one to 17. He was in charge when I was there, and had dragged Penrith up by its bootlaces and helped make it what it is now. He went through each nominee for each position and before naming the legend for that position he said a little something about the winner, who then went on stage to shake his hand and acknowledge the acclaim from the crowd.

It seemed like a lifetime as time ticked by until it came to number 11. Roger said "And the next one, number 11. This guy, I couldn't believe it what he did on the field but I couldn't get him to do anything off it. I couldn't get him to go to work." I knew at that instant I had won the position because he went on to talk about exploits at work, or lack of them to the great amusement of the audience.

Bill wearing his Penrith legend shirt, one of only 17 made,
in front of a banner celebrating the Legends team in 2006.

Bill celebrating at the Legends evening, with Tim Sheens, Bruce Ward,
Graham Moran, Glenn West, Ray Blacklock and Terry Geary.

I loved the next thing he said: "I watched this guy, first thing he put this 60 yard kick in and then he put a little kick over the top and scored. I thought that's 'arsey' ('lucky' in Australian English) and then he did it again, and again, and again. I thought, 'That's not luck, what a player we've signed here'. There's no more to say. Bill Ashurst."

What an introduction. I walked onto the stage to a standing ovation, shook Roy's hand, hugged him, took the applause of the crowd and waved to them. It was like the crowd acknowledging one of my tries all over again. I was made up with an indescribable incredible feeling of emotion that I had not had for many years. To come up and get my award from Roger and as a Pom at that, it was superb.

My second row partner was announced next and it was John Cartwright. I would have been really chuffed to put my arm around him in a pack and play. We were very similar; he was a very good player.

The Penrith Panthers Legends team announced that night by Roy was: Bob Landers, Grahame Moran, Ryan Girdler, Alan McIndoe, Brad Fittler, Greg Alexander, Terry Geary, Royce Simmons, Tim Sheens, Bill Ashurst, John Cartwright, Colin van der Voort. Substitutes: Craig Gower, Brad Izzard, Mark Geyer, Tony Puletua.

This Legends team was a very good side. When I spoke to Roy Masters and Max Cowan they told me that when they came to the second row positions, everyone on the panel said Bill Ashurst. There was no discussion, so I was clearly revered at Penrith. I'm not saying I deserved to get that respect from my peers, I think I opened a few eyes – a Pom from Higher Ince.

It was a great honour. In all the great Australian club legends teams there are only a handful of Poms that have got into their respective sides. I got in that Penrith team, Dick Huddart at St George, Dave Bolton at Balmain and Malcolm Reilly at Manly. It was one heck of a recognition and one heck of an honour.

On the Saturday, Penrith Panthers chairman Barry Walsh, a great friend and person, took me to the Kangaroo Reunion at the New South Wales Leagues Club. It's like the British Lions Dinner they have over here and is always on the day before the Grand Final. I had never been and I met lots of brilliant wonderful players. I remember standing there with Bob Reilly, Tommy Bishop, Ted Goodwin, Bobby Fulton and Tommy Raudonikis.

Arthur Beetson came over. He looked at Bob Reilly and said "Bear, you've played with this Pommie bastard and you have played with us. Where would you rate this Pom?"

Bob just looked at him and without hesitation said "Top three".

I thought "Wow, that's some recommendation."

I had a discussion with Tommy Raudonikis who had a go at me for not signing for Cronulla instead of Penrith.

Anyway I had another fantastic time and went back to the hotel, because next day was Grand Final Day. I went to the Grand Final with Barry Walsh. He had been invited by the sponsors; I was there with the bigwigs. A few former players and coaches I had played against and locked horns were there, I didn't know a lot of the other people though. Before the game there was a pre-match dinner and we met up with Terry Quinn who I had played with. He was now in charge of Country Rugby.

Anyway, I was sitting there with Barry and went to the bar for a couple beers. As I was coming back I noticed that my shoelaces were undone. I saw this guy stood in front of me in this busy large room. He was a small, bald headed guy with specs and a suit on. I said "Excuse me mate, can you hold these please while I tie my shoelace?"

He looked at me and said "Yeah, not a problem."

I handed him the beers, bent down, tied my shoelaces and got the beers back. I said "Thanks, mate." I walked back to our table. Barry, Terry and this couple who were with us were laughing their heads off. I said "What's the matter?"

Barry said "Do you know who that was?"

I said "Who?"

He said "The Prime Minister of Australia." I burst out laughing as they started laughing again and said "Well I didn't know did I, he never told me. Anyway, he's only same as us."

I didn't know who he was, I didn't ask him his name. I only found out then that it was John Howard, who was the second longest serving Prime Minister in Australian history. I thought to myself how privileged it must have been to hold two pints for Bill Ashurst.

I spent a week with Barry Walsh, Terry 'Dollar' Geary and met up friends Wayne Brain, Hodgsy, Reggie Walton, Terry Wickey, and Ray Blacklock. I went up for a weekend in Newcastle with Ross Gigg and went to the Newcastle Trots. We found that Mal Reilly was home in Newcastle so we rang him up and had a fantastic night. I also met up with the one armed golfer, Jack Newton.

I went to Dave Bolton's house and had a couple of barbecues there. One night at Dave's though in the middle of a barbecue we got a phone call from back home. It was that Keith Holden had killed himself. That sadly flattened the night because Dave had played with him at Wigan in the 1950s and 1960s.

Greg Maledis looked after me all the time I was there. He and his wife were wonderful people, took me to their home and invited me for dinner. Greg took me to a couple of 'do's at Koogie, posh places like. Thanks to his generosity I came home with £300 more than I'd gone with; that's how much he looked after me.

Finally the stay came to an end as time whistled by. I had had a fantastic time and the icing on the cake was to be named as a Penrith Panthers legend. I think it was a phenomenal achievement with some great players named in that side and those that didn't make it. Many thanks are due to Max and all at Penrith who looked after me and those who contacted me and came to see me. My thoughts are there for all those have passed on and I'm waiting for my computer to ping when the club celebrates its golden anniversary.

33. Talking about Bill Ashurst

As Bill outlines in this book, he has spent a lifetime in rugby league. For over 25 years he has been an active Christian, and has known his wife Sheila for 50 years. Here, various people who have been involved with Bill over the years have their say about him.

Sheila Ashurst

All those years ago when we first met, I said to Bill I wanted to finish it before it even started, not because I didn't like the look of him, I thought he was a nice handsome man, which I still do to this day. Even my dad when he I took him home on the third date, I said this is Bill and my dad said "Nay here that's something like a Mon". Bill was nearly touching the top of the door frame.

He was so sporty. He took me to Ince Park and he was playing a game of football, I was sitting watching on the bench and I saw him kick this lad's head as if he was kicking a football. I got up as I was disgusted, I walked off and I said 'That's it for me I don't want anybody as violent as that'. He ran off the pitch, caught me up and pleaded with me to stay with him and I was crying.

Anyway, he talked me round and we got married in 1966 and in a life of ups-and-downs and split-ups because of Bill's womanising we have known each other for 50 years. We are still together and are two years off our golden wedding anniversary.

With everything that Bill has done, I have always thought you don't love a person if you want to hold onto a person. I couldn't put up with it and hold onto him that way. I used to say if he wants somebody else I'll let him go because there is more love in that, I'm letting him please himself what he wants to do.

I'd get on with my life after he'd gone, I'd get over it that's what I used to think. If they're going to be better than me, let him have his own life with somebody who won't hold him back from rugby. I felt at those times I supported Bill throughout his rugby playing and coaching over all these years from when he started.

I've allowed him to do it, but not been actually here, there and everywhere with him, I missed going on trips and letting him enjoy me being on his arm and stuff like that. On that side and when I look at his life now, I should have been the woman on his arm. It's my own fault that I've not been and it's so because we are totally different. That's what I've said right at the beginning when I said to him: we're not compatible Bill.

I like craftwork, knitting, sewing, making a house a home. This is the worst house I have ever lived in, I can't get this one how I really like it because it's too small. Our other homes were larger than this one and I was a lot happier in those places. Bill is happier here and always liked the area. Most of our children have moved in around us now.

So we're alright now, but I've always been that type of person, wanting to make a home, wanting my husband Bill to be happy and wanting my children to be happy. I wanted my children to have their own dad, I didn't want them having another dad, I loved doing all that so I'm a proper homely person. I wanted to be a good wife, good mother and he'll tell you himself, he's not really short of anything, when he out he's easily led. If he can be happy with somebody else, can get on with his life better than he can with me, go for it, he can get wealthy. He will never get wealthy with me because I can't go with him on that sort of thing.

My wealth is the love, the support, the being there for each other and I have always known that with everything we have been through and Bill knows that. He has always said it "It doesn't matter what has happened, it's you that's the number one you'll always be my number one." I didn't used take him on at the time he used to say it, I do know deep down I am number one for him. I know that and he is number one for me.

There was only one lad for me before I met Bill and as it happened I never went out with him as Bill came along all those years ago. I've never even let myself even go and have a look for anybody else, even when at times we have been separated, I never thought of looking for anybody else. I've always said to myself even if anything happened to him I wouldn't want anybody else. I would go the rest of my life on my own I'm happy with him and the times I had had with Bill. I have no regrets, it's gone, it's over, it's been forgiven, if I had to do all this again I would only make one change. I would be the woman on his arm, I wouldn't let him go on his own to places where he had to have another woman to show the other men he had a women. I would do it; I would put myself out that bit more for him yeah that's my regret, my only regret

Throughout everything Bill has been a really good dad to his children, they think the world of him as do our grandchildren to us both. I did think that after he walked out with Wigan St Patricks that year he was done really retired from the game, done his time. We was going here there and everywhere go on the train to places spending days together you know, as life's short really.

Bill's 66 now, I'm 67 this month [July 2014] so I thought this last two years we'd have been here there and everywhere but we're not. We do get out a little bit, but we don't do as much as what we thought we would. Hopefully in the years to come we can have that contentment rather than rugby league back in our lives. He has just come back from Malta and is talking about going to Canada with a BARLA team next year. I hope in my heart that that is it now, it can now be about us, I want us to do it together and now have our time.

With what we have both been through together all these years I know that one thing is for sure and it's the final words from me. God's in control, there is only God could have put us two together. He has still kept us together 50 years later and if God wants to use this book that what it's all about.

Alan Purcell
Bill and I have one thing in common we both started Rose Bridge Secondary Modern School, Bill as a pupil I as a teacher. I didn't know him for months until I re-introduced rugby league to the school.

In a training session this lad came out lanky, no weight on him, he had this tremendous skill with a ball, I put Bill in the middle and had kids running round in a circle.

He could pass the ball like any professional footballer boom, boom, boom. I tried with him with the boot, after watching him I he was somebody very special and would go far in rugby football.

Sid Ollershaw, who was coming to the end of his career, was my mentor. He taught me everything I know about teaching, he told me about Johnny Lawrenson, who went onto to play for Wigan, England and Great Britain. Who at 14 at this school had ball in hand, punted over the heads, caught it, under the sticks, before anybody else could move. Nobody else will be able to do it he said.

I saw this tactic being used by Bill. Sid came and watched his next game. In the first few minutes Bill punted over the heads, caught it and flew away under the sticks. To quote Sid 'Bloody hell, I never thought I'd see it again in a boy.'

I didn't teach him everything I knew. I taught Bill the rules of the game, tactics, discipline, which he failed many a time, not at school but in later years. Regarding his skills no, Bill could teach anybody the natural skills of a rugby player even as a young boy.

He had a great career but sadly the end was sad, no player of his ability should have had to leave the game in such a sad way. It must have been sheer frustration because the real Bill Ashurst would not have done that.

The real end of his career came in the number of years he put into junior rugby league, I believe that there are many kids playing professional rugby league now who could say thank you to him.

I challenge anybody who has followed Wigan over the years to go back to the Bill Ashurst era and name the team; I'll guarantee that 99.9% will say the same first one: Bill Ashurst.

Shaun Wane

When I was about six or seven my dad used to take me to Central Park to watch Wigan. At that time I was a fanatical Wigan fan. Bill was the main man, he had great skills for a big man and had a big body, a great kicking game and was a great ball-playing handling forward.

A great tackler, he had the mongrel in him and he'd always get in a bit of trouble as well as sometimes getting sent off. I always looked up to him, so I can understand why he went to Australia – he would have been a fantastic player over there then.

When I was at Wigan as a youngster I got chance to be coached by him, he came down to the club as assistant to Alex Murphy. Bill was fantastic and I got on with him really well.

He looked after me; he took me under his wing, two born and bred Wigan lads as well obviously appealed to him. I was only young and he invited me into the first team dressing room from the 'A' team. It was unbelievable that as in those days it was a big thing. It made me feel at ease, made me feel at home and he always gave me some good advice and treated me well.

As a player and a coach I have played and worked with some great coaches to where I am today, Bill was one of them; I took bits from all of them which has built my own coaching philosophy. Part of that was from what Bill instilled in me in those early days and what I started doing with my own players coming through the coaching ranks.'

Chris Middlehurst

As far as I'm concerned Bill Ashurst was a good coach, I was at the end of my career, he came down to Halton Simms Cross were I was playing still playing as an amateur and he asked me to come over to Runcorn. He ended up making me captain and it was good, Bill was a footballer, certainly a football coach he wasn't a 'bash at them' and that and we never concentrated much on defence; it was all on attacking play.

We had some good footballers in the side as well and I was a big part of that being in the middle and playing loose-forward at that stage. It was one the best most enjoyable clubs I have been with, to be honest, under Bill. That was even though I had been at Warrington, Widnes and Swinton in the past, going there finishing my career, I really enjoyed the 18 months I was there.

The first season he was involved, when he took over we were joint top of the league in November I think we won seven out of the first eight. It fell away at the end because of the small squad, but Bill had some good ideas because he had played in Australia at Penrith.

He came back with that knowledge so after he had finished playing he put it into practice. He was good with camaraderie, squad building and had good man management. As far as I am concerned he was one of the best coaches around then and he was only at Runcorn, who had always finished bottom of the league and were thrashed every week.

We just missed out on getting into the play-offs that year because of tailing away, but what we did do we went away at the end of the season as well. All the players saved up each week; Bill came away with us and we spent a weekend in Blackpool which was a great end to that first season.

I thought it was the best season the club had ever had, with the people running it that year. After that, things changed and I thought the club went to pot again, including the well-publicised strike.

I was captain at the time; I took a bit of flak for that after the players asked for a bit of extra money after we had been drawn to play mighty Wigan in the Cup. They switched the game to Wigan for a bigger gate, more income in their coffers. Everything else is history. Bill turned out himself and got sent off for having a go at Andy Goodway.

I was disappointed when that happened and I never played for them again after that. I was kept out of the game for 18 months after that because the club held my registration, and stopped me playing and finishing my amateur career in Widnes at Simmies.

I saw Bill play a couple of times when he came to play at Widnes for Wakefield when I was a kid growing up and in the 1979 Challenge Cup Final. I saw videos of him in Australia when I was over there in 1985. A lot people talked about him over there and the Aussie players said that he was a good footballer and had a good time at Penrith.

He was, is a great man and I still speak to him now and when I go to St Pats to watch a game. He's always there and we always have a laugh and a joke about Runcorn. That was the best time for me, I was playing well a big part of the set up and I have a lot of respect for Bill and think he was a great player and coach.

Peter Carroll

Bill is a great friend of mine and I saw him play many, many times for Wigan and Wakefield Trinity. I first got to know him when I was a taxi driver and used to pick him up at the pub and take him home. It was 'I've just taken the great Bill Ashurst home' – me a lifelong Wigan supporter.

Bill was a fantastic player, the money he would be on in today's game. The players' fitness is totally different to Bill's day, but I think he would cope with it, but probably he couldn't have a fag.

Bill didn't like training, but he did it and when we used to watch him playing he looked as fit and fast as anyone on that field whether playing centre or second row. He was a bit like Shaun Edwards; you can't coach people like that, they have got it built in them. With his kicking game Bill would have had a field day with 40/20s with the length he got kicking the ball downfield and into touch

A phenomenal player of the good players at the time, he could kick the ball, dummy and run, although if he could get someone to run for him he would do it with his sublime passing. He would make the break and give it to somebody else. He was certainly a character both on and off the field barking out the orders to everyone.

He is a belting person and will do anything for you, I know that if I'm in trouble I can phone him up and he will be here. It works both ways between us over the years and we have had some great times together. He is a very good friend and his wife Sheila is the salt of the earth. He is a family man, anyone hurts his family they hurt Bill and I would not like to get on the wrong side of him.

Roy Masters

To understand how good Bill Ashurst was as a rugby league player, consider this: he played about half as many games he could for Penrith, returned to the UK without informing the club and still was selected in the Panthers team of the half century.

Bill was a great tactical kicker at a time when coaches in Australia threatened to cut off the leg of a forward who booted the ball. He was also at the vanguard of the round-the-corner goalkicking method, now the universal approach.

If interchange has been allowed in Bill's era, he would have been sensational. He reserved his energy for attack rather than defence, prompting many a player to say to him "You set up the tries and I'll do your tackling for you."

Bob McCarthy

I remember Bill Ashurst as a great forward, before he even came over to Australia we used to get a lot of television coverage of the English game and Bill was always standout for Wigan and Great Britain.

I never really clashed with him until he came over to Australia to play for Penrith and I remember once there the newspapers were saying 'The world's best two second rowers were up against each other today: Bill Ashurst and Bob McCarthy.'

I was the best second row in Australia in the game then and Bill obviously the best in England and when we played them Bill was standing back a bit. I didn't know much about him and the Mike Stephenson thing.

I said to him 'You're not taking the ball up much today Bill' and he didn't say much you know, we just got the ball moving on and he sort of came right into the game right on half time. We were leading and he got the ball three or four metres the other side of halfway and went whack with this powerful field goal straight between the posts. I was walking off and thought 'Oh, what a kick' as he went past me he said 'That's why I don't run the ball'.

Bill and I were good. We respected each other and like all good players we didn't go and try and bash each, we just appreciated each other's ability. Unfortunately for us, the Australian game didn't see much of Bill because he took off back to the UK.

I think Bill was a very cagey forward and to be the status he reached in England he had to be pretty good. Bill wasn't backward at coming forward with the way he played the game on the field and he certainly took no prisoners on the pitch

Bill is definitely up there with the best English players that I played against, he wasn't like a magnificent runner, a running forward, more constructive, a constructive forward. He would have been good with me I would have been running off his passes and he could have dummied and done all that sort of stuff.

Tommy Raudonikis

I didn't have much to do with Bill, but I played against him a number of times. He was a great attacker with the football, could unload a ball, hit a line and go through a line, and offload. Plus he didn't mind doing the hard work, but the big thing about him was that he wouldn't take a backward step and he was a dirty bastard too sometimes. But he was from his reputation a bit of a wild man and he liked having a good time and a few beers.

Ronnie Coote

Bill came over to Australia to play in the 1970s and the great thing that I can remember about him I played against him and Stevo at Penrith. It was always a tough afternoon when you had to go and play against them as they were both really good players.

One year in the Amco Cup, Bill scored this magnificent try from a chip kick and chase, which he used to do on occasions. He followed up, got the ball and finished up scoring a try. In scoring that try he won a car for the 'try of the season' in the Amco Cup; not a bad prize.

That's the sort of player Bill was: a big tall bloke, rangy, hard to handle and had a good kicking game. He used to kick field goals, as well as goals to go with his try scoring exploits. He was a good player in those areas and departments.

I don't know what happened to make him leave Australia he took off one time and I don't know the story there, all of a sudden he was just gone.

Bill has always been thought of as a great character in Australia, he was a good player in a tough team and without a doubt a match winner on his day, when he had a day on you had to be wary of him.

Jim Hartley

What to say about Bill, in my opinion Britain's most skilful rugby league forward ever? If I was to pick a Great Britain all-time side of the players I have seen — and I have been watching the game since I was a young boy in 1959 — Bill would be in my second row. Quite a compliment considering the outstanding forwards he played with and against, and who have played since.

His great attributes were football skills. His kicking game which was the best I have ever seen from the hand. The distance that he could achieve would make the modern day 40/20 rule embarrassingly easy for Bill. He would probably have to have that rule rewritten, it would have to be something like a 20/10 rule. He could drop a goal from any angle, including his own body angle. In the Championship final at Station Road against St Helens, which St Helens won, he did two drop goals from under a mountain of defenders, but still got the ball over the crossbar at an impossible angle.

His handling skills really had to be seen to be believed; modern day players like Jamie Lyon, Matt Gidley and quite a few others have developed reverse passes, flipping the ball out with the back of the hand. Bill could take the ball into a forward pack, drive it through and get the pass out to anybody. His great physique and physical strength certainly helped him in that respect, but the belief in himself that he could do it and do it every time was, I think, what gave him that advantage over his opponents.

His aggressive defence could be brutal at times, and I think Alex Murphy and one or two others remember the tackles he made on them. The only weakness in his game was his left hook, which wasn't quite as strong as his right cross to the chin, but his aggression was usually tempered by good humour. He was one of those old fashioned players who believed that you could take out a bit of retribution on the field, that it was the right thing to do and that you didn't need to bother the referee or the judiciary, but that's not the modern way.

Well, I remember his last ever game for Wigan in Challenge Cup against Bradford Northern, I was standing, as an ordinary fan then not involved with any club, on the Spion

Kop end. Bill had broken the line from the halfway line and reached about five metres from the tryline right under the posts. He was carrying two or three Bradford defenders with him and couldn't make any more yards, wouldn't have got to the line and looked for a support player to give the pass to.

He turned and looked over his left shoulder and every single one of his teammates were still in their own half, no-one had supported him. So he took retribution out on the four Bradford players that were within reach of him. Four punches later there were four unconscious Bradford players. The referee stood there astounded and before he could send him off, Bill just turned around on his heels and marched 95 yards down the field and down the tunnel sending himself off, never played for the club again. In his last ever game for Runcorn against Wigan he was sent off, that's Bill for you; he didn't do anything by halves.

I think the reputation he built for himself in Australia where he was reputed to be able to pick up the man-of-the-match award anytime he wished to simply by outplaying everybody else on the field probably says it all about him. Nobody has ever done that, Bill could do it more often than most and his career in Australia earned the respect of every rugby league fan and coach in Australia.

On the 40th Anniversary of the Penrith Panthers he became one of their 17 legends of the club, something that is usually just restricted to Australians. They very much have a belief that they are the best which quite often they are, but we've had some outstanding players over here and Bill for me comes right at the top of the list.

I think Malcolm Reilly did the British game great credit in his time in Australia. We all know about that; Bill did just the same and should be given all the recognition that he deserves for the time he played in Australia. In this day and age, if a Tomkins or a Graham or the Burgess brothers playing in Australia we can watch every one their games, but unfortunately in those days we couldn't, so they were lost to the British game. We could read the occasional report on a match and we lost touch with some of our great players that went over to play out there.

Andy Kelly

When Bill came to Wakefield it was just the magnitude of the man, he was someone I knew about as a back-row forward and he had already put himself on the map. There was two back-row forwards who I had as my role models if you like and they were Phil Lowe from Hull KR and Bill Ashurst from Wigan. To have him at the club where I was starting out my career was like an unbelievable thing in some aspects and I learned so much from him.

As a back-row forward there was a uniqueness about him, he had the size of a back-row forward, the speed of a back-row running forward, but the skills of a halfback; he could read a game and in a lot of instances was just telling you where to run. He would say 'You just run to that space and I'll put the ball there'. He would create the opening for you to run into and made a lot of things for me.

It sort of modelled me as a player, but that was because of his understanding of the game which was just second to none. He just encapsulated lots of different attributes that fitted lots of different players across the park all in one player. I was lucky I got the opportunity to play with him. I thoroughly enjoyed that period. It was a fantastic time, I learned so much from him and he moulded and fashioned me as a player.

The year he coached, we had a really tough season. The club had sold all its star players at the end of the season as he took over. I broke my arm playing in November on my 21st birthday. It was a tough period for me, but Bill worked really, really hard in the background and with me. Even in 1981 he was setting me goals.

He put a few incentives in place for me, he had his Penrith shirt and at that time we didn't see Australian shirts in this country and I admired that shirt. He said you play for me before the end of the season and I'll give you my shirt. As good as his word, he gave me that shirt and I have treasured it for a long time.

As a player Bill is among the greats, he probably hasn't received the accolades that he deserves for the era he played at; he was ahead of his time. In terms of players that I played with, such as Ray Price, Mark Graham and Steve Ella, I have played with a lot of good players at the front or back end of their careers and Bill rates just as highly as any of them. He was an incredible, thoughtful, supportive person and for a young player coming through at the start of his career I found him a very giving person with respect to his experience and knowledge.

Neil White

Time can play tricks with memories, enhance ordinary moments into great ones, turn decent players into legends, but I know that isn't the case with Bill Ashurst. It's not because I remember particular moments, like a spectacular try or match-winning tackle, but because remember the excitement and awe I felt when I first saw him play.

Very few players evoke a certain sense of anticipation, that when they have the ball something special is about to happen. Ellery Hanley, Martin Offiah, Jason Robinson, Sam Tomkins. Those are the more recent examples, of players who make you hold your breath for a second. For me, as a skinny young kid from Wakefield, Bill Ashurst was one of those players too. When the ball was in his hands, there was always the chance of some magic. He'd either break the line himself, running strong, a shimmy in the tackle, his greased black hair flapping around, muddy bandages around his knees, or else he'd find the killer pass for someone else, one of the little men.

I remember the fuss when he signed for the Trinity, my father pointing it out in the *Evening Post*, a world record signing from Wigan, £18,000, a sign of the club's rebirth. I'd missed out on the glory years at Wakefield; I saw just the tail-end of Neil Fox's career at the top and my only experience of Harold Poynton was collecting the newspapers from him when I did my paper round from Harold's shop on my estate. David Topliss had sustained my need for a hero, but when Bill Ashurst came along it felt like my Sunday afternoons had been dusted in glamour.

The first game I saw Bill Ashurst play in Trinity colours was at Featherstone on Good Friday. I can remember peering through the railings at Post Office Road as he did something I'd never seen before: he almost won the game single-handedly; absolutely on his own. That's how I recounted it afterwards, to those friends who were more interested in the round ball, that Wakefield had signed a genius. He ran hard like I expected from a forward, but what I remember is how he took charge. Big and strong, uncompromising, but he organised everything; always the first to receive the ball, directing, leading. I left Featherstone that day knowing I'd witnessed something special.

He repeated it on Easter Monday, this time at Belle Vue, his first home game. Bill Ashurst was a maestro, conducting the team like they were there just for him, dominating the game. It was the start of something big, a sign that the club could become great again. Wakefield had a star.

We didn't quite reach the top, a Wembley appearance being the peak, and those dodgy knees got to him in the end, but through the eyes of that skinny kid from Wakefield, watching in the mud and gloom of the 1970s, I can say that Bill Ashurst stands out as a bright spot, one of the most naturally-gifted rugby players I have ever seen.

Terry Fanning

That day 26 years ago I saw Bill come into our Pentecostal Church, we had a balcony in the church and from what I saw he actually cried throughout the service. We are in the habit of inviting people to accept Jesus as their saviour and Bill came forward to do that, he was very, very moved. It wasn't just an emotional thing.

I had worked with Bill at Heatstore for two or three years so I knew him beforehand and that morning; yes he was genuine but we do wait and see and test. So when I say he was genuine then he was because it has lasted until now.

We baptised by full emersion on confession of their faith so they have to confess that they are believers which Bill did and we baptised him. Bill being the size he was we baptised the first three rows. He has given his time, Christianity is not a religion for us it is a lifestyle and the proof of the pudding is in his lifestyle now.

I saw Bill play and he would rank with the greatest in his position that I have ever seen, starting at centre and moving into the second row and he was phenomenal second row forward. A great player, great ball handler, could see an opening, made openings and sometimes he did keep his temper, the rest of the time he got sent off.

We have been friends, one thing I like about Bill is we are different personalities, but Bill is genuine and he has never lost his background, never gone from his roots, he's a changed person but is a genuine guy and I like genuine people.

34. The epilogue

After leaving Runcorn Highfield, my professional playing and coaching days were over and I went on another journey. This incorporated my church, my testimonies and my return to grassroots rugby league. For the last 26 years I became involved in a new area of the game to me, youth and junior rugby league.

This has seen me put thousands of hours into the game I will always love, in rain, hail, sun and snow in the day and evening to try and help players on their pathway into the game. I am not the only one; there are thousands of unpaid volunteers over all of the country preaching our game to youngsters taking it up.

Without these volunteers and amateur or community clubs – which is the fashionable term these days – to gain grants for them, there would be no professional game. The professional game thrives on these roots and without that source; our game would wither and die.

My son Billy was playing at St Williams then, so I got involved at the club with a good friend of mine, Tommy Young. I started off coaching the under-9s side. I did a number of years there before moving onto Hindley, because one of my sons, Andrew, wanted to play for them.

I moved to Hindley when Andrew was aged 10 and coached there until he was 16. I had a fantastic time with the kids and club there. I worked with two great assistant coaches, Gary Hankinson and Andy Brummell; all the young lads were great. Some had joined me from St Williams.

I then packed coaching in for a little while, although I still watched some youth and junior games while I was involved with my church. However, after watching my grandson Billy training one night at Wigan St Pats, I got involved with that club for the next few years, initially with Alan Rimmer – a great bloke – and his assistant.

Building that team up, I got two other coaches involved with him, Ian Gildart and Peter Williams. Peter was possibly the best skills coach I have ever seen. We got involved with a breast cancer campaign and wore a pink kit. People laughed when we went onto the pitch. They didn't laugh when we were coming off after they had been beaten.

Among other successes, we reached the under-14s BARLA National Cup Final at Lytham St Anne's and beat West Hull 24–22. Two years later, we reached the under-16s BARLA National Cup Final, at the same venue, and beat Bold Miners 26–4.

That final should have been my last involvement in the amateur game, or so I thought. Over that period they were the best youngsters side that I have ever seen play rugby league; arguably the best youth and junior side ever to turn out for St Pats in any era.

I had the honour of leading that side out onto the field with a great friend of mine, the greatest winger ever to play rugby league, Billy Boston. Irony of ironies, my first steps into rugby league were watching him on telly in the 1958 Challenge Cup win over Workington Town and my last steps were with him in 2012.

Tim Sheens, Dale Cherry Evans, Cameron Smith, Peter Williams and Bill, who was presenting the Australians with a Wigan St Pat's shirt.

Wigan St Pat's team that won the BARLA National Youth Cup in 2010.
Bill coached young players at the club for many years.

In June 2014, I was asked by tour manager Stuart Prior to be involved with the BARLA Great Britain under-17s side which toured Malta. He was also involved with that Wigan St Patricks team. It was another great opportunity to meet young people, talk to them and help the coaches.

On the match day of the team's test match, I had a sad job that needed to be done after sitting in at the team selection. With my years of experience, it was me who could console and tell the kids who were not in the team for the game. It was a bit sad, but yet again we had a few laughs afterwards to cheer them up and keep them together as one team on-and-off the field.

We had a great coaching staff and I think that they learned from my experience from what I've done in the game. I really enjoyed it the mentoring side. Great staff, great tour, good kids, great tour manager and a 90–0 win.

People may ask why do it, why play it with a score like that, but it is great for the game. The kids got the experience, they learned what it was like to be together on a tour, they were from different clubs and different environments.

The coaches of the Malta team we beat all had the opportunity to learn. They will continue to do so after videoing the game. They have learned from British coaches and are learning from the best game in the world, British rugby league, and that for me was a success.

I always said that I would never do a book, for Sheila's sake at the end of the day. I hope I have not disrespected any players or coaches or anyone else. I've said how I saw things. Sheila encouraged me to do it. She said "You have lived a life, there are other people who have never been in your class at rugby league who have written books and you need to tell your story."

She pushed me and is totally behind me doing it now. I was surprised when Sheila said that, given she has never been a sports lover and what I put her through over the years. I am glad I have done it and that I worked with Steve Manning. It's been a wonderful experience to tell it all as it was.

However, the experience that has been most wonderful in my life is my missus, Sheila, and my very large family. I want to dedicate everything in this book to Sheila, my children and grandchildren. Ever since I first met her at 16, and said I would never play rugby again and I'd never play sport again, all my life I've always enjoyed playing and coaching sport.

Sheila has hated rugby league all her life, but she has supported me and let me do what I do and I did the wrong thing by her quite a number of times. For the things I've done wrong, I can only say sorry to her, nothing was meant. Sheila has always been the only love of my life; she has been throughout and always will be.

She has been a fantastic mother, to have our first three children in Wigan, then to come across to Australia with me even though she brought her mam, she's been fantastic. She has put up with a lot; she said that she never wanted to go to a game. Well Sheila, I'll tell you this, you said that it was because you didn't want to see me injured. I'm glad you didn't go to a lot more games because every time you came to a game I got hurt, so whether that was an omen or not I don't know.

Sheila has been fantastic, we have had our ups-and-downs, we've been separated, we're back together and she is a wonderful grandma, superb Nan and has so much love for everybody. Our favourite song, all the way mine and you wouldn't believe it even through all the wrong I've done, has always been the Bette Midler song *The Wind beneath My Wings*.

I couldn't have done all this without her and the way that she brought up my kids and grandkids, I want to say that everything is down to Sheila and my family; I love her and every one of them. I love you to the end of the earth and I thank you for being in my life and want to say 'thank you' to all of you. I love you all and I am so proud of being able to say here we're all still part of each other.

To all the people that have helped me in rugby league at Wigan, Penrith, Wigan again, Wakefield Trinity, Runcorn Highfield as a professional player and coach; St Williams, Ince Rose Bridge, Hindley and Wigan St Patrick's, thank you for everything in the game. It's the best and greatest game in the world.

I've loved every minute of it and many people at one time or another have said to me, and I'll finish with this, "Would you change anything if you could go back?" I reply "Definitely, I would have gone for goal against Barrow instead of kicking for touch because it cost us the game."

That's it. Hope you enjoyed it.

Appendix: Statistics and records

Representative honours

Great Britain:
1971–72
New Zealand, 25 September 1971, at Salford, lost 13–18.
France, 6 February 1972, at Toulouse, won 10–9
France, 12 March 1972, at Odsal, won 45–10, 2 tries
Summary: Played 3, won 2, lost 1, scored 2 tries.

Lancashire:
1971–72
Yorkshire, 29 September 1971, at Leigh, lost 22–42
1972–73
Yorkshire, 11 October 1972, at Castleford, lost 18–32.
Summary: Played 2, lost 2.

The Rest:
versus Kangaroos
15 February 1974, lost 0–26.

Clubs in Great Britain

Wigan

	App	Sub	T	G	DG	Pts
1968–69	27	0	15	1		47
1969–70	34	5	14	14		70
1970–71	36	0	17	49		149
1971–72	33	1	15	52		149
1972–73	28	1	6	26		70
1977–78	21	0	7	4	6	35
Totals	**179**	**7**	**74**	**146**	**6**	**520**

Wakefield Trinity

	App	Sub	T	G	DG	Pts
1977–78	4	0	2	7	2	22
1978–79	11	0	2	1	1	9
1979–80	8	0	0	0	4	4
1980–81	6	0	1	0	0	3
1981–82	1	1	0	0	0	0
1983–84	1	0	0	0	1	1
Totals	**31**	**1**	**5**	**8**	**8**	**39**

Runcorn Highfield

	App	Sub	T	G	DG	Pts
1988–89	0	1	0	0	0	0

Penrith

NSWRL	App	T	G	DG	Pts
1974	13	8	0	4	28
1975	16	2	42	1	91
1976	17	9	9	1	46
Totals	**46**	**19**	**51**	**6**	**165**

Amco Cup	App	T	G	DG	Pts
1974	1	2	5	0	16
1975	2	2	3	0	12
1976	1	1	0	0	3
Totals	**4**	**5**	**8**	**0**	**31**

Summary

Team	App	Sub	T	G	DG	Pts
Great Britain	3	0	2	0	0	6
Lancashire	2	0	0	0	0	0
The Rest	1	0	0	0	0	0
Wigan	179	7	74	146	6	520
Wakefield Trinity	31	1	5	8	8	39
Runcorn H	0	1	0	0	0	0
Penrith	50	0	24	59	6	196
Totals	**266**	**9**	**105**	**213**	**20**	**761**

Club honours

Wigan

Winners:
BBC2 Floodlit Trophy 1968–69
Lancashire League 1969–70
League Leaders Trophy 1970–71
Lancashire Cup 1971–72

Runners Up:
Challenge Cup 1969–70
BBC2 Floodlit Trophy 1969–70
Lancashire Cup 1977–78

Wakefield Trinity

Runners Up:
Challenge Cup 1978–79

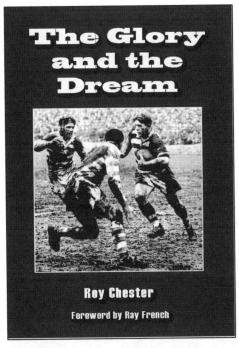

The Glory and the Dream

Roy Chester

Foreword by Ray French

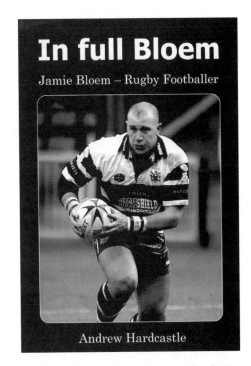

In full Bloem

Jamie Bloem – Rugby Footballer

Andrew Hardcastle

The Glory and the Dream is a great new rugby league novel. It tells the story of a young boy's rite of passage. It is full of rich characters, and is played out against a backdrop of social upheaval in the austere post-war years of rationing and shortages. But it was a time when communities pulled together. Walking days, royal visits, Sunday School outings to the seaside and communal bonfire nights were annual highlights. It was a time when youngsters had to make their own entertainment, including playing rugby league.

It is about Johnny Gregson, the young star of the Garton rugby league team, whose dream is to follow his dad's success in the sport. Johnny lives with his mother in Four Locks, a poor working class area in a grimy northern town. His father died in the Second World War. The story starts in 1945, when Johnny is aged 10. It follows his rise from junior rugby league through playing rugby union as a schoolboy to turning professional with Garton.

Johnny faces challenges at every turn, including when he wins a scholarship to a local public school and is labelled as a 'slum kid;' by the class bully. His prowess at rugby helps him deal with this boy. Also, at the tender age of 16, he meets a young woman who becomes very important to him. This is a story about sport, romance and working class life. It includes many humorous incidents, insights and even tragedy in a young man's development.

Published in March 2014 at £9.95. Order for just £9.00 post free in the UK from www.llpshop.co.uk from London League Publications Ltd, PO Box 65784, London NW2 9NS

In full Bloem is an authorised biography of Jamie Bloem. From being a young South African rugby union player, he developed into a star rugby league player. From 1992 to 2005 he played every position on the field in a career that took in Castleford, Oldham, Doncaster, Widnes and Huddersfield, but primarily Halifax. He later became a coach, commentator and Grade 1 referee. He was never far from the headlines, be it for drug taking, an accusation of biting, charges of abusing referees, declining pay cuts, or even sometimes for scoring spectacular tries or kicking touchline goals. This is a frank account of when he was in the wrong and when he was not. Published in 2013 as a hardback @ £14.95, now available direct from London League Publications Ltd at www.llpshop.co.uk for just £8.95 post free in the UK from London League Publications Ltd, PO Box 65784, London NW2 9NS.

Soldiers' League
The story of Army Rugby League
By Sean Fanning

"Rugby league epitomises all of the qualities required of a soldier – skill, fitness, courage, teamwork, determination and a strong sense of discipline."

Lieutenant General Sir Scott Grant, former President Army Rugby League.

Rugby league only became a recognised sport in the Army in 1994. However, since then it has thrived, overcoming many obstacles on the way. This book is the first to be published about rugby league in the Armed Forces. It covers the growth and development of the sport, including:

- Inter-Services matches
- The Army in the Challenge Cup
- International matches and tours
- The Lawson and Yeoman Cups
- Combined Services rugby league
- Profiles of players, coaches and managers and officials
- Rugby league and the Army prior to 1994
- A tribute to Jack Harrison, the only professional rugby league player to win the Victoria Cross who was playing when he enlisted.

Sean Fanning played professional rugby league for Leigh and Highfield. He was a Staff Sergeant in the Army Medical Service until 2014, and was on active duty in Afghanistan in 2012. He has played for and coached the Army Rugby League team, played for the Great Britain Armed Forces team in the 2008 Armed Forces World Cup and has played for Combined Services.

Sean Fanning's share of the profits from this book will be paid directly to Soldiers' League, which raises money for service charities, including the Royal British Legion, Blesma and Combat Stress.

Published in 2013 @ £14.95, now available direct from London League Publications Ltd at www.llpshop.co.uk for just £14.00 (£10 for current or serving members of the Armed Forces) post free in the UK or by post from London League Publications Ltd, PO Box 65784, London NW2 9NS.

London League Publications Ltd books are also available on www.Amazon.co.uk both in print and as E-Books for Kindle readers.